Electronic Markets

Electronic Markets

Benefits, Costs and Risks

Edited By

Craig Standing
Professor of Strategic Information Management,
School of Management, Edith Cowan University

palgrave
macmillan

First published 2009 by
PALGRAVE MACMILLAN

Palgrave Macmillan in the UK is an imprint of Macmillan Publishers Limited,
registered in England, company number 785998, of Houndmills,
Basingstoke, Hampshire RG21 6XS.

Palgrave Macmillan in the US is a division of St Martin's Press LLC,
175 Fifth Avenue, New York, NY 10010.

Palgrave Macmillan is the global academic imprint of the above companies
and has companies and representatives throughout the world.

Palgrave® and Macmillan® are registered trademarks in the United States,
the United Kingdom, Europe and other countries

ISBN 978-1-349-31058-6   ISBN 978-0-230-27423-5 (eBook)
DOI 10.1057/9780230274235

This book is printed on paper suitable for recycling and made from fully
managed and sustained forest sources. Logging, pulping and manufacturing
processes are expected to conform to the environmental regulations of the
country of origin.

A catalogue record for this book is available from the British Library.

A catalog record for this book is available from the Library of Congress.

10 9 8 7 6 5 4 3 2 1
18 17 16 15 14 13 12 11 10 09

Contents

Tables and Figures

Tables

Figures

Notes on the Contributors

Alison Yacyshyn, currently a Visiting Assistant Professor at the University of Alberta School of Business, has a PhD from the Department of Sociology at the University of Western Ontario. Her research interests include Sociology of Health, Aging, Disability, Research Methods and Statistics, and Demography.

Amir Parssian is an associate professor of information systems at IE Business School in Madrid. His main areas of research cover knowledge quality assessment, information quality, green IT, and data mining where his work has been published in *Management Science* and *Information Systems Research* journals among others.

Avi Noy, PhD, is a researcher and an adjunct instructor at the University of Haifa. His research focus is information systems, social computing, online auctions, recommender systems and simulation and gaming, especially in electronic-commerce and educational settings. He received a BSc in Computer Engineering and an MBA from the Technion, Israel Institute of Technology; LLB from the University of Haifa, Israel, and a PhD from the University of Haifa, Israel.

Aviv Shoham (PhD Marketing, University of Oregon) is a senior lecturer and marketing department head at the Graduate School of Management at the University of Haifa, Israel. His main research interests are international marketing strategy and international consumer behaviour. His research has been published in numerous journals and conferences, including the *Academy of Marketing Science, Journal of International Marketing,* and *International Marketing Review.*

Bela Florenthal is Assistant Professor of Marketing, College of Business, Butler University, USA. She has a Ph.D., (Marketing), from Smeal College of Business Administration, Pennsylvania State University. She also has Master of Science in Business Administration, Technion-Israel Institute of Technology, Haifa, Israel. She research interests include e-tailing/retailing and shopping behaviour, the impact of cultural differences on shopping behaviour, green (Eco-friendly) marketing, and internet technologies and their impact on consumer behaviour.

Craig Standing is Professor of Strategic Information Management at Edith Cowan University, Australia. His current research interests are in the areas of electronic markets and mobile commerce. He has published in the *European Journal of Information Systems, IEEE Transaction on Engineering Management, Information and Management and European Journal of Operational Research.*

Denise E. Gengatharen is currently teaching in MIS and Project Management at the School of Management, Edith Cowan University. Her research interests are in the areas of SMEs and e-commerce, e-marketplaces and knowledge management. She is currently on the editorial board of *Electronic Markets – The International Journal on Networked Business.*

Dr Helen Cripps was awarded her PhD for research focusing on business relationships and the role of IT in a Marine, Defence and Resources cluster south of Perth. She recently won a state government research contract to continue her research in the marine industry. She currently lectures in the School of Marketing Tourism and Leisure at Edith Cowan University. Prior to entering academia Helen was a practitioner in government economic policy, community development, relationship building and marketing. Helen research interests included adoption and evaluation of IT, business relationships and regional economic growth through clusters and networks.

Ian Sims holds professional qualifications as a Chartered Accountant, a CPA with a specialist designation in Information Systems and MCIPS. He has managed complex information systems in both the public and private sectors. Ian has published widely in information systems journals and has presented at international conferences. He is a lecturer at Southern Cross University, Australia, and course coordinator for the Master of Supply Chain Management.

Dr. Paul McElhone is the Executive Director of the School of Retailing at the University of Alberta. His research interests include specialty retail environments, customer service and electronic mediums. Paul also teaches Retailing and Channel Management, Selling and Sales Management, and Principles of Real Estate as well as managing McElhone Consulting, an international retail consultancy.

Dr. Rolf T. Wigand is Maulden-Entergy Chair and Distinguished Professor of Information Science and Management at the University of Arkansas at Little Rock. He researches information management, electronic commerce and markets, and the strategic deployment of information and communication technology. Current research on vertical IS standards in three industries (mortgage, retail, automotive supplies) as well as online gaming behaviour is funded by the National Science Foundation.

Rosemary Stockdale is currently senior lecturer in information systems at Massey University in Auckland New Zealand. Rosemary has published widely in leading information systems journals and has presented at international conferences. She is associate editor of the *Journal of Systems and Information Technology* and is currently researching online health-related support systems.

Dr. Samar I. Swaid is an Assistant Professor of Computer Science at Philander Smith College. Prior to being awarded the PhD in 2007, she worked in the IT industry for 10 years. Her research interests are information systems adoption and implementation, e-commerce, and e-health. Her work was published in different conferences and journals.

Susan Standing is a research fellow in the School of Management at Edith Cowan University. She is researching the benefits, costs and risks associated with electronic auctions. Other research topics include the managing strategic alliances in the biotechnology sector and mobile technology in the health care sector. Susan has published widely in information systems journals and has presented at leading information systems conferences.

Yuval Dan-Gur's professional experience is in planning and monitoring large-scale working plans, managing and integration of high-risk projects and evaluation of new technologies in computers and telecommunication fields. He graduated with a Bsc. in Electrical Engineering from the Technion of Haifa (1987) and an Msc. in Industrial Engineering (Technion, 1996). His research deals with Recommender Systems.

1

Online Retailing, Electronic Marketplaces and Electronic Collaboration

Craig Standing

The growth in electronic business with the rise of the internet has been nothing short of phenomenal. This has created unprecedented access to markets in the form of consumers and companies. The nature of the internet has enabled organisations to develop extended relationships with consumers and for organisations to further interact with their business partners, suppliers and other organisations. Electronic markets are characterised by the buying and selling of goods and services but, in addition, the internet has become a vehicle for electronic collaboration through electronic markets that exchange information and knowledge. These electronic markets are the theme for this book.

What are electronic markets?

Throughout the book, the terms electronic markets and electronic marketplaces are used interchangeably. Electronic markets are the activities associated with particular goods, services or knowledge. Electronic markets can be composed of a range of transaction mechanisms or modes of doing business. They can be local, national, regional or global. However, an electronic marketplace (sometimes referred to as exchanges, auctions and catalogue aggregators) can be defined as an interorganisational information system that allows the participating buyers and sellers in a market to exchange information about prices and product offerings (Bakos, 1997). In other words, they are more specific and identify a particular trading space. An electronic market is typically made up of many such marketplaces.

Markets and marketplaces and hierarchies

Electronic markets have a strong theoretical basis. The two mechanisms for conducting business activity are hierarchies and markets (Williamson, 1975). The term 'hierarchy' in this context refers to organisations that take on a hierarchical form through the procurement and selling of goods and services in the supply chain. Markets, on the other hand, are seen as horizontal. Markets are viewed as being more efficient from a transaction cost perspective. Transaction costs are the costs associated with finding someone with whom to do business, reaching an agreement about the price and other aspects of the exchange, and ensuring that the terms of the agreement are fulfilled. Electronic markets have the potential to streamline and manage these activities and reduce the transaction costs associated with conducting business compared with hierarchies where a company has to manage its suppliers and procurement processes. It has been noted, however, that market efficiencies may be related to certain types of non-recurrent transactions (Williamson, 1979) and some organisations develop closer relationships with their suppliers to obtain supply-chain efficiencies as a form of competitive advantage (Clemons et al., 1993).

Drivers of electronic markets

The benefits of electronic market participation include: improved efficiencies, cost savings, exposure to global markets, improved service, reduced communication costs, accelerated flow of news and information and improved market information. Electronic markets can also be used as knowledge-sharing networks with the potential for product and service innovation. The expectations of consumers have also changed. Web sites that provide a means for customers to interact directly with bricks and mortar companies have become an expectation and often the more the consumer can accomplish online the better the perception of service.

Globalisation

The internet has accelerated the process of globalisation. The concept of globalisation has given rise to a diversity of arguments. The arguments range from globalisation as solely an economic force to globalisation as a term to describe the changes on social, political, cultural as well as economic levels (Giddens, 1999). In its broadest sense, globalisation can be thought of as 'the widening, deepening and speeding up of worldwide interconnectedness in all aspects of contemporary social life from the cultural to the criminal, the financial to the spiritual' (Held et al., 1999, p. 2). This interconnectedness can be seen in the increasing trend of companies to exploit international markets and procure internationally. Multinational companies have used the internet to integrate their organisations better and share knowledge both internally and with their alliance partners.

The key areas of electronic markets are:

1. Online retailing
2. Knowledge sharing and electronic collaboration
3. Electronic marketplaces and portals

Online retailing

Online retailing has gone from strength to strength. Although security issues are still a factor in adoption and use, consumers are increasingly turning to the internet, not only to make comparisons and find out information but also to make purchases. Despite the success of online retailing, the factors that enable a company to be successful online are still a topic of research. One of the main reasons for this because the internet has become crowded with companies offering similar products and services and it has become difficult for consumers to make comparisons. Companies often bundle products and services to make it difficult to compare on price alone. Developments in this area are also being driven by increasing consumer sophistication and expectations.

An organising framework for e-tailing strategies is presented by Florenthal and Shoham (Chapter 2) according to three levels of interaction based on product, process and partnership. The product level includes strategies of personalisation, customisation and pricing. The process level examines electronic agents that support customers in the online shopping experience. The partnership level focuses on strategies that develop long-term relationships with customers which result in loyalty, commitment and trust.

Noy and Dan-Gur focus specifically on recommender systems to enhance trust. Recommender systems generate and present recommendations on various items, locations, organisations and people. A multi-tiered design approach is presented that involves humans and software agents to overcome some of the limitations of existing designs.

The chapter by Swaid and Wigand examines the customer perspective of e-service quality. Most e-service evaluation instruments focus on the quality of the web site whereas Swaid and Wigand examine the entire shopping experience. A range of factors influence the perception of e-service quality and include: web site usability, information quality, service reliability, responsiveness, assurance and personalization.

McElhone and Yacyshyn investigate the value of web sites for consumers where companies have established brick and mortar offerings. They found that consumers value information and product descriptions provided on these web sites. However, the web sites need to be well designed and provide a breadth of information that is continually being updated.

Knowledge sharing and electronic collaboration

The internet has enabled new ways of sharing knowledge and has created an electronic knowledge market. The many forums and technologies for collaborating are examples of knowledge marketplaces and although financial transactions are not central, there is an exchange of knowledge that takes place.

Parssian and Standing suggest that despite the breadth of research on knowledge management the issue of knowledge quality has not been properly examined. Knowledge quality is influenced by information quality and the value of knowledge can be determined by the type of knowledge, its scarcity and depreciation rate and its quality. They outline a method for building knowledge value into organisational systems.

Electronic clusters that collaborate and share knowledge are investigated by Cripps. This leading researcher on the topic asks the question 'why do some e-clusters work and others don't?' From her research she has found that issues related to secrecy, security and low levels of IT sophistication are substantial barriers to e-collaboration.

Electronic marketplaces and portals

Stockdale examines the importance of community and social networking as a feature of electronic marketplaces. Using a New Zealand example, the chapter explores how a sense of belonging and community values can contribute to a sustainable consumer-to-consumer entity.

An often overlooked area within electronic markets is the business-to-business (B2B) sector. This is where organisations trade with other organisations as part of buying and selling within the supply chain. Trading between companies reflects substantial markets and the role of e-marketplaces and electronic auctions should not be underestimated. Many firms find it difficult to assess the potential benefits, costs and risks of participation during the e-marketplace selection process and also during participation. It has been acknowledged that decisions in the B2B arena are usually more complex than in the business-to-consumer (B2C) arena where decisions are more likely to be based on price and transaction costs. Trust, frequency of the transaction, complexity of the transaction, firm reputation, managerial skill, service, delivery scheduling and switching costs are some of the factors that make strategic decisions on firms' participation in B2B e-markets more difficult (Glassberg & Merhout, 2007). In an analysis of the adoption of an e-marketplace in the Australian beef industry it was found that social and political factors also played a significant role in determining levels of adoption (Driedonks et al., 2005). In particular, Driedonks et al., found loss of social capital, the nature of industry supply chain communication channels, and not recognising power brokers in the supply chain all had an impact on the adoption and success of the e-marketplace.

In addition to strategic decisions, firms have problems managing the tactical (Soh et al., 2006) and operational (Gengatharen & Standing, 2005) aspects of their participation in e-marketplaces. In B2B markets, sellers are often concerned about information transparency and, in particular, price transparency, since they fear this will reduce prices. Buyers are usually concerned about a lack of price transparency and if this is not available they typically require other compensatory benefits to participate (Soh et al., 2006). Price transparency is enabled by information technology (IT) mechanisms such as electronic catalogues with posted prices, electronic forward or reverse auctions or electronic price negotiation (Bichler et al., 2002). Firms also find pricing decisions for their products and services complex (Bergen et al., 2005). Although e-markets generally provide lower search costs than physical markets, decisions on competitive prices are confused by the tactics of sellers who may make frequent small price increases more often than small price decreases or can change their pricing in a random fashion so that it is difficult for buyers to determine their true prices (Oh & Lucas, 2006). Bakos et al., (2005) found that although the Internet promotes transparency in what can be termed the visible side of the market, for example commission rates, it can also make it more difficult for buyers to determine value for money. Oh & Lucas (2006) call for more qualitative research on the pricing tactics employed by managers in B2B e-marketplaces and their impact on sales volume and overall profitability because of the capabilities of interviews to uncover the complexity behind the decision making.

Connection to a B2B e-marketplace may involve a significant investment in hardware, software and employee training and this can impose significant switching costs for participants. In addition, buyers may be analysing sellers they have likely never dealt with before and information available in the electronic market may not reveal the size of the firm or its reputation, thus increasing risk (Glassberg & Merhout, 2007). Research has shown that many organisations entering B2B e-marketplaces are passive members that rarely conduct transactions (Gengatharen & Standing, 2005). Active trading in e-marketplaces by participants has been shown to depend upon a range of factors such as the scope of the individual marketplace, the motivations of the participating buyers/sellers and the IT and information system (IS) capabilities of participants (Stockdale & Standing, 2006).

Standing and Standing examine the relationship between strategy and structure in electronic markets. In particular, e-marketplace structures create operating environments that engender particular power relations and economic conditions. The factors to be considered are economic, relational, service and community based.

Decisions related to electronic market participation are usually influenced by institutional structures. These are the behaviours, norms and values created by forces in the environment and within organisations. They lead to decisions being taken because of legitimating forces rather than rational cost-benefit decision making. Standing, Sims and Standing review the ways that institutional theory impacts on electronic markets and electronic marketplace adoption and use.

Governments worldwide have moved into the electronic market space. Gengatharen examines the success and failure of regional portals, particularly in relation to the implications for small and medium enterprises. Studies conducted by Gengatharen highlight the importance of trust between those involved for the eventual success of regional portals.

This book should serve as an excellent resource for those interested in electronic markets. The authors are all leading researchers in their respective fields and are based in Australia, United States, Canada, Spain, New Zealand and Israel. The examples and cases used are all highly relevant to the theme of the book. Although electronic markets are dynamically changing, the principles approach used by the authors will ensure the material stays current for many years to come. Happy reading!

References

Bakos, J. Y. (1997). Reducing buyer search costs: implications for electronic marketplaces. *Management Science, 43*(12), 1676–1692.

Bakos, Y., Lucas, H., Oh, W., Simon, G., Viswanathan, S. & Weber, B. (2005). The impact of e-commerce on competition in the retail brokerage industry. *Information Systems Research, 16*(4), 352–371.

Bergen, M., Kauffman, R. & Lee, D. (2005). Beyond the hype of frictionless markets: evidence of heterogeneity in price rigidity on the internet. *Journal of Management Information Systems*, 22(2), 57–90.

Bichler, M., Kalagnanam, J., Katircioglu, K., King, A. J., Lawrence, R. D., Lee, H. S., Lin, G. Y. & Lu, Y. (2002). Applications of flexible pricing in business-to-business electronic commerce. *IBM Systems Journal*, 41(2), 287–302.

Clemons, E. K., Reddi, S. P. & Row, M. C. (1993). The impact of information technology on the organization of economic activity. The 'Move to the Middle' hypothesis. *Journal of Management Information Systems*, 10(2), 37–53.

Driedonks, C., Gregor, S., Wassenaar, A. & van Heck, E. (2005). Economic and social analysis of the adoption of B2B electronic marketplaces: a case study in the Australian beef industry. *International Journal of Electronic Commerce*, 9(3), 49–72.

Gengatharen, D. & Standing C. (2005). A framework to assess the factors affecting success or failure of the implementation of government-supported regional e-marketplaces for SMEs. *European Journal of Information Systems*, 14(4), 417–433.

Glassberg, B. C. & Merhout, J. W. (2007). Electronic markets hypothesis redux: where are we now? *Communications of the ACM*, 50(2), 51–55.

Giddens, A. (1999). *Runaway world: how globalisation is reshaping our lives*. London: Profile.

Held, D., McGrew, A., Goldblatt, D. & Perraton, J. (1999). *Global transformations: politics, economics and culture*. Cambridge: Polity Press.

Oh, W. & Lucas, H. C. (2006). Information technology and pricing decisions: price adjustments in online computer markets. *MIS Quarterly*, 30(4), 705–724.

Soh, C., Markus, M. L. & Goh, K. H. (2006). Electronic marketplaces and price transparency: strategy, information technology, and success. *MIS Quarterly*, 30(4), 705–724.

Stockdale, R. & Standing, C. (2006). An interpretive approach to evaluating information systems: a content, context, process framework. *European Journal of Operational Research*, 173(3), 701–1188.

Williamson, O. E. (1979). Transaction cost economics: the governance of contractual relations. *Journal of Law and Economics*, 22(2), 233–261.

Williamson, O. E. (1975). *Markets and hierarchies, analysis and antitrust implications: a study in the economics of internal organization*. New York: Free Press.

Part 1
Online Retailing

2
Matching E-tailing Strategies to Customers' Behaviour: Three Levels of Interaction

Bela Florenthal and Aviv Shoham

Introduction

Several frameworks have been suggested to describe the range of business strategies that companies may employ in the fast-evolving electronic marketplace. These have included descriptions of strategies such as the use of recommendation agents and e-customisation (Ansari et al., 2000; Ansari & Mela, 2003; Häubl & Murray, 2003). However, these frameworks have not distinguished between strategies that are specific to e-tailing and those which may be used in a more general business context, for example by manufacturers who have an online presence. This distinction is important because innovative and unique e-tailing modes of operation (exemplified by companies such as Priceline.com) have recently emerged to improve competitiveness in this volatile market (Kalyanam & McIntyre, 2002; Yadav & Varadarajan, 2005).

An organising framework is proposed to better understand how e-tailers can compete with e-manufactures (manufactures that have online stores). The framework suggests three levels of interaction – product, process and partnership – to assess online strategies. At the product level, personalisation of product attributes based on customer preferences is addressed. At the process level, recommendation agents are evaluated. Finally, at the partnership level, long-term relationships with customers are examined.

The framework addresses not only e-business strategies but also the preferences and perceptions of customers. The hierarchical structure of the framework makes it possible to examine e-business strategies across the three levels. For example, a certain product-related strategy (e.g., introducing a new product category) might require a specific process-related strategy (e.g., redesigning the search engine). The product level is the primary level, embedded in the process level, which, in turn, is embedded in the partnership level.

This chapter is structured in four sections. In the first section, the differences between e-tailers and e-manufacturers are discussed in terms of online strategies. In the second section, the proposed organising framework is presented, which provides a way of examining online interactions between e-tailers and their customers. In the third section, e-tailing strategies and the perceptions and preferences of customers for these strategies at each level of interaction is examined. The chapter concludes with a discussion and suggestions for new research opportunities and lessons for practitioners with respect to the proposed framework.

E-tailer strategies vs. e-manufacturer strategies

With the introduction of the internet, many manufacturers who used to sell their products only through retailers now sell through their web sites directly to customers (Varadarajan & Yadav, 2002). At the same time, some off-line retailers have established an online presence (i.e., multi-channel strategies) and some new modes of e-tailing have emerged (e.g., Shopping.com and mySimon.com) (Kalyanam & McIntyre, 2002; Yadav & Varadarajan, 2005). To maintain their competitiveness, some e-tailers have offered customers strategies that are different from those of online manufacturers. For instance, mySimon.com offers price comparisons across manufacturers. Compared to e-manufacturers, e-tailers are usually able to offer their customers a greater variety of product alternatives, a wider range of prices, and more product-related information. E-manufacturers, on the other hand, can offer other advantages, such as the opportunity to customize products, that e-tailers cannot offer.

Multi-channel retailers (retailers with both on – and off-line presence) have also built their competitive advantage in recent years. Blockbuster, for instance, offers mail-in rentals and in-store exchange of movies. However, the number of e-tailers (retailers with online presence only) has been increasing and they have developed unique ways of delivering value to customers (i.e., movie downloads). These e-tailers not only compete with e-manufacturers and with multi-channel retailers (i.e., Netflix.com is in direct competition with Blockbuster).

The proposed framework classifies e-business strategies into three business-customer interaction levels but focuses on e-tailers and their ability to compete with other businesses on each level. The three levels of interaction and the hierarchical structure of the framework are presented next.

An organising framework for e-business strategies

The framework organizes e-business strategies into three interaction levels and suggests a hierarchical structure of dependencies among the strategies across these levels (Figure 2.1). For example, product personalization strategies are categorized into a product level, but influence the strategies of electronic agents, whose activities are categorized at the process level.

The three levels of interaction

As illustrated in Figure 2.1, the interactions between e-businesses and customers can be categorized into three levels: (a) product, (b) process,

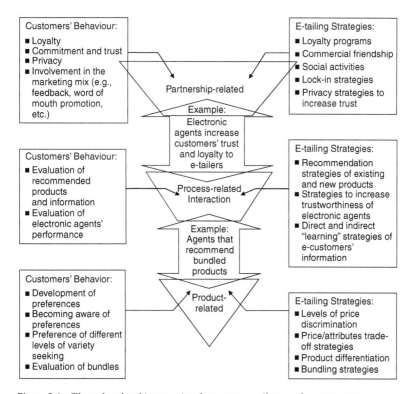

Figure 2.1 Three levels of interaction between e-tailers and e-customers

and (c) partnership. The product level includes strategies of product personalization/customization that match customer preferences. Physical products, services, and information can be personalized/customized as separate products, bundles, or both. Price strategies are included in this level, as price may be considered an attribute of the product.

The process level includes e-business strategies that facilitate product-level activities. Different types of electronic agents that assist customers in the online shopping process are classified into this level. For example, an attribute-based search agent that helps customers sort through product alternatives in a short period of time is considered a process-level strategy. Customers' perceptions of information provided by the electronic agents and their perceptions of the agents are also included in this level.

The partnership level focuses on e-business strategies that develop long-term relationships with customers and result in loyalty, commitment, and trust. Different types of partnerships can be estab-lished with customers, depending on the amount of information they are willing to share. Customers who share their preferences, for example, are more likely to develop a stronger partnership with e-businesses than those who do not. A weaker partnership can be formed with customers through indirect collection of information about their past purchases or browsing patterns. The relationships between the e-business strat-egies are examined through the hierarchical structure of the framework depicted in Figure 2.1.

The hierarchical structure

An inverse triangle with connecting arrows between interaction levels is proposed as the framework's structure (Figure 2.1). This structure serves several purposes. First, it suggests a hierarchy among the three levels. The inverse triangle starts with product-level strategies as its base. The process level is built on the product level and the partnership level is at the top of the triangle relating directly to the process level and indirectly to the product level. For example, customers can customize and evaluate product alternatives (product level) using recommendation agents (process level). Repeat purchases and other product-related activities using recommen-dation agents (i.e., reading reviews by other customers) could increase a customer's commitment and loyalty to that e-business (partnership level). Thus, each level of interaction depends on the lower levels.

Second, the structure suggests that each level of interaction involves additional shopping activities that are not directly related to the lower level. At the process level, for instance, customers can view reviews or ratings by other customers, which broadens the basis for their interaction with the e-business. This level draws in recreational shoppers, who have no intention to purchase, but want to broaden their product-related knowledge. Similarly, partnership-level interactions are based initially on e-customer activities at the process level, but also involve broader shopping-related activities, such as electronic word-of-mouth.

Finally, the arrows connecting levels of interaction are bi-directional and indicate that each level enhances the possible interactions of the related level/s and benefits from interactions with those levels. For example, process-level interactions can benefit from partnership activities, such as loyalty programs and product activities, such as past purchases of personalized products. On the other hand, process-level interactions (e.g., using recommendation agents) can enhance product-level interactions (e.g., product customization) and partnership-level interactions (e.g., loyalty) when e-customers perceive the recommendations to be reliable. The structure suggests that the partnership level does not have a direct relationship with the product level; the two levels are connected through the process level. In most cases, partnership activities, such as loyalty shown through repeat purchases, involve some process-level activities (e.g., the use of recommendation agents) although they relate to product-level activities, such as evaluation of the product.

E-business strategies and e-customers' perceptions and preferences that relate to the three levels of interaction are presented next. The competitive advantage of e-tailing is examined in relation to e-manufacturers at each level of interaction. Relationships of strategies across levels are discussed.

Product-related interactions

The literature identifies a variety of product-related strategies that can be used in the marketplace. E-tailers can employ some of them to compete better with e-manufacturers. Table 2.1 summarizes the definitions of e-tailing strategies and gives examples for preference elicitation, price discrimination and price/attribute trade-offs, product differentiation and bundling.

Product personalization strategy based on preference elicitation

Customers do not always have stable or well-developed preferences, and, even if they do, they may not be aware of them (Simonson, 2005). Simonson (2005) identified four customer groups based on their

Table 2.1   Summary of product-related e-tailing strategies

Subject	References	Concepts Related to E-tailing	Examples of E-tailing Strategies
Preference elicitation and product personalization strategy	Simonson (2005)	Four groups of customers identified: (a) Group 1: poorly developed, unstable preferences and poor awareness of them (b) Group 2: poorly developed, unstable preferences and good awareness of them (c) Group 3: stable, well developed preferences and poor awareness of them (d) Group 4: stable, well developed preferences and good awareness of them	(a) Group 1 and 4: offer large assortment of personalized product alternatives. (b) Group 2 and 3: do not offer personalized product alternatives.
Price discrimination and price/ attributes trade-offs	Murthi & Sarkar (2003)	Three types of price discrimination strategies identified: (a) First degree – different prices to different individual customers for the same product (b) Second degree – different models of the same product for different prices (c) Third degree – different prices to different segments	(a) First degree – e-mail personalized prices (e.g., e-coupons) for a limited time period. (b) Second degree – offer personalized high price/high quality alternatives separately from other alternatives. (c) Third degree – within a segment, expose customers to other customers' choices of high price/high quality alternatives.

Continued

Table 2.1   Continued

Subject	References	Concepts Related to E-tailing	Examples of E-tailing Strategies
Product differentiation	Tirole (1988); Murthi & Sarkar (2003)	Two types: (a) Horizontal – product attribute differentiation (b) Vertical – price discrimination	(a) Horizontal: • In 'product' space, allow customers to personalize attributes of technologically advanced products that correspond to product performance. • In 'information' space, offer customers personalized information that corresponds to their involvement. (b) Vertical: see price discrimination strategies above.
Price vs. product bundling	Stremersch & Tellis (2002); Bakos & Brynjolfsson 1999	Differentiated between: (a) Price bundling – two or more products offered as a package at a discounted price (b) Product bundling – integrated package of two or more products offered at a higher price than when sold separately	(a) Price bundling – offer unlimited possibilities of price bundles across product categories, manufacturers, and brands. (b) Product bundling – offer integrated packages of products, services, and information.
Pure vs. mixed bundling	Stremersch & Tellis (2002)	Differentiated between: (a) Pure bundling – offering only the bundle and not each product separately (b) Mixed bundling – offering the bundle and each product separately	(a) Pure bundling – offer personalized packages of product, services, and related information. (b) Mixed bundling – offer personalized packages at price discounts *and* each product at regular price.

Continued

Table 2.1 Continued

Subject	References	Concepts Related to E-tailing	Examples of E-tailing Strategies
E-customers' perception of bundles	Stremersch & Tellis (2002); Yadav & Monroe (1993); Yadav (1994); Harris (1997)	E-customers' perceptions and evaluations of bundles: (a) Price perceptions – customers perceive price as a loss and savings as a gain (b) Product perceptions – customers perceive product quality based on product combinations (c) Three-stage evaluation process – • Scanning – determine which product alternatives are included in the bundle • Anchor selection – select a product alternative that is most important for the evaluation • Anchoring and adjusting – other alternatives are evaluated according to the anchor selection. Upward and downward adjustments are made	(a) Price perceptions – • A price bundle: present one price bundle and not a breakdown of prices. • A price promotion bundle (discounted price): present separate savings and not an aggregate saving of the bundle. (b) Product perceptions – when offered price promotion bundles customers might perceive the quality of the products in the bundle as low. (c) Three-stage evaluation process – offer bundles of same quality products as the anchoring and adjusting stage can devalue the quality of a bundle with various levels of quality.

preference awareness and stability. Not every group can be approached using a product personalization strategy (Table 2.1). When using a product personalization strategy to target Groups 1 and 4, e-tailers usually can outperform e-manufacturers when they carry a large assortment of product options in a single product category. This strategy may not be successful with customers in Group 2, who need first to develop their preferences, or with Group 3 who are inclined to make emotion-laden purchases and end up dissatisfied with them (Simonson, 2005).

Price discrimination and price/attribute trade-offs

Online price discrimination strategies (Varadarajan & Yadav, 2002) can be classified into three degrees (Murthi & Sarkar, 2003). First-degree discrimination strategies can be suitable for customers in Groups 1, 2 and 3. Because these groups have not yet developed their preferences and/or are not aware of them, they will be more inclined to accept a one-time, personalized price offer from a trustworthy e-business (Garbarino & Johnson, 1999; Simonson, 2005). This is especially true for passive deal-prone consumers who will accept price promotions without much consideration for low-price products (DelVecchio, 2005). Second-degree strategies are more suitable for customers in Group 4, where retailers can capitalize on a customer's preference for high-priced, high-quality product options. The first – and second-degree strategies can provide a competitive advantage for e-tailers only when they offer personalized price/product options that e-manufacturers do not offer.

Third-degree strategies can be used with Group 2 customers who are receptive to recommendations from others purchasing similar items (Simonson, 2005). Amazon is an example of the use of this technique. It constantly exposes customers to the purchasing decisions of other customers with the same profile during the shopping process. E-tailers are usually more competitive than e-manufacturers with respect to this strategy. For the same product option, e-manufacturers usually have less heterogeneous data about a customer's purchases (brand variety) than e-tailers do. Therefore, they seldom provide customers with such information because they might be perceived as unreliable when promoting their high-price products.

Horizontal product differentiation

As indicated in Table 2.1, retailers can practice horizontal and vertical product differentiation strategies online. Vertical product differentiation is considered to be a price discrimination strategy because it offers different product/price combinations. Horizontal product differentiation strategies can be practiced in 'product' or 'information' space (Murthi & Sarkar, 2003; Varadarajan & Yadav, 2002).

With reference to 'product' space, one option is to differentiate products based on the trade-off between risk and return (e.g., existing vs. alpha version of a product). Customers are inclined to prefer a high-risk, high-performance product alternative to a low-risk, low-performance alternative if they are highly involved in the product category or if they can observe similar purchases by other customers (Simonson et al., 2004). Capitalizing on this, e-tailers can outperform e-manufacturers by offering a larger variety of high-risk, higher performance alternatives to Groups 2 and 4 (more involved customers), and low-risk, lower performance alternatives to Groups 1 and 3 (less involved). For customers in Group 2 they can use the 'information' space to provide evidence of high-risk, high-performance purchases by similar customers.

Bundling strategies

With the development of the internet, e-businesses have discovered the almost unlimited possibilities of bundling strategies that can be offered to meet customers' preferences. In this section, bundling strategies will be differentiated in terms of product bundles as opposed to price bundles and mixed bundles as opposed to pure bundles. This section will conclude with a discussion of customers' perceptions of the various bundling strategies.

Price bundling and product bundling strategies

Stremersch & Tellis (2002) differentiate between price and product bundling strategies (Table 2.1). E-tailers can be more competitive than e-manufacturers in offering customers personalized price bundles, as they can create bundles across product categories, manufacturers and brands. For instance, airlines usually limit themselves to only a few hotel chains and car rental companies whereas Priceline.com can offer customers a wider variety of packages.

With reference to product bundling strategies, e-tailers will usually be less competitive than e-manufacturers in offering personalized bundles of physical goods. This integration process is usually a manufacturing decision (Stremersch & Tellis, 2002). However, e-tailers can be more competitive than e-manufacturers in offering personalized services and bundles of information goods (Bakos & Brynjolfsson, 1999). Offering personalized information/service bundles, even when these are provided free, can be a useful strategy for e-businesses when customer information is gathered through registration, preference elicitation or browsing patterns (Ansari & Mela, 2003; Murthi & Sarkar, 2003). Customers' use of information bundles (e.g., personalized e-mails) could also increase purchases of physical goods (Ansari & Mela, 2003).

Hybrid bundles of physical goods, information goods and services can be personalized to suit a customer's interests, hobbies, and ad hoc needs. For example, a monthly subscription package of mail-in movie rentals, coupled with access to online movie previews and e-mail notification of special product offers (e.g., CDs, MP3s, books and T-shirts) can be personalized to different segments so that higher profits are earned by the e-business (Bakos & Brynjolfsson, 1999; Stremersch & Tellis, 2002). The package can be modified when customer preferences change or new ad hoc needs emerge (e.g., substituting music downloads with software downloads).

Pure bundling and mixed bundling strategies

Stremersch & Tellis (2002) also differentiate between pure and mixed bundling strategies (Table 2.1). In highly competitive environments, mixed bundling strategies are more effective (Stremersch & Tellis, 2002). To better differentiate themselves in the marketplace, e-tailers are able to offer unique product bundles at price discounts that e-manufacturers cannot match, in addition to offering the products separately at a regular price (e.g., book bundles at Amazon.com).

Evaluation of bundles

Customers' perceptions of and preferences for different bundle types should determine not only the way in which e-businesses present the prices and savings of the bundles but also what products should be bundled together (Table 2.1). For example, customers may perceive the quality of a new product as low if it is a brand extension of the more established product in the bundle (Harris, 1997).

Yadav (1994) identified a three-stage bundle evaluation process (Table 2.1), which allows customers to evaluate more complex or larger scale bundles. E-businesses should be sensitive to the processes that customers use in anchoring and adjustment, as a bundle that has a strong anchor with moderate additional alternatives is likely to be evaluated as a poorer bundle. However, this process is not symmetrical. A weak anchor with moderate alternatives does not improve the overall bundle evaluation as much (Harris, 1997; Yadav, 1994). E-tailers that compete for market share of vacation packages should anchor themselves

Table 2.2   Summary of process-related e-tailing strategies

Subject	References	Concepts Related to E-tailing	Examples of E-tailing Strategies
Electronic agents	Häubl & Trifts (2000); Häubl & Murray (2003); Ansari et al., (2000)	Can be defined as: (a) Shopping aids (b) Recommendation aids (c) Personal assistants	Offer shopping aids to: (a) Compare prices across online stores (e.g., MySimon.com); (b) Find products within an on-line store (e.g., Amazon.com); (c) Provide recommendations for new or existing products (e.g., RealMovieCritic. com); (d) Assist in the task of product personalization (e.g., Landsend.com).
Direct and indirect 'learning'	Murthi & Sarkar (2003); Ansari et al., (2000)	(a) Direct 'learning' – asking customers to provide personal information (e.g., name, address, e-mail) and attribute-based preferences (b) Indirect 'learning' – can be done in several ways: • Learning individual customer's past behaviour • Aggregating data across customers (e.g., collaborative filtering) • Using both individual level and aggregate level information	(a) Direct 'learning': • Subscriptions generate personal information from customers. • Offer customers a list of attributes to choose from for their purchases. (b) Indirect 'learning': • Individual level – 'learning' – customers' past purchases, the price paid, and browsing behaviour. • Aggregate level – predicting customers' preferences based on past behaviour of similar customers.
Variety seeking preferences	Simonson (2005)	Three levels of behaviour: (a) No variety seeking – prefer the same product for each purchase	(a) No variety seeking – personalize the same offer based on customers' past purchases.

Continued

Table 2.2   Continued

Subject	References	Concepts Related to E-tailing	Examples of E-tailing Strategies
		(b) Moderate variety seeking – switch among a small group of products (c) High variety seeking – switch among a large group of products	(b) Moderate variety seeking – offer a personalized list of alternatives where customers' past purchases are listed first. (c) High variety seeking – offer a large list of alternatives personalized by price, attributes, brands, or other filtering information.
E-customers' evaluation of recommended alternatives	Häubl & Murray (2003); Huffman & Kahn (1998); Cooke et al., (2002)	Includes: (a) Attribute-based evaluation process (b) Recommendation of unfamiliar products	(a) Attribute-based evaluation process – influence the attributes customers consider in their evaluation process. (b) Recommendation of unfamiliar products – promote unfamiliar products when mixing them with familiar products.
E-customers' evaluation of electronic agents	Gershoff et al., (2001); Gershoff et al., (2003); Bechwati & Xia (2003)	Includes: (a) Agent's diagnosticity – determined by how much the agents provided variation in past recommendations (e.g., movie ratings) and how much the agent's past recommendations are in agreement with e-customer's evaluations (b) Agent's ability to save customers cognitive effort	(a) Agent's diagnosticity – agent's reliability can be increased when it makes more extreme recommendations and incorporates customers past opinions in its recommendations. (b) Agent's ability to save customers cognitive effort – provide customers with cues about the types and the number of databases the agent is searching through.

to the most important alternative in their bundle. If the anchoring alternative is the hotel chain, for example, they might want to match the offer of the car rental to the perceived quality of the hotel chain.

Process-related interactions

The process level focuses on the methods e-businesses use to ensure a match between customers' preferences and product offerings. E-tailers can successfully compete with e-manufacturers when employing electronic agents to aid customers in their purchasing decisions. Customers' evaluations of recommendations and electronic agents are presented for this level. Table 2.2 summarizes e-tailing strategies and customers' perceptions at the process level.

Electronic agents

Electronic agents have become popular for different shopping tasks online. They are mostly used to assist customers with making purchasing decisions and/or conducting information searches (Alba et al., 1997; Ansari et al., 2000; Häubl & Trifts, 2000). In employing electronic agents, e-tailers can be more competitive than e-manufacturers, in providing product-related information (e.g., price comparisons) across brands, manufacturers, and/or web stores. In order for electronic agents to perform these shopping tasks, they need first to 'learn' a customer's preferences (Häubl & Murray, 2003; Murthi & Sarkar, 2003).

Direct and indirect 'learning' methods

Electronic agents can 'learn' customer information directly, indirectly, or as a combination of both (Ansari et al., 2000; Murthi & Sarkar, 2003). The more relevant the information these electronic agents collect, the more appropriately they can assist consumers with their purchases (Ansari et al., 2000). In direct 'learning', the agents need to know the customer's attribute-based preferences in order to recommend relevant product alternatives (Ansari et al., 2000). Therefore, these agents are more suitable for customers that have stable preferences and are aware of them (Group 4) and less suitable for customers who cannot express their preferences (Groups 1–3; Ansari et al., 2000). Additionally, agents frequently present a limited number of attributes, because (a) customers tend to consider a small number of attributes for each product category (Häubl & Murray, 2003; Huffman & Kahn, 1998) and (b) the agents need to find common attributes, which could be few in number, across product alternatives (Häubl & Murray, 2003).

When customers have undeveloped preferences, are not aware of them and/or refuse to reveal them, an indirect 'learning' method can be employed (Häubl & Murray, 2003; Murthi & Sarkar, 2003; Simonson, 2005). Indirect 'learning' of customer preferences can be done at the individual and aggregate levels (Table 2.2). At the individual level (e.g., past purchases) 'learning' customers' preferences indirectly is 'fast, accurate and unobtrusive to the customers' (Murthi & Sarkar, 2003, p. 1353). The drawback is that data are collected within a single web store and the reason why customers prefer one web store to another, for instance, cannot be examined (Murthi & Sarkar, 2003).

At the aggregate level, e-businesses can predict customers' product and browsing patterns based on the behaviour of similar customers (Ansari et al., 2000; Murthi & Sarkar, 2003). However, when customer heterogeneity is not adequately taken into account, predicting customer preferences using aggregate data can be problematic (Ansari et al., 2000; Murthi & Sarkar, 2003). In addition, this method cannot provide the customer with any explanation to support the recommendations (Ansari et al., 2000; Murthi & Sarkar, 2003). This can reduce customer confidence in the agent and its recommendations (Bechwati & Xia, 2003; Cooke et al., 2002; Häubl & Murray, 2003). A more sophisticated method that uses the individual *and* aggregate levels of 'learning' was developed by Ansari et al., (2002) to overcome some of the problems mentioned above.

E-tailers can increase their competitiveness compared to e-manufacturers by using indirect and direct 'learning' agents. Usually, e-tailers have access to larger aggregate data sets than e-manufacturers and can therefore provide better suggestions for their customers. They can also provide customers with comparative information on a larger scale than e-manufacturers can (e.g., attribute-based comparison of brands across manufacturers). The customers will determine the range and the type of options that are recommended, based on the strategies they use to seek options.

Variety seeking preferences

Different strategies can be used to cater to a customer's specific level of variety seeking behavior (Table 2.2). Customers who do not have a preference to seek variety can be classified as Group 4 in terms of preference formation (well-developed/highly aware). E-tailers can compete for this segment by offering them the same products using one of the price discrimination strategies. Customers who have a moderate preference for variety seeking can be also be classified in Group 4, but their preferences may not be successfully predicted by e-businesses (Simonson, 2005). To compete for this segment, e-tailers might use electronic agents that suggest a few unfamiliar alternatives (e.g., brands) that were purchased by similar customers, coupled with familiar alternatives that were purchased in the past.

Customers with a high preference for variety seeking can be classified as Groups 1, 2 or 3 in terms of preference formation (undeveloped and/ or unaware of preferences). E-tailers can compete for these segments by using electronic agents that offer unique bundles of product alternatives ('product' space) and product information ('information' space). For example, Priceline.com allows customers to personalize a list of alternatives based on price and dates. In addition, customers can receive information about places to eat, shop, or tour during their vacation. The large number of options the search agent provides, coupled with detailed information for each option, can help variety-seeking customers develop, or become more aware of, their preferences.

Customer evaluation of recommended alternatives

The form in which information is presented affects the formation of customers' preferences, product evaluations and purchasing decisions (Cooke et al., 2002; Häubl & Murray, 2003). In terms of product evaluation, customers most frequently use attribute-based rather than alternative-based processes to evaluate products (Häubl & Murray, 2003; Huffman & Kahn, 1998). An attribute-based evaluation process may be of great service to customers in Groups 1, 2 and 3 (undeveloped and/or unaware of preferences; Huffman & Kahn, 1998; Simonson, 2005). The attribute-based process can help these customers learn or develop their preferences to reduce the number of options they evaluate. It may result in increased satisfaction with the process and a greater readiness to make a purchase (Huffman & Kahn, 1998). When customers use this process, they also increase their perception of covering all possible options in the consideration set (Huffman & Kahn, 1998).

Attribute-based recommendation agents can help e-tailers increase their competitiveness when they reduce the need for customers to search for pre-purchase information across web stores (Häubl & Trifts, 2000) and can influence the attributes customers consider when making a purchase (Häubl & Murray, 2003). Customers are more likely to consider the suggested attributes if a rationale is provided, which will further reduce their desire to extend the search (Cooke et al., 2002; Häubl & Murray, 2003).

Selling new or unfamiliar products is a challenge for e-businesses (Cooke et al., 2002). Customers usually do not have well-established preferences and thus may rely heavily on the agent's recommendation (Cooke et al., 2002; Simonson, 2005). On the other hand, customers may be averse to unfamiliar recommendations that an agent suggests (Cooke et al., 2002). The agent usually provides customers with additional information about these products to reduce this aversion. But when information about unfamiliar options creates a contrast between familiar and unfamiliar choices, a lower evaluation of the unfamiliar options could result (Cooke et al., 2002). In order to overcome this problem, agents should provide a mix of unfamiliar and familiar products in addition to the information about unfamiliar products (Cooke et al., 2002).

Customers' evaluation of electronic agents

The reliability and trustworthiness of agents have been researched, as were customers' satisfaction with agents' performance. Table 2.2 summarizes possible e-tailing strategies to improve the customer perception of agents' diagnosticity and their ability to save cognitive effort.

Customers usually evaluate agents based on their past performance because agents might contradict each other in providing recommendations (Cooke et al., 2002; Gershoff et al., 2001; Gershoff et al., 2003). An agent's diagnosticity is of particular importance to customers when unfamiliar products are recommended. Agents are considered more diagnostic and hence more reliable when they provide less uniform recommendations (West & Broniarczyk, 1998) and when they provide recommendations that are in agreement with a customer's past opinions (Cooke et al., 2002; Gershoff et al., 2001). In becoming more competitive, e-tailers may need to have better information about a customer's past opinions (especially the extreme ones) than e-manufacturers, so that they can calibrate their recommendation agents better (Gershoff et al., 2003).

Customers also evaluate agents on how much cognitive effort the agents can save them. When searching for product information, customers usually make trade-offs between the cognitive effort they exercise and the accuracy of the information they receive (Bechwati & Xia, 2003). Therefore, customers will be more satisfied with an agent that saves them significant cognitive effort without compromising on the quality of the information (Bechwati & Xia, 2003). E-tailers can increase their competitive advantage and customer satisfaction when designing agents that signal the extensive search that they have performed (e.g., number of databases) and provide highly accurate information.

Partnership-related interactions

The third level of the framework focuses on short – and long-term e-business strategies that increase the trust, loyalty and commitment of new and existing customers. It is named the partnership level because customers are encouraged to participate in operation-based activities of the e-businesses (e.g., word of mouth, feedback). The Customer Relationship Management (CRM) literature identifies three levels of partnership-based interactions. These are presented below, and the relationships to the previous two levels (product and process) are discussed.

Three levels of partnership

'Customers vary in their relationships with a firm on a continuum from transactional to highly relational bonds' (Garbarino & Johnson, 1999, p. 70). Transactional customers buy products or services without tying themselves to the business physically, mentally or emotionally (Garbarino & Johnson, 1999; Noble & Phillips, 2004). They may, for instance, refuse to join a loyalty program, and forgo the opportunities to receive coupons via e-mail.

Relational or collaborative customers are physically, mentally or emotionally involved with the business they buy from (Bettencourt, 1997; Garbarino & Johnson, 1999; Price & Arnould, 1999). Collaborative customers, for example, might promote an e-business through electronic word-of-mouth (Bettencourt, 1997) or give suggestions on how to improve its operation. Few customers are purely transactional (Garbarino & Johnson, 1999); most are collaborative to various degrees (Garbarino & Johnson, 1999; Noble & Phillips, 2004). Therefore, e-businesses need to personalize their customer relationship programs to accommodate different degrees of collaboration. Berry (1995) suggested three levels of partnership-based interactions (basic, medium, and high). Table 2.3 summarizes the e-tailing strategies that can be offered at each partnership level.

Basic level partnership

At the lowest level of commitment, e-tailers can increase customers' repeat purchases and satisfaction through unique loyalty programs that offer more tangible benefits (e.g., points for online purchases) than e-manufacturers. Customers might not commit to a program that requires a substantial effort (e.g., a detailed registration form) and provides limited tangible benefits (e.g., small price discounts; Noble & Phillips, 2004). Customers who are highly satisfied with an e-tailer's loyalty program might become medium-level partners (Rodgers et al., 2005).

Table 2.3 Summary of partnership-related e-tailing strategies

Subject	References	Concepts Related to E-tailing	Examples of E-tailing Strategies
Basic level	Noble & Phillips (2004); Garbarino & Johnson (1999); Bettencourt (1997)	This level includes: (a) Loyalty programs (b) Tangible benefits (c) Overall satisfaction	(a) Simplify the initiation of loyalty programs (e.g., fewer stages of online registration). (b) Offer substantial tangible benefits (e.g., less frequent but more substantial price discounts). (c) Well-planned loyalty programs increase overall customer satisfaction with the purchase.
Medium level	Noble & Phillips (2004); Ansari & Mela (2003); Price & Arnould (1999); Garbarino & Johnson (1999) Harris & Goode (2004)	This level includes: (a) Commitment and loyalty (b) Social bonds and commercial friendship (c) Customer's trust in retailer's activities	• Send personalized e-mails that reflect customers' preferences and interests. • Recognize customers as an elite or preferred group. • Offer online social interaction with the e-tailer (e.g., feedback) and other customers (e.g., chat rooms) • Establish trust by offering substantial benefits through the loyalty programs.
High level	Noble & Phillips (2004); Garbarino & Johnson (1999); Harris & Goode (2004); Hoffman et al., (1999); Murthi & Sarkar (2003)	This level includes: (a) Enduring trust and commitment (b) Privacy policies	• Use lock-in strategies (e.g., ask for personal information) to increase switching costs. • Provide customers with higher control over their personal information. • Make customers aware of the different uses they make of their private information.

Medium-level partnership.   Customers at the medium level have developed some commitment and loyalty to the e-business. Developing social bonds with customers and enhancing their trust in the e-tailer's unique activities can deepen medium-level partnerships (Tsai et al., 2006). A unique online newsletter that is personalized to customers' interests is an example of strengthening medium-level partnerships. However, over-communicativeness might lead to the customer being annoyed and to the termination of the relationship (Noble & Phillips, 2004).

Developing commercial friendships with customers, which include self-disclosure activities, cooperation, and repeated social interactions can also be used (Price & Arnould, 1999). A commercial friendship can be practiced online (e.g., feedback and chat rooms). Many customers might feel comfortable giving feedback to e-businesses and networking with other customers online (Kalyanam & McIntyre, 2002). E-tailers can foster stronger commercial friendships with customers compared to e-manufacturers when they set up unique social interactions among them. An example might be the online party for the launch of the new Harry Potter book.

Medium-level activities should increase customers' trust in the partnership (Garbarino & Johnson, 1999). Establishing trust with e-businesses is particularly important because physical contact is impossible (Harris & Goode, 2004). Transaction uncertainty can be reduced if an e-tailer is perceived as trustworthy (Grabner-Kraeuter, 2002). E-tailers can lose customer trust and loyalty when they offer hollow loyalty programs and customers may feel 'cheated or deceived by the benefits of the relationship program' (Noble & Phillips, 2004, p. 297). Once trust is established, customers can become higher level partners (Berry, 1995; Noble & Phillips, 2004).

High-level partnership

Trust can lead to higher levels of loyalty and a commitment to a relationship (Garbarino & Johnson, 1999; Ha, 2004; Harris & Goode, 2004). However, to establish enduring trust online, privacy policies need to meet customer preferences. Table 2.3 presents examples of e-tailing strategies that can meet these preferences (e.g., increased perception of privacy) and thus establish enduring trust.

Two online privacy issues may concern customers: (1) how e-businesses use private information about customers; and (2) whether e-businesses sell customer information to other organizations. E-businesses usually record customers' browsing patterns (Hoffman et al., 1999). Though the information can be used to make personalized recommendations, customers might perceive this activity as a breach of privacy and feel that this information can be used against them (Hoffman et al., 1999; Noble & Phillips, 2004). For instance, price discounts might not be offered to customers, who usually search for premium products. E-businesses also view customers' personal information as an asset and hence may trade it with other e-businesses (Kalyanam & McIntyre, 2002; Laudon, 1996). To increase customer trust in online activities, e-tailers might develop innovative privacy policies (e.g., compensate customers for selling their private information). These policies can increase the perception that customers have of their own control over their personal information, might provide a competitive advantage over e-manufacturers and can increase switching costs.

Discussion

Based on an extensive review of e-business literature, this chapter presents an organizing structure of competitive strategies e-tailers can practice in response to customer expectations and e-manufacturers' capabilities. The organizing framework suggests a three-level hierarchical structure that associates concepts within and across levels. For example, association between price discrimination and price bundling can be seen within the product level. A relationship between preference formation (product level) and indirect 'learning' strategies (process level) can be recognized. This representation of e-tailing strategies opens possibilities for new research opportunities and new modes of e-tailing practices.

New research opportunities

Within the product level, researchers have examined bundles of goods separately from bundles of information. This framework suggests that bundles of goods and information may be valued by customers. Potential research could involve the examination of (a) customers' willingness to pay and (b) competitive price differentiation and personalization strategies of these online bundles. A research opportunity across levels could be to assess customers' perceptions of recommendation agents (second-level interaction) that deliver mixed bundles of goods and information (first-level interaction). So far, researchers have examined recommendation agents either for goods or for information, but many e-tailers deliver mixed bundles.

In relation to the process level, customers' perception of and preference for the different 'learning' strategies (direct vs. indirect) have been under researched. Customers might prefer direct over indirect 'learning' of their preferences so they can have more control over their privacy. Furthermore, these second-level preferences may affect third-level customers' trust and commitment to e-tailers. Thus, examining customers' preferences for the type of learning e-tailers use and their impact on trust and commitment are additional future research avenues.

In relation to the partnership level, few scholars have evaluated the competitive advantage provided by lock-in strategies that are based on the amount of information customers reveal to e-tailers. Different lock-in strategies might result in different levels of commitment. Assessing perceptions of these strategies and their impact on commitment could be a contribution to the existing marketing literature.

E-tailers can offer customers different levels of privacy (Murthi & Sarkar, 2003). Research could examine how the levels of privacy affect customers trust in and commitment to e-tailers. In connecting the process and the partnership levels, customers' perceived control over privacy could be assessed in terms of their preferences for direct or indirect 'learning' strategies.

Lessons for practitioners

The framework presented in this chapter describes competitive strategies e-tailers can use within and across levels of interaction to leverage e-consumers' perceptions and internet technologies (Figure 2.1 and Tables 2.1–2.3). Understanding how e-tailing strategies on one interaction level influence customer responses on other interaction levels could enhance the relationship between e-tailers and their customers. For example, e-tailers who provide information about the search process used by recommendation agents could enhance customers' perceptions of the accuracy of the product information (product level), reduce search activities (process level) and increase e-tailers' trustworthiness (partnership level). Another example is of e-tailers allowing customers to choose the method of 'learning' they prefer. This strategy refers to the process level, but may impact customers' willingness to commit and form a stronger partnership with e-tailers. At the product level, this may increase customer satisfaction with product options that were personalized according to their preferred method.

Limitations

Although the review of the literature related to the online marketplace has not been exhaustive, many papers related to online research were examined. The proposed framework organizes existing and potential e-business strategies into three levels of interaction emphasizing the competitiveness that can be secured by using these e-tailing strategies. Particular attention has been given to customer perceptions and preferences in relation to these strategies.

It can be argued that sometimes a clear distinction between the three levels is hard to maintain. Even so, the hierarchical structure proposed in this chapter can help scholars and practitioners in examining specific e-tailing strategies in the context of other e-tailing strategies, and evaluate their impact on one another. Connections and distinctions between e-tailing strategies across and within levels of interaction can be easily identified using the proposed framework.

Some strategies examined in this chapter can be practiced by e-manufacturers *and* e-tailers. However, suggestions to differentiate between them have been made in order to show how e-tailers can offer added value to customers to a greater extent than e-manufacturers can (e.g., bundles across brands). The strategies that can set e-tailers apart from e-manufacturers will create the competitive advantage e-tailers are looking for in the online marketplace.

References

Alba, J., Lynch, J., Weitz, B., Janiszewski, C., Lutz, R., Sawyer, A. & Wood, S. (1997). Interactive home shopping: consumer, retailer, and manufacturer incentives to participate in electronic marketplaces. *Journal of Marketing*, 61(3), 38–53.

Ansari, A., Essegaier, S. & Kohli, R. (2000). Internet recommendation systems. *Journal of Marketing Research*, 37(August), 363–375.

Ansari, A. & Mela, C. F. (2003). E-customization. *Journal of Marketing Research*, 40(2), 131–145.

Bakos, Y. & Brynjolfsson, E. (1999). Bundling information goods: pricing, profits, and efficiency. *Management Science*, 45(12), 1613–1630.

Bechwati, N. N. & Xia, L. (2003). Do computers sweat? The impact of perceived effort of online decision aids on consumers' satisfaction with the decision process. *Journal of Consumer Psychology*, 13(1 & 2), 139–148.

Berry, L. L. (1995). Relationship marketing of services-growing interest, emerging perspectives. *Journal of Academy of Marketing Science*, 23(4), 236–245.

Bettencourt, L. A. (1997). Customer voluntary performance: customers as partners in service delivery. *Journal of Retailing*, 73(3), 383–406.

Cooke, A. D. J., Sujan, H., Sujan, M. & Weitz, B. A. (2002). Marketing the unfamiliar: the role of context in electronic agent recommendations. *Journal of Marketing Research,* 39(4), 488–497.

DelVecchio, D. (2005). Deal-prone consumers' response to promotion: the effect of relative and absolute promotion value. *Psychology & Marketing*, 22(5), 373–391.

Garbarino, E. & Johnson, M. S. (1999). The different roles of satisfaction, trust, and commitment in consumer relationships. *Journal of Marketing*, 63(April), 70–87.

Gershoff, A. D., Broniarczyk, S. M. & West, P. M. (2001). Recommendation or evaluation? Task sensitivity in information source selection. *Journal of Consumer Research*, 28(December), 418–438.

Gershoff, A. D., Mukherjee, A. & Mukhopadhyay, A. (2003). Consumer acceptance of online agent advice: extremity and positivity effects. *Journal of Consumer Psychology*, 13(1&2), 161–170.

Grabner-Kraeuter, S. (2002). The role of consumers' trust in online-shopping. *Journal of Business Ethics*, 39(1/2), 43–50.

Ha, H.-Y. (2004). Factors influencing consumer perceptions of brand trust online. *Journal of Product & Brand Management*, 13(5), 329–342.

Harris, J. (1997). The effects of promotional bundling on consumers' evaluations of product quality and risk of purchase. Paper presented at the Advances in Consumer Research.

Harris, L. C. & Goode, M. M. H. (2004). The four levels of loyalty and the pivotal role of trust: a study of online service dynamics. *Journal of Retailing*, 80(2), 139–158.

Häubl, G. & Murray, K. B. (2003). Preference construction and persistence in digital marketplaces: the role of electronic recommendation agents. *Journal of Consumer Psychology*, 13(1&2), 75–91.

Häubl, G. & Trifts, V. (2000). Consumer decision making in online shopping environments: the effects of interactive decision aids. *Marketing Science*, 19(1), 4–21.

Hoffman, D. L., Novak, T. P. & Peralta, M. A. (1999). Information privacy in the marketspace: implications for the commercial uses of anonymity on the web. *Information Society*, 15(2), 129–139.

Huffman, C. & Kahn, B. E. (1998). Variety for sale: mass customization or mass confusion? *Journal of Retailing*, 74(4), 491–513.

Kalyanam, K. & McIntyre, S. (2002). The e-marketing mix: a contribution of the e-tailing wars. *Journal of Academy of Marketing Science*, 30(4), 487–499.

Laudon, K. (1996). Markets and privacy. *Communications of the ACM*, 39(9), 92–104.

Murthi, B. P. S. & Sarkar, S. (2003). The role of the management sciences in research on personalization. *Management Science*, 49(10), 1344–1362.

Noble, S. M. & Phillips, J. (2004). Relationship hindrance: why would consumers not want a relationship with a retailer? *Journal of Retailing*, 80(4), 289–303.

Price, L. L. & Arnould, E. J. (1999). Commercial friendships: service provider-client relationships in context. *Journal of Marketing*, 63(October), 38–56.

Rodgers, W., Negash, S. & Suk, K. (2005). The moderating effect of on-line experience on the antecedents and consequences of on-line satisfaction. *Psychology & Marketing*, 22(4), 313–331.

Simonson, I. (2005). Determinants of customers' responses to customized offers: conceptual framework and research propositions. *Journal of Marketing*, 69(1), 32–45.

Simonson, I., Kramer, T. & Young, M. (2004). Effect propensity. *Organizational Behavior and Human Decision Processes*, 95(November).

Stremersch, S. & Tellis, G. J. (2002). Strategic bundling of products and prices: a new synthesis for marketing. *Journal of Marketing*, 66(January), 55–72.

Tirole, J. (1988). *The Theory of Industrial Organization*, The MIT Press, Cambridge, MA, 1988.

Tsai, H.-T., Huang, H.-C., Jaw, Y.-L. & Chen, W.-K. (2006). Why on-line customers remain with a particular e-retailer: an integrative model and empirical evidence. *Psychology & Marketing*, 23(5), 447–464.

Varadarajan, P. R. & Yadav, M. S. (2002). Marketing strategy and the internet: an organizing framework. *Journal of Academy of Marketing Science*, 30(4), 296–312.

West, P. M. & Broniarczyk, S. M. (1998). Integrating multiple opinions: the role of aspiration level on consumer response to critic consensus. *Journal of Consumer Research*, 25(1), 38–51.

Yadav, M. S. (1994). How buyers evaluate product bundles: a model of anchoring and adjustment. *Journal of Consumer Research*, 21(September), 342–353.

Yadav, M. S. & Monroe, K. B. (1993). How buyers perceive savings in a bundle price: An examination of a bundle's transaction value. *Journal of Marketing Research*, 30, 350–358.

Yadav, M. S. & Varadarajan, P. R. (2005). Understanding product migration to the electronic marketplace: a conceptual framework. *Journal of Retailing*, 81(2), 125–140.

3

The Customer Perspective of E-Service Quality: An Empirical Study

Samar I. Swaid and Rolf T. Wigand

Introduction

At their core, networked software applications create services that are able to perform businesses' activities and communicate with others creating value for the firm and its customers. Currently, services delivered through the network and especially the web (termed here e-service) redefine the conceptualization of services (Hofacker et al., 2007) and thereby impose new challenges to the concept of e-service quality.

As electronic markets are found to be competitive environments (Reichheld & Schefter, 2000), meeting customer needs has become the new battleground. Successful electronic retailers recognize that the key to retaining customers and generating profits is providing superior service quality and meeting customers' expectations. Service marketing literature finds that traditional service quality – that takes place in physical facilities such as stores, restaurants and clinics – is an elusive and complicated concept and difficult to measure (Cronion & Taylor, 1992; Parasuraman et al., 1988).

Unlike products, services are 'intangibles' and their output is viewed as an activity rather than a tangible object (Johns, 1999) – an issue that makes managing service quality a difficult task. Parasuraman et al., (1988, p. 15) define service quality as the 'global judgment, or attitude, relating to the superiority of the service'. In this regard, Parasuraman et al., (1988) proposed that service quality can be evaluated using five dimensions forming what is called the SERVQUAL model (Parasuraman et al., 1988). The five dimensions of the SERVQUAL model are

- tangibles (physical facilities, equipment and appearance of personnel);
- reliability (ability to perform the promised service dependable and accurately);
- responsiveness (willingness to help customers and provide prompt service);
- assurance (knowledge and courtesy of employees and their ability to inspire trust and confidence); and
- empathy (caring and individualized attention, the firm provides its customer) (Parasuraman et al., 1988).

The SERVQUAL model was conceptualized based on the function of the difference scores or gaps between perceptions and expectations (Q = P – E). The use of the gap model has been challenged by different studies in that the perception-only index can be sufficient as a measure of the service quality (e.g., Cronin & Taylor, 1992; Teas, 1993). Cronin & Taylor (1992) found that using the perception index only (SERVPERF) gives a better measure of service quality. The SERVQUAL model is now widely tested in traditional settings such as industrial marketing, higher education, restaurants, hotels, real estate, hospitals, the legal profession, employees and service providers (e.g., Lee et al., 2000; Lim & Tang, 2000; Stodnick & Rogers, 2008; Juwaheer, 2004; Fick & Ritchie, 1991; Roses et al., 2008; Wisniewski, 2001; Brysland & Curry, 2001).

As businesses increasingly adopt the web to deliver their services (e-services), the question of how to manage the quality of e-services rises. Service quality is a subjective issue and a contextualized construct (i.e., industry and context dependent) (Parasuraman et al., 1988). Therefore, it is expected that in judging service quality in the setting of e-retailing, customers use cues that are different from those that are used in the setting of other web sites (e.g., news websites, portal websites and university websites). This chapter is dedicated to understanding how online shoppers value e-retailing e-service quality when they buy tangible products that need to be delivered.

What is electronic service quality?

Service delivered via the web (e-service) is an area that has become of interest to e-businesses and researchers in many disciplines. But what exactly is e-service?

E-service has been interpreted by service marketing researchers as the 'provision of service over electronic networks such as the internet and includes the service product, service environment and service delivery that comprise any business model, whether it belongs to a goods manufacturer or a pure service provider' (Rust & Kannan, 2003, p. 561). Similarly, de Ruyter et al., (2001) composed the conceptualization of e-service as 'an interactive content-centered and Internet-based customer service, driven by customer and integrated with related organizational customer support processes and technologies with the goal of strengthening the customer-service provider relationship' (p. 185). In the same vein, Boyer, Hallowell & Roth (2002, p. 175) defined e-services as 'interactive services that are delivered on the Internet using advanced telecommunications, information and multimedia technologies'. On the other hand, computer and information scientists view e-service as a self-contained, web-enabled application capable of not only performing business activities on their own, but also possessing the ability to communicate and engage with other e-services in order to complete higher-order business transactions (Umpathy & Purao, 2004).

As this chapter views e-services through the marketing lens, we define e-service quality as the extent to which the web facilitates efficient shopping, purchasing and delivery of products and services (Zeithaml et al., 2002). Service marketing literature has found that understanding service quality is whatever the customer perceives it to be – and other criteria in understanding the construct of service quality are essentially invalid (Grönroos, 2007; Rust & Miu, 2006; Zeithaml et al., 1996). In the setting of e-services, quality measurement is more challenging due to the special characteristics of e-services, as discussed below.

Challenges in measuring E-service quality

Developed instruments that measure traditional service quality are not appropriate to assess e-service quality for three main reasons: (i) the e-service delivery environment (ii) the characteristics of online shoppers; and (iii) the characteristics of e-services.

Service delivery environment

Traditional services are delivered in human-based environments, where face-to-face interactions take place in service delivery and consumption. Therefore, customers use cues from the physical environment of service delivery, the appearance of the service employee and the performance of the customer service representative. On the other hand, e-services are delivered with little or no direct human intervention mediated in a computer. Therefore, technology-based cues are mainly used to judge the quality of e-service. As a result, traditional service quality instruments are not directly applicable in the setting of e-services.

Behaviour of the online shopper

As is the case in shopping in physical facilities, shopping online depends on the shoppers' motivations. Motivations in online environments are classified into experiential or goal-oriented (Hoffman & Novak, 1996). Customers with experiential behavior go shopping when they have an ongoing interest that is associated with playfulness and fun (Wolfinbarger & Gilly, 2003). On the other hand, goal-oriented shoppers are task-oriented and have planned purchases (Wolfinbarger & Gilly, 2003). Online shoppers are considered goal-oriented shoppers rather than entertainment seekers (Zeithaml et al., 2000) who go online shopping when they have a specific purchase in mind (Hoffman & Novak, 1996). Simply put, consumers are seeking to complete their task with the use of little effort – decreasing the monetary and non-monetary costs (e.g., time, effort and psychological cost) and resulting in task accomplishment (Dholakia & Uusitalo, 2002)

Characteristics of e-services

Services have five unique characteristics that make them different from goods. These characteristics are generally summarized as intangibility, heterogeneity, perishability, inseparability of production and consumption (Zeithaml & Bittner, 2003; Lovelock & Gummesson, 2004). Bateson (1979) explains intangibility of services as physical intangibility and mental intangibility. Physical intangibility means that services cannot be touched, tasted, smelt or seen. In addition, services can also be difficult for the mind to grasp and thus can be mentally intangible. Berry & Parasuraman (1991) conceptualized intangibility as 'that which can't be touched, impalpable,' and 'that which cannot be easily defined, formulated, or grasped mentally.' Intangibility is considered the most substantial differentiating attribute between services and products and the main source of difficulty faced by customers when trying to evaluate service quality (Zeithaml et al., 1985). In addition, services are described by their inseparability which means the simultaneousness of production and consumption of services (Zeithaml et al., 1985). Another characteristic is heterogeneity which may be explained by the differences in staff performances or the unique demands of each customer (Zeithaml & Bitner, 2003). Services are also perishable in that they cannot be saved, stored, resold or returned. Lovelock & Gummesson (2004) proposed to identify services by purchases that do not lead to ownership for the buyer, but result in benefits that occurred through access to services or temporary possession.

As e-services are delivered and consumed in technology-based environments, their characteristics apply differently and are found to be highly flexible. E-services are found to be less intangible, more homogeneous, inventoried, separably consumed, owned and copyrighted (for more details see Hofacker et al., 2007). As the web is the service environment for service delivery and consumption – totally or partially – online shoppers have limited capabilities of information processing which makes e-services less intangible. Hofacker et al., (2007) explain that e-services are more homogeneous given that they are not labour intensive and depend mainly on networked software. In regards to inseparability of the production and consumption, e-services can be consumed at the time of production (e.g., online ticket reservation) or consumed partially later (e.g., online purchasing for physical products such as books). E-services are not necessarily perishable, for example, when a song is downloaded online, it can be stored by the consumer. Also, ownership cannot be transferred in e-services – a property that uniquely identifies services (Lovelock & Gummesson, 2004).

As noted above, the attributes of the e-service delivery environment, online shoppers behaviour and e-service characteristics introduce difficult challenges on how to conceptualize and evaluate e-service quality. The next section demonstrates prior research on e-service quality and the gaps in academic literature.

Prior research on e-service quality

With the increasing use of e-commerce, a number of attempts have been made to understand the concept of e-service quality in the virtual world. Previous studies on e-service quality can be classified into two main types: (i) studies that focus on the technical quality of the web site in terms of web site design and interactivity and (ii) studies that focus on the service delivered through the web site that consider customer service and order fulfillment as core components.

Research on website technical quality

In this vein, e-service quality relies heavily on the interface design and web site interactivity. For example, Aladwani & Palvia (2002) measured web quality using four dimensions: specific content, content quality, technical adequacy and perceived web quality. Similarly, Iwwarden et al., (2004) reworded the measures of the SERVQUAL model to measure the service quality of different websites (e.g., university websites, stock exchange information, banking, chat rooms, electronic libraries, e-shops and e-games). Their work identified e-service quality as composed of fast access, ease of navigation, presentation of a complete overview of the order before final purchase decision, assurance and a simple registration process.

Barnes & Vidgen (2002) focusing on the e-bookstores developed the WebQual scale including the five factors of: usability, design, information, trust and empathy. In this research, participants were not engaged in a complete purchasing transaction that includes purchasing and receiving products (e.g., books) or any after-sale services. Another study by Liu & Arnett (2000) found that e-service quality consists of information and service quality, system use (including ease of use and privacy), playfulness and system design quality (including processing speed and balance between security and ease-of-use for the payment method). A study which focused on online travelling websites conducted by van Riel et al., (2004) resulted in having service quality, navigation, design accessibility, reliability and customization as the dimensions of e-service quality.

Loiacono et al., (2007) developed the WebQual instrument for measuring web quality on the dimensions of: informational fit-to-task, interactivity, trust, response time, ease of understanding, intuitive operations, visual appeal, innovativeness, flow/emotional appeal, consistent image, online completeness and better than alternative channels. This realm of research exhibits primarily web interactivity orientation. However, many failures in e-services have been related to order fulfilment and back-office operations (Sousa & Voss, 2006), which suggest e-service quality should be evaluated using cues that go beyond website quality.

Research on e-service quality

On the other hand, a few other studies extend the scope of e-service quality to include core customer service components. For example, Wolfinbarger & Gilly (2003) developed a scale for measuring e-service quality on four factors: website design, reliability/fulfilment, privacy/security and customer service. Their work was conducted using focus group research and survey study, however, some of the identified factors do not show strong face validity (Parasuraman et al., 2005). In addition, today's customers demand more sophisticated services such as personalized offerings and promotions that adapt to their preferences. As a result, personalization should be one of the key factors of e-service quality. Another comprehensive study that focused on e-service quality is the one conducted by Parasuraman et al., (2005) developing two scales. Parasuraman et al., (2005) established the E-S-QUAL for core services quality and E-RecS-QUAL for service recovery quality. E-S-QUAL consists of efficiency, system availability, fulfilment and privacy, while the E-RecS-Qual consists of responsiveness, compensation and contact. Although the study was conducted comprehensively, we believe the e-service quality should be conceptualized to include all encounters that occur before, during and after the purchase transaction. Therefore, the responsiveness factor should be included in the core factors of e-service quality. In this chapter, we follow a systematic framework for constructing an instrument to measure e-retailing service quality when shoppers buy tangible products that need to packaged and delivered, as shown next.

Scale development

In this section, we discuss the process of developing and validating a scale for measuring e-service quality. Measurement scales are defined by Devellis (2003) as 'measurement instruments that are collections of items intended to reveal levels of theoretical variables, not readily observable by direct means' (p. 8). We follow a multi-step process in constructing a scale to measure e-service quality. We start by defining e-service quality as the extent that the web facilitates effective shopping, purchasing and delivery of products and services (Zeithaml et al., 2000). In this study, we followed Voss's (2003) recommendation by restructuring the dimensions of the SERVQUAL model to suit the setting of online environments.

Dimensions of e-service quality

Website design

Website design is the tangible aspect of e-service quality that is partially comparable to the appearance of a storefront of a service counter (Zeithaml et al., 2002). Website design refers to the way the site is designed and information is presented in terms of color use, layout, quality of pictures and font style. The need to have a well-designed and good-looking website is essential to satisfy customers (Swaid & Wigand, 2007), attract new customers (Zhang & Prybutok, 2004) and retain existing ones (Swaid & Wigand, 2009). A great number of customers abandon their online shopping carts because they get frustrated with the technology and the site interface. Therefore, we suggest the website design is one factor of e-service quality.

Website usability

The functionality and the efficiency of the user interface can enable and facilitate the exchange of information between online shoppers and e-retailers. Online shoppers value a well-functioning website that can easily be navigated. Online shoppers abandon a website when it is difficult to get an overview of its structure and when it is time consuming to find the required information (Aladwani & Palvia, 2002). Usable websites should be friendly and equipped with product search features, sorting functions and comparison engines. Hence, we propose that website usability is a key factor of e-service quality.

Information quality

Content of the website refers to the way the information is presented, combining text, video, pictures, graphics, audio and 3D simulations. Online shoppers rely on the information presented on the website to make an informed decision (Li et al., 2002). Therefore, presenting information that is accurate, current, relevant and updated improves the perception of web quality (Aladwani & Palvia, 2002). Doll & Torkzadeh (1988) define four dimensions for information quality in computer-mediated systems: accuracy, format, timeliness and content. Online shoppers rely on websites to deliver information such as product description, price, product comparisons, delivery times and policies and instruction. Accordingly, we propose that information quality is one of the factors of e-service quality.

Reliability

Reliability in the offline context is defined as 'the ability to perform the promised service dependably and accurately' (Parasuraman et al., 1988, p. 23). Reliability is perhaps the most important dimension of service quality in traditional stores (Parasuraman et al., 1988). Wolfinbarger & Gilly (2003) found that reliability is the strongest predictor of customer satisfaction and the second strongest predictor of loyalty. Reliability in e-stores is defined as a dimension that deals with providing the service on time and as promised. As a result, we suggest that reliability is one of the important dimensions of e-service quality.

Responsiveness

The responsiveness dimension refers to answering online shoppers' questions via providing accurate, quick, error-free and prompt responses. Online shoppers require a 'Frequently Asked Questions' page, communication mechanisms to ask and receive answers from customer service representatives such as emails, message board, chat rooms, discussion forums, or a toll free number. Advanced technologies enable the retailer to be more innovative in delivering services. For example, features such as click-to-call and click-to-chat help customers to find answers online and provide a channel to air complaints. Hence, we suggest that responsiveness is one of the dimensions of core e-service quality.

Assurance

Assurance in traditional stores is defined by 'knowledge and courtesy of employees and their ability to convey trust and confidence' (Parasuraman et al., 1988). In e-stores, assurance is '...the degree to which customers believe the site is safe from intrusion and personal information is protected ... involves the confidence the customer feels in dealing with the site and is due to the reputation of the site and the products or services it sells' (Zeithaml et al., 2000, p. 16). Assurance is considered one of the most important drivers of customer loyalty in e-stores (Parasuraman et al., 2005; Swaid & Wigand, 2009). Online shoppers are concerned about dealing with virtual organizations that may not have a physical location, where they could be tracked. Therefore, cues such as security and privacy policies, third-party seals, affiliation with a known retailer or organization (e.g., TrustE and Better Business Bureau) inspire trust. Online shoppers look for a clear and detailed specification of how the e-store is applying security technologies and how that will protect their information. In addition, online shoppers feel more comfortable dealing with retailers that have a good general reputation. Therefore, we propose that assurance is a key dimension of e-service quality.

Personalization

Since one of the important reasons for conducting online shopping is convenience (Zeithaml et al., 2000), offering customized products and personalized recommendations enhance the perception of e-service quality. When recommendation agents suggest products to online shoppers based on their profile or on the profiles of like-minded users (e.g., using collaborative filtering), they are more satisfied (Swaid & Wigand, 2007). Personalization can be defined as the ability of the shopper to configure a website, product or service according to his or her preferences and the ability of the website to be tailored to these configurations and preferences (Zeithaml et al., 2000). Since e-service is delivered through a technology-based environment where collecting customers' information is possible, personalization forms one of the key features that differentiate the web from other traditional service delivery channels.

Accordingly, we suggest the following hypothesis:

H1: e-service quality is a multidimensional construct that is composed of website design, website usability, information quality, reliability, responsiveness, assurance and personalization (see Figure 3.1).

Service quality in traditional settings was found to influence customer satisfaction (Oliver, 1980), perceived value (Zeithaml et al., 2000)

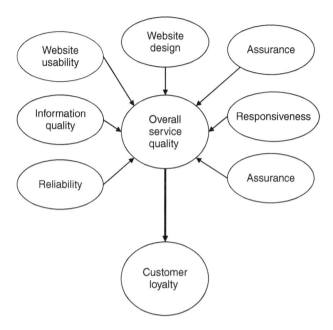

Figure 3.1 Research conceptual model

and customer loyalty (Bloemer et al., 1998; Zeithaml et al., 1996). In the setting of e-retailing service quality, we focus on customer loyalty. But why is customer loyalty important to e-service quality models?

The quest of the dependent variable

As e-markets are competitive environments (Reichheld & Schefter, 2000), where the competitor is a click away, retaining customers is extremely difficult (Srinivasan et al., 2002), but when achieved is rewarding. According to Balabanis et al., (2006), around one half of sales is accounted for by repeat online customers. Customer loyalty is essential for maintaining profitability and market share (Jarvis & Mayo, 1986; Kotler & Singh, 1981). In addition, acquiring new customers costs more than generating profits from existing customers (Reichheld & Schefter, 2000). Loyal customers not only promote positive word-of-mouth, but also provide opportunities for revenue generation via cross-selling (selling new products and services to existing customers) or upselling (enhances customers' use of existing products or services). Therefore, studying the relationship between e-service quality and customer loyalty advances our understanding of the drivers of customer loyalty. Oliver

(1999, p. 34) defines customer loyalty as 'a deeply held commitment to rebuy or repatronize a preferred product/service consistently in the future thereby causing repetitive same-brand or same-brand-set purchasing despite situational influences and marketing efforts having the potential to cause switching behavior'. Accordingly, we propose that (see Figure 3.1).

H2: Overall service quality influences customer loyalty.

An empirical study

Phase I: Conceptualization and operationalization

As we have conceptualized constructs of e-service quality based on the original dimensions of the SERVQUAL model, we adopted valid scales from prior research to operationalize the constructs. Latent constructs can be operationalized using formative (also known as cause measures) or reflective indicators. Formative indicators are measures that form or cause the creation or change in a latent variable (Chin, 1998). On the other hand, reflective (effect) measures are viewed as affected by the same underlying construct and are measures that co-vary to the extent that they measure this underlying construct (Chin, 1998).

The current research uses reflective indicators for two main reasons. First, one of this study's objectives is to develop a multi-item scale to measure e-service quality. As Bollen (1989, p. 22) points out, 'unfortunately, traditional validity assessment and classical test theory do not cover cause indicators'. Therefore, reflective measures were used to represent latent constructs of e-service quality. Second, conducting structural equation modeling (SEM) becomes problematic when formative measures are included (Chin, 1998; MacCallum & Browne, 1993). Following constructs' conceptualization and operationalization, we organized the generated measures in a questionnaire instrument preparing for data collection. Additionally, measures of two dependent variables of overall service quality and customer loyalty were adopted from Wolfinbarger & Gilly (2003) and Parasuraman, Zeithaml & Malhotra (2005) respectively. Items were measured using the seven-point Likert-type scales ranging from (1) strongly disagree to (7) strongly agree. The questionnaire instrument was pre-tested using a sample of subjects from the same population of online shoppers.

Participants were screened to ensure that they had sufficient online shopping experience. In this study we tested our model using the population of college students that was found to resemble the online shopping population (McKnight et al., 2002). In addition, EMarketer (2009), found that college students are the most active web users and conduct more personal business online than the overall web audience. More importantly, using the population of college students decreases the effect of variance when not exposed to all factors (structure, roles, and responsibilities) of the real world environment (Greenberg, 1987). Therefore, we invited college students at a mid-size university to participate in our study. The criterion for participating in the study was to have used the Internet at least 12 times during the past three months and having made at least one online purchase transaction within that last three months, as used by Parasuraman et al., (2005). Eight women (38%) and thirteen men (61%) participated in the pre-test study. The questionnaire was first pre-tested focusing on its format, layout and length. Second, the questionnaire's items were tested aiming to identify ambiguous questions and items with meanings. Pre-testing the instrument resulted in maintaining 47 items to measure e-service quality on dimensions of website design, website usability, information quality, reliability, responsiveness, assurance and personalization. Next, the questionnaire instrument was emailed to students explaining the research objectives. Due to missing data, eight cases were eliminated resulting in a total of 605 complete cases to be used for statistical analysis. The age profile of participants reflects a representation of most age groups, with the majority (54%) being in the 21–35 age range. Sixty-eight per cent of the respondents were men. Thus the sample is more representative to the US Internet users studies that found Internet users are mostly men and young (EMarketer, 2009). Typical products and purchases were books (24%), computer hardware and accessories (21%) (see Figure 3.2). Data collected were split randomly into two datasets to be used for exploratory factor analysis phase and psychometric properties assessment in terms of reliability and validity.

Phase II: Analytical work

Exploratory Factor Analysis (EFA) is one of the multivariate analysis techniques that are described as complex and as a multi-step process (Hair et al., 1998). To ensure the applicability of the factor analysis to the data, a number of statistical tests are needed. According to Hair et al., (1998) two measures can be used to examine the entire correlation matrix: the Bartlett test of sphericity and the Measure of Sampling Adequacy (MSA). The Bartlett test of sphericity is a statistical test for the presence of correlations among variable. The Bartlett test of sphericity was significant indicating that there is a significant correlation between the variables. In addition, the MSA value was 0.905 which can be interpreted as meritorious. Therefore, we conclude that the

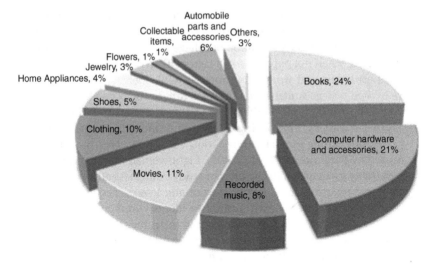

Figure 3.2 Descriptive statistics of products purchased online

inter-correlation matrix contains sufficient common variance to make factor analysis worthwhile. Principal Axis Factoring (PAF) extraction method was used in conducting factor analysis and Varimax rotation was used as the orthogonal method in rotating the factors. Items were factor analyzed using the scree test and the rule of thumb of eigenvalues greater than the value of one to retain stable factor structure. The first phase of factor analysis resulted in identifying six factors: website quality, information quality, reliability, responsiveness, assurance and personalization (see Table 3.1). At this exploratory stage of factor analysis, constructs reliability was tested using Cronbach's Alpha test. As shown in Table 3.1, Alpha values ranged from 0.767 to 0.882, exceeding the 0.70 recommended by Nunnally & Bernstein (1994).

Conducting exploratory factor analysis resulted in purifying data and developing an initial instrument for measuring e-service quality on six dimensions of website quality, information quality, reliability, responsiveness, assurance and personalization. As Churchill (1979) recommends testing the scale using another dataset, we apply structural analysis in testing the stability of the dimensions of e-service quality and evaluate the reliability and validity of the instrument.

Phase III: Structural analysis

Structural Equation Modeling (SEM) is a comprehensive statistical approach for testing hypotheses about relations among observed and

Table 3.1 Factor solution of e-service quality based on exploratory analysis

Dimension	Label	Item	Reliability Coefficient Alpha	Factor Loadings of Items on Dimensions	
				Items	Loadings
Website usability	F1	4	.767	WUS1	.773
				WUS2	.768
				WUS3	.745
				WUS4	.739
Information quality	F2	6	.882	INQ1	.900
				INQ2	.877
				INQ3	.872
				INQ4	.842
				INQ5	.840
				INQ6	.808
Reliability	F3	6	.872	REL1	.846
				REL2	.824
				REL3	.823
				REL4	.787
				REL5	.755
				REL6	.640
Responsiveness	F4	5	.843	RES1	.823
				RES2	.789
				RES3	.785
				RES4	.735
				RES5	.702
Assurance	F5	4	.859	ASS1	.891
				ASS2	.838
				ASS3	.786
				ASS4	.780
Personalization	F6	3	.810	PER1	.911
				PER2	.896
				PER3	.871

latent constructs (Hoyle & Panter, 1995). The main advantage of SEM is answering a set of questions in a single and systematic analysis by modeling the relationships among multiple independent and dependent constructs simultaneously (Anderson & Gerbing, 1988; Gefen et al., 2002).

A two-step procedure described by Anderson & Gerbing (1988) to conduct SEM is followed. First, a measurement model that describes the relations among the latent constructs and their items is developed and assessed using Confirmatory Factor Analysis (CFA). Second, a structural model was built testing the relations among the latent constructs of e-service quality and dependent variables of overall service quality and customer loyalty.

Developing a measurement model

A measurement model consisting of dimensions of e-service quality as exogenous variables and overall service quality and customer loyalty as endogenous variables was constructed using Confirmatory Factor Analysis (CFA). This model was modified by deleting variables with insignificant factor loadings, variables with high normalized residuals and variables indicated to be problematic by modification indices such as the Wald test and Lagrange Multiplier test (Hatcher, 1994). Insignificant variables with an absolute t-value less than 1.96 $(p<0.05)$ or near-zero standard errors were eliminated. Once all the problematic variables were eliminated, the model was evaluated for goodness-of-fit, reliability and validity. As shown in Table 3.2, factor structure of e-service quality indicates stable factor solution. Loadings were high and items loaded on its dimensions. Further, we examined the measurement model using the test of normed chi-square $(X^2/df$: *the ration of chi-square to the degree of freedom*), Goodness of Fit Index (GFI), Bentler Comparative Fit Index (CFI), Bentler & Bonett (1980) Normed Fit Index (NFI) and the Root Mean Square Error of Approximation (RMSEA) test. The observed normed X^2 for the measurement model was 1.73, less than the value of three recommended by Bagozzi & Yi (1988). The value of the Goodness of Fit Index (GFI) was 0.96 indicating an overall good fit. In addition, fit indices of Bentler Comparative Fit Index (CFI) and Bentler & Bonett Normed Fit Index (NFI) and the RMSEA suggest good fit for the measurement model. Both the CFI and NFI may range in value from 0.0 to 1.0, where a fit index of 0.0 is associated with the model that specifies no correlations exist among items (null model) while a fit index of 1.0 is the one associated with a model that reproduces the original covariance matrix (Hatcher, 1994). Results of CFA reveal that both CFI (0.95) and NFI (0.92) are greater than 0.90, indicating a very good fit of the data (Hatcher, 1994). Conversely, the value of RMSEA of less than 0.05 suggests a good fit of data. The developed measurement model reveals the value of 0.047 for RMSEA suggesting that the model is a good fit of data. The reliability of scale was assessed using the composite reliability test

Table 3.2   Confirmatory factor analysis

Construct/ Item	Loadings (a)	t-value (b)	Std Err	Cronbach's Alpha	Composite reliability	Variance extracted estimates
Information	0.888	19.47	0.07	0.867	0.920	0. 750
Quality	0.839	17.75	0.08			
INQ1	0.888	19.48	0.07			
INQ3	0.925	20.87	0.06			
INQ4	0.800	16.51	0.08			
INQ5	0.855	17.99	0.06			
INQ6	0.854	17.95	0.07			
Usability	0.819	16.84	0.06	0.859	0.908	0. 718
WUS1	0.806	16.43	0.07			
WUS2	0.876	16.03	0.05			
WUS4	0.832	17.46	0.06			
WUS5	0.840	17.70	0.06			
WUS3	0.757	15.16	0.07			
Reliability	0.855	18.20	0.06	0.893	0.905	0.722
REL1	0.712	14.89	0.06			
REL2	0.903	19.93	0.06			
REL4	0.845	17.84	0.06			
REL5	0.841	17.76	0.06			
REL3	0.814	16.87	0.06			
Responsiveness	0.880	19.11	0.06	0.872	0.910	0.735
RES1	0.936	21.26	0.07			
RES2	0.948	21.76	0.08			
RES3	0.888	19.49	0.08			
RES4	0.881	19.23	0.08			
RES5	0.8260	16.06	16.60			
Assurance	0.8449	17.12	17.12	0.889	0.914	0.855
ASS1	0.8626	17.63	17.63			
ASS2						
ASS3						
ASS4						
Personalization				0.858	0.841	0.712
PER1						
PER2						
PER3						
Goodness-of-fit statistics	$X^2 = 453.3$ $X^2/df = 1.73$ GFI = 0.96			CFI = 0.95 NFI =0.92 RMSEA = .047		

and the variance extracted test (Hatcher, 1994). Calculated composite reliability index ranged from 0.841 to 0.920 (see Table 3.2), exceeding the recommended value of 0.70 (Hatcher, 1994). The variance extracted index is usually used to assess the amount of the variance that is captured by an underlying factor in relation to the amount of variance due to measurement error. The variance extracted ranges from 0.712 to 0.855 (see Table 3.2), exceeding the 0.50 cut-off (Hatcher, 1994).

Reliability and validity assessment

Before proceeding to the structural analysis, we tested the reliability and validity of the developed scale. Both of Cronbach's alpha and composite reliability values of e-service quality constructs are greater than the cut-off value of 0.70 (Nunnally & Bernstein, 1994) (see Table 3.2). Validity of scale is based on content validity, convergent validity and discriminant validity. Focus group research ensured the content validity of our scale. Convergent validity was assessed based on the factor's loading on its factor. According to Bagoozi & Yi (1988), factor loadings exceeding the value 0.70 indicate strong convergent validity. The discriminate validity was evaluated using the confidence interval test (Hatcher, 1994). The test involves calculating the confidence interval of plus or minus two of the standard error around the correlation between the factors (Hatcher, 1994). Confidence interval values indicated the discriminant validity since no confidence interval included the value of one (Hatcher, 1994). Finally, we tested the nomological validity testing the relationships among the dimensions of e-service quality and the construct of overall service quality, as shown in the next section.

Developing a structural model

As we have confirmed the dimensionality of e-service quality, we developed an advanced measurement model that incorporates the dimensions of e-service quality and the two dependent variables of overall service quality and customer loyalty. This step was necessary to build the structural model that incorporates the links among dimensions of e-service quality and overall service quality and customer loyalty. Fit indices for the developed measurement model were as follows: the value-normed chi-square test was 1.89, while GFI value was 0.91. Both CFI and NFI were 0.92. Value of RMSEA was 0.048. Fit indices indicate that the measurement model is accepted and can be used for developing the structural model. The structural model incorporates the relationships among constructs of e-service quality, overall service quality and customer loyalty.

The first step in structural model testing is to estimate the goodness-of-fit of the hypothesized model (see Figure 3.2). Typically, this is done using the chi-square test (X^2), however, due to the sensitivity of this test to sample size, the normed chi-square test (X^2/df) was used (Bagozzi and Yi, 1988). The value of the normed chi-square was 2.2 less than the value of three (Bagozzi and Yi, 1988). Additionally, tests of Goodness of Fit Index (GFI), Bentler Comparative Fit Index (CFI) and the Normed Fit Index (NFI) were conducted. Generally, these tests indicate good fit if the value is greater than 0.90. The GFI test was 0.98, while tests of CFI and NFI were 0.93 and 0.92 respectively. The second step of model estimation is to examine the path significance of each link in the theoretical model and the variance explained of each path. Standardized path coefficients and path significances are shown in Figure 3.3 (the measurement models are left out for purposes of clarity). All of the hypothesized associations were strongly significant at p =.0001. Given the strong loadings of all dimensions on a higher order quality construct, this study illustrates that service quality should be evaluated using attributes of website usability, information quality, reliability, responsiveness, assurance and personalization; construct of reliability being the strong predictor of the perception of overall service quality (β =.056) which explained 42 per cent of the variance in overall service

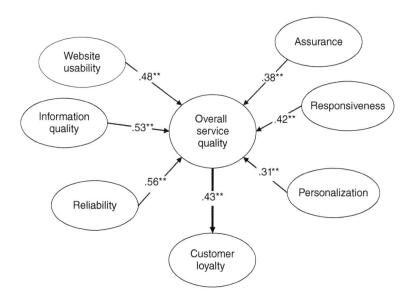

Figure 3.3 Modeling e-service quality as higher order factor
Notes: ** p<0.01

quality. In addition, results indicate that one driver of customer loyalty is the perception of e-service quality. A significant relationship between overall service quality and customer loyalty ($\beta = .41$) was found.

Discussion and conclusion

This chapter presents an empirical study on the conceptualization of e-service quality. The first issue of this chapter looked at how customers evaluate electronic service quality. Results of analytical work indicate that online shoppers require: (1) a website that is easy to navigate and supported with search and comparison features; (2) rich and accurate information in different formats of text and multimedia; (3) orders fulfilled accurately as promised and service delivered accurately; (4) customer questions are answered promptly and accurately via human and automated agents; (5) security and privacy policies are clearly specified and trust cues are managed; and (6) personalized attention is provided via product recommendations and customized offers. The study suggests that shoppers associate attractive websites with website functionality. Websites are an endless shelf space for retailers that should be well-designed presenting a wide selection of products and services. However, managers are encouraged to design their websites to be more than online catalogs guiding the customer to an interactive experience. Features such as search functions, site maps and price comparisons are now a must for interactive websites that help shoppers make informed decisions.

Our results also indicate the importance of information quality in affecting the perception of e-service quality. Online shoppers value the depth of information found on the web that reduces their search cost and enhances their decision making. Details of product information, order fulfilment, pricing, and handling returns should be accurate and updated. Nevertheless, during and after the purchase transaction, problems can occur. Websites should provide shoppers with answers to their questions and concerns. Mangers should provide the necessary mechanisms to receive customers' questions and to respond promptly. A number of advanced technologies enable shoppers to contact the e-retailer online. For example, features such as click-to-call and click-to-chat can be used enabling shoppers to communicate with customer service representatives online. Using these technologies may introduce some challenges on how to ensure the quality of this factor. Forester found that only 14 per cent of online shoppers were satisfied with the help they received while chatting with a customer service representative online (Internet Retailer, 2008). Therefore, managers should evaluate the responsiveness dimension on the aggregate level and on the attribute level to capture any weakness that may result in shoppers' dissatisfaction.

Similar to service quality research in a traditional setting, the reliability dimension is a strong predictor of overall service quality and customer loyalty. Managers should especially focus on issues of delivery fulfilment and order tracking. Nevertheless, effective personalization requires more than off-line stored information that is collected via surveys and registration forms. E-retail managers are required to use advanced technologies to capture shoppers' behaviour and browsing activities in real-time fashion. Capturing users' click-stream data as they navigate through the site is encouraged to create personalized experiences where websites are adapted in content and layout to the shopper's preferences. However, managers are advised to apply personalization strategies carefully. Online shoppers are unwilling to trade their privacy and security for personalized services or offerings. E-retailers are encouraged to sharpen their image and brand to inspire trust. Also, managers can educate their shoppers about what technologies have been used and how to secure data and transactions. As the web now moves to web 2.0 generation, managers can utilize virtual communities and social applications (e.g., peer-to-peer forums and blogs) to promote positive word-of-mouth and thereby inspire confidence.

Limitations

The instrument construction processes applied in this chapter were systematic, however, as is the case in any empirical study, there are a number of limitations that should be addressed. First, the discussed findings and their implications are obtained from a sample of students. Although a number of industry reports show the significance of this segment of online shoppers (e.g., EMarkter, 2009), re-testing the instrument using other populations is recommended. In addition, it is imperative to test the developed scale using minority populations such as African American and Hispanic populations, especially as the online shopping of these minorities increases (Media Audit, 2008). In this chapter, we explored the conceptualization of e-service quality and tested its relation to customer loyalty. It is also beneficial to test research models incorporating other variables such as perceived risk, perceived control, trust, and customer delight. The current study focused on e-service quality for business-to-customer markets. It would be interesting to investigate the conceptualization of service quality in business-to-business e-markets.

This chapter presents work that aims to understand the concept of e-service quality from the perception of online shoppers. Feigenbaum (1983) defines quality as 'Quality is a customer determination, not an engineer's determination, not a marketing determination, [n]or a general management determination. It is based upon the customer's actual experience with the product or service, measured against his or her requirements' (as cited in Hoyer & Hoyer, 2001, p. 56).

References

Aladwani, A. & Palvia, P. (2002). Developing and validating an instrument for measuring user-perceived web quality. *Information and Management*, 39(6), 467–476.

Anderson, J. & Gerbing, D. (1988). Structural equation modeling in practice: a review and recommended two-step approach. *Psychological Bulletin*, 103(3), 411–423.

Bagozzi, R. & Yi, Y. (1988). On the evaluation of structural equation models. *Journal of Academy f Marketing Science*, 16(1), 74–94.

Balabanis, G., Reynolds, N. & Simintiras, A. (2006). Bases of e-store loyalty: perceived switching barriers and satisfaction. *Journal of Business Research*, 59(2), 214–224.

Barnes, S. & Vidgen, R. (2002). An integrative approach to the assessment of e-commerce quality. *Journal of Electronic Commerce Research*, 3(2), 114–127.

Bateson, J. (1979). Why we need service marketing, in Ferrell, O.C., Brown, S.W., Lamb, C.W. Jr. (Eds.), *Conceptual and Theoretical Developments in Marketing*, Chicago: American Marketing Association, 131–146.

Bentler, P. M. & Bonett, D. G. (1980). Significant tests and goodness of fit in the analysis of covariance structures. *Psychological Bulletin*, 88(3), 588–606.

Berry, L. & Parasuraman, A. (1991). *Marketing Services: Competing Through Quality*, New York: The Free Press.

Bloemer, J., de Ruyter, K. & Wetzels, M. (1998). Linking perceived service quality and service loyalty: a multi-dimensional perspective. *European Journal of Marketing*, 33(11/12), 1082–1105.

Bollen, K. (1989). *Structural Equations with Latent Variables*. New York: Wiley.

Boyer, K., Hallwell, R. & Roth, A. (2002). E-service: operating strategy – a case study and a method for analyzing operational benefits. *Journal of Operations Management*, 20(2), 175–188.

Brysland, A. & Curry, A. (2001). Service improvements in public services using SERVQUAL. *Business Research*, 48(3), 233–246.

Chin, W. (1998). Issues and opinion on structural equation modeling. *MIS Quarterly*, 22(1), vii–xvi

Churchill, G. (1979). A paradigm for developing better measures of marketing constructs. *Journal of Marketing Research*, 16(1), 64–73.

Cronin, J. & Taylor, S. (1992). Measuring service quality: a reexamination and extension. *Journal of Marketing*, 56, 55–68.

De Ruyter, K., Wetzels, M. & Kleijnen, M. (2001). Customer adoption of e-service: an experimental study. *International Journal of Service Industry Management*, 12(2), 184–207.

Devillis, R. (2003). *Scale Development* (2nd ed.). Thousand Oaks, CA: Sage Publications.

Dholakia, R., & Uusitalo, O. (2002). Switching to electronic stores: consumer characteristics and the perception of shopping benefits. *International Journal of Retail & Distribution Management*, 30(10), 459–469.

Doll, W. & Torkzadeh, G. (1988). The measurement of end-user computing satisfaction. *MIS Quarterly*, 12(June), 259–274.

EMarketer. (2009). College Students Online: Driving Change in Internet and Mobile Usage. Retrieved from: http://www.emarketer.com/Report. aspx?code=emarketer_2000524, accessed on 15 March 2009.

Feigenbaum AV. (1983). *Total quality control*: 3rd edition. McGraw Hill: NY, USA.

Fick , G. & Ritchie J. (1991). Measuring service quality in the travel and tourism industry. *Journal of Travel Research*, 30(2), 2–9.

Gefen, D. (2002). Customer loyalty in e-commerce. *Journal of the Association for Information Systems*, 3(1), 27–51.

Gefen, D. Straub, D. & Boudreau, M. (2002). Structural equation modeling and regression: Guidelines for research practice. *Communications of the AIS*, 4, 1–77.

Greenberg, J. (1987). The college sophomore as guinea pig: setting the record straight. *Academy of Management Review*, 12(1), 157–159.

Grönroos C. (2007). *Service Management and Marketing: Customer Management in Service Competition* (3rd ed.), Chichester: Wiley.

Hair, J., Anderson, R., Tatham, R. & Black, W. (1998). *Multivariate Data Analysis* (5th ed.), Englewood Cliffs, NJ: Prentice–Hall.

Hatcher, L. (1994). *A Step-by-Step Approach to Using the SAS System for Factor and Structural Equation Modeling*, Cary, NC: The SAS Institute.

Hofacker, C., Goldsmith, R., Swilley, E. & Bridges, E. (2007). E-services: a synthesis and research agenda. *Journal of Value Chain Management*, 1(1/2), 13–44.

Hoffman, D. & Novak, T. (1996). Marketing in hypermedia computer-mediated environments: conceptual foundations. *Journal of Marketing*, 80(4), 50–68.

Hoyer, R. & Hoyer, B. (2001). What is quality. *Quality Progress*, 34(7), 53–62.

Hoyle, R. & Panter, A. (1995). Writing about structural equation models. In Hoyle, R. (ed.), *Structural Equation Modeling: Concepts, Issues, and Applications*, Thousand Oaks, CA: Sage Publications, 158–176.

InternetRetailer. (2008). Consumers like live chat feature but want more from it, study says. Retrieved from: http://www.internetretailer.com/dailyNews. asp?id=25764, accessed on 15 March 2009.

Iwaarden, J., Wiele, T., Ball, L. & Millen, R. (2004). Perceptions about the quality of web sites: A survey among students at Northeastern and Eastern University. *Information and Management*, 41, 947–959.

Jarvis, L. & Mayo, E. (1986). Winning the market-share game. *Cronell Hotel Restaurant Administration Quarterly*, 27(3), 72–71.

Johns, M. (1999). What is this thing called service? *European Journal of Marketing*, 33, (9/10), 958–973.

Juwaheer, T. (2004). Exploring international tourists' perceptions of hotel operations by using a modified SERVQUAL approach – a case study of Mauritius. *Managing Service Quality*, 14(5), 350–364.

Kotler, P. & Singh, R. (1981). Marketing warfare in the 1980's. *Journal of Business Strategy*, 1(3), 30–41.

Lee, H., Delene, L. & Bunda, M. (2000). Methods of measuring health-care service quality. *Journal of Business Research*, 48(3), 233–246.

Li, Y., Tan, K. & Xie, M. (2002). Measuring web-based service quality. *Total Quality Management*, 13(5), 685–700.

Lim, P. & Tang, N. (2000). A study of patients' expectations and satisfaction in Singapore hospitals. *International Journal of Health Care Quality Assurance*, 13(7), 290–299.

Liu, C. & Arnett K. (2000). Exploring the factors associated with web site success in the context of electronic commerce. *Information and Management*, 38(1), 23–33.

Loiacono, E., Watson, R. & Goodhue, D. (2007). WebQual: an instrument for consumer evaluation of web sites. *International Journal of Electronic Commerce*, 11(3), 51–87.

Lovelock, C. & Gummesson, E. (2004). Whither services marketing? In search of a new paradigm and fresh perspectives. *Journal of Service Research*, 7(1), 20–41.

MacCallum, R. & Browne, M. (1993). The use of causal indicators in covariance structure models: some practical issues. *Psychological Bulletin*, 114, 533–541.

McKnight, D., Choudhury, V. & Kacmar, C. (2002). Developing and validating trust measures for e-commerce: an integrative typology. *Information Systems Research*, 13(3), 334–359.

MediaAudit. (2008). Online Shopping By Minorities Increase. Retrieved from: http://e-commerce news.internetretailer.com/search?p=Q&ts=custom2&isort= date&mainresult=mt_inrg_f&w=customer+service&x=10&y=10, accessed on 15 March 2009.

Nunnally, C. & Bernstein, I. (1994). *Psychometric Theory*, (3rd ed.). New York: McGraw-Hill.

Oliver, R. (1980). A cognitive model of the antecedents and consequence of satisfaction decision. *Journal of Marketing Research*, 17, 460–469.

Oliver, R. (1999). Whence consumer loyalty? *Journal of Marketing*, 63, 33–44.

Parasuraman, A., Zeithaml, V. & Berry, L. (1988). SERVQUAL: a multi-item scale for measuring consumer perception of service quality. *Journal of Retailing*, 64, 2–40.

Parasuraman, A., Zeithaml, V. & Malhotra, A. (2005). E-S-Qual: a multiple-item scale for assessing electronic service quality. *Journal of Service Research*, 7(3), 213–233.

Reichheld, F. & Schefter., P. (2000). E-loyalty: your secret weapon on the web. *Harvard Business Review*, 78(4), 105–113.

Roses, L., Hoppen, N. & Henrique, J. (2008). Management of perceptions of information technology service quality. *Journal of Business Research*, article in press.

Rust, R. & Kannan, P. (2003). E-service: a new paradigm for business in the electronic environment. *Communications of the ACM*, 46(6), 37–42.

Rust, R. & Miu, C. (2006). What academic research tell us about services? *Communications of the ACM*, 49(6), 49–54.

Sousa, R. & Voss, C. (2006). Service quality in multichannel services employing virtual channels. *Journal of Service Research*, 8(4), 356–371.

Srinivasan, S., Anderson, R. & Ponnavolu, K. (2002). Customer loyalty in e-commerce: an exploration of its antecedents and consequences, *Journal of Retailing*, 78(1), 41–50.

Stodnick, M. & Rogers, P. (2008). Using the SERVQUAL to measure the quality of the classroom experience. *Journal of Innovative Education*, 6(1), 115–133.

Swaid, S. & Wigand R. (2009). Measuring the quality of e-service: scale development and initial validation. *Journal of Electronic Commerce Research*, 10(1), 13–28.

Swaid, S. & Wigand, R. (2007). Key dimensions of e-commerce service quality and its relationships to satisfaction and loyalty. *Proceedings of the 20th Bled Electronic Commerce Conference*, 1–15.

Teas, R. (1993). Expectations, performance evaluation and consumers' perception of quality, in Olorunniwo, F., Pennington, J. & Hsu, M. (2002), Developing a service quality construct: a pedagogical approach. *Proceedings of the Association of Marketing Educators*, First Annual Conference of Federation of Business Disciplines, 179–190.

Umpathy, K. & Purao, S. (2004). Services-oriented computing: an opportunity for the language-action perspective. *Proceedings of the 9th International Working Conference on the Language-Action Perspective on Communication Modeling*, 41–58.

Van Riel, A., Semeijn, J. & Pauwels, P. (2004). Online travel service quality: the role of pre-transaction services. *Total Quality Management*, 15(4), 475–493.

Voss, C. (2003). Rethinking paradigms of service: service in a virtual environment. *International Journal of Operations & Production Management*, 23(1), 88–104.

Wisniewski, M. (2001). Using SERVQUAL to assess customer satisfaction with public sector services. *Managing Service Quality*, 11(6), 380–388.

Wolfinbarger, M. & Gilly, M. (2003). e-TailQ: dimensionalizing, measuring and predicting etail quality. *Journal of Retailing*, 27, 183–198.

Zeithaml, V. (1981). How consumer evaluation processes differ between goods and services, in Donnelly, J.H., George, W.K. (Eds.), *Marketing of Services*, Chicago: American Marketing Association, 186–190.

Zeithaml, V. & Bitner, M. (2003). *Service Marketing: Integrating Customer Focus Across the Firm*. New York: McGraw-Hill.

Zeithaml, V., Parasuraman, A. & Berry, L. (1985). Problems and strategies in services marketing. *Journal of Marketing*, 49, 33–46.

Zeithaml, V., Parasuraman, A. & Berry., L. (1996). The behavioral consequences of service quality. *Journal of Marketing*, 60, 31–64.

Zeithaml, V., Parasuraman A. & Malhorta A. (2000). A conceptual framework for understanding e-service quality: implications for research and managerial practice. *Marketing Science Institute (MSI)*, Report # 00–115.

Zeithaml, V., Parasuraman, A. & Malhotra, A. (2002). Service quality delivery through the web sites: a critical review of extant knowledge. *Journal of the Academy of Marketing Science*, 30(4), 362–375.

Zhang, X. & Prybutok, V. (2004). An empirical study of online shopping: a service perspective. *International Journal of Services Technology and Management*, 5(1), 1–13.

Appendix: Final Version of E-Service Quality Measures

E-service quality

Respondents were asked to rate each of the scales items using a 7-point Likert scale ranging from 1 (strongly disagree) to 7 (strongly agree). Items of e-service quality measures were presented in random order to respondents. The items presented below are grouped by dimension.

Information quality

INQ1: Information contained on the website is current and timely.
INQ3: Information contained on the website is accurate and relevant.
INQ4: Information contained on the website is at the right level of detail.
INQ5: Information contained on the website is pretty much what I need to carry out my tasks.
INQ6: Information contained on the website is easy to understand.

Website usability

WUS1: Finding your way on the website is easy.
WUS2: Navigation is consistent and standardized.
WUS4: Scrolling through pages is kept to a minimum.
WUS5: Graphics and animation do not detract me from use.

Reliability

REL1: The website when it promises to do something in a certain time it does so.
REL2: All relevant order confirmation details are sent to my email within 24 hours.
REL3: Order cancellation and returns are confirmed within three days.
REL4: Order tracking details are available until delivery.
REL5: The website service performs the service right the first time.

Responsiveness

RES1: When you have a problem, the website service shows a sincere interest in solving it.

RES2: Automated or human email responses on serving pages give customers prompt service.

RES3: Email responses are relevant and accurate.

RES4: Email content is appropriate to customer requirements.

RES5: Website addresses are included in all existing documentation, publicity and advertising channel.

Assurance

ASS1: The website has adequate security and privacy policies.

ASS2: The website has a good reputation.

ASS3: I feel I can trust this website.

ASS4: The company behind the site is reputable.

Personalization

PER1: The website gives me personal attention.

PER2: The website enables me to order the product in a way that meets my needs.

PER3: The website understands my specific needs.

4
Consumer Value within a Click-and-Mortar Construct

Paul McElhone and Alison Yacyshyn

Introduction

Rapid technological advances affect the daily decisions retailers make and the impact is seen in the quality, value and loyalty chains (Parasuraman & Grewal, 2000). The discussions around channel conflict (Tsay & Agrawal, 2004), conflict issues, the impact on channel efficiency (Rosenbloom, 1973), the level of cooperation needed (Bonoma, 1976) and leadership required (Filser et al., 2001) to create retailer value are complex and research suggests that further analysis is required to assist the retailer in creating multi-channel strategies (Rosenbloom, 2007). In a relentless pursuit of creating value for the consumer, (one may ask) will technology improve efficiencies and reduce cost (Chircu & Mahajan, 2006)? There are also many questions which are now beginning to emerge about online shopping (Carpenter & Fairhurst, 2005), and more specifically at the store level, the use of radio-frequency identification (RFID) (Napolitano, 2005) which are now begining to emerge.

As research data continue to give more focus on global trends, even small retailers are looking for more cost-effective ways to create an online presence (Hoffman & Novak, 2000). The value of extending market reach has never been more important to retailers (Sharma & Mehrotra, 2007), but more research is needed to define business models for online strategies.

In recent years there has been much research dedicated to the evolutionary process that has lead to the demise of the traditional department store anchors, the emergence of 'Big Box' formats, and the growing gap between specialty retailers and deep discount merchants (Levy et al., 2005). Since value for the retailer (all the reasons for wanting to run a retail business) and consumers (the benefits received in the exchange process) is the driver behind retail development, growth and the future of retail (Berry, 1996), an investigation of retail trends and format development is of importance.

Retailing is a set of business activities that add value to the products and services sold to consumers for their personal or family use (Levy et al., 2005). The exchange process, whether face-to-face or electronic, links consumers and retailers in a buyer-seller relationship (Peppers & Rogers, 2004). Since retail relationships are bilateral and interdependent in nature, customer value and retailer value is a logical focus for contemporary research and analysis.

Much of the research on retailer value has been conducted in parallel with the majority of the research dedicated to consumer value (Carpenter & Fairhurst, 2005). Retailer value has not received the same level of attention and much of the literature addresses issues of channel management (Rosenbloom, 2007) and channel conflict (Tsay & Agrawal, 2004). Research investigating the introduction of click-and-mortar as a concept, the link of click-and-mortar to customer value (Adelaar et al., 2004), and examination of service and cost benefits of click-and-mortar integration (Bendoly et al., 2007) are quite current. Integrating a discussion linking both consumer value and retailer value will enrich a more in-depth discussion around a state-of-the-art click-and-mortar strategy.

The changing face of communication in retail

Advances in technology have changed the face of communication creating a variety of t touch points between consumers, retailers, and distribution channels. Internet merchants have invested millions of dollars into new technologies to make their sites more user friendly, but consumers are expecting more from the internet than it has delivered (Tedeschi, 2007). Astute companies are starting to encourage the growth of online communities in order to enhance the value proposition of their goods and services. In today's very competitive global marketplace, product exclusivity has been marginalized. Traditionally, retailers created a competitive advantage through product selection (SteenKamp, 1989), environmental design (Backstrom & Johansson, 2006), and the implementation of human resource strategies that focused on hiring quality sales associates (Harrison-Walker & Coppett, 2003) who were committed to the relationship selling process as part of their value-added proposition. Today, this is not enough. Retailers need to benefit from an e-commerce strategy and there are advantages and synergies (Saeed et al., 2003) that arise when firms have a combination of physical and electronic channels. The changes in communication inherently affected the concept of value and thus, the theory of value has evolved historically.

Historical changes in the theory of value

Axiology (or the study of value) has been the interest of philosophical discussion for several decades. Value is a very complex concept, inextricably linked to economic thought (Jevons, 1957), marketing strategies (Stern et al., 2006) and sociological theory (Denzin, 1978). However, value as a concept has evolved over time. The earliest axiological discussions by thinkers such as Ricardo (1817) and Marx (2005) viewed value as linked to profits. Ricardo (1817), in his essay on profits, argued that value was determined by labour embodied, while Marx (2005) expanded Ricardo's theory with the belief that relative prices were determined by value. Marx saw value as a social relation, which manifests itself in a relationship between commodities. Smith (2001) expanded the concept developing a cost of production or adding up theory. For him, the word 'value' had two different meanings and sometimes was expressed as utility of some particular object and sometimes as the power of purchasing other goods, which the possession of the object conveys. Smith developed the concepts of 'value in use' and 'value in exchange'. The things which had the greatest value in use frequently had little or no value in exchange; and on the contrary, those which had the greatest value in exchange, frequently had little or no value in use.

The earliest roots of the discussion of 'value' as a concept started with the agrarian period (16th century). Throughout the 18th century, classical political economists defined value as a product of labour. During the 19th century and in the years leading up to and during the Industrial Revolution economists wrestled with the concepts of 'value in use' and 'value in exchange' and issues of labour power (Marx, 2005) and the value of production. The post-industrial period saw a more functional perspective as economists began to examine value in terms of marginality (Pareto, 2007). Literature reviews suggest the term 'value' was seldom used during the 1930s and the years leading up to WWII (as a result of the Great Depression). Economic discussions were concerned more about the equilibrium between money, interest rates, investment in infrastructure and the economic roles of the state and the private sector (Keynes, 1971). The optimism of the post-war years of the 1950s brought with it the value of innovation at every level from the introduction of plastics and television to the redesign of the North American automobile and a proliferation of modern furniture (see the website, American History: 1900–1909, http://kclibrary.lonestar.edu/decade00.html, for additional information). By the 1960s, marketing (as a business term) was introduced by the president of General Electric, Fred J. Borsch (Lamont, 1955), and researchers began examining consumer value as a concept that underpinned the strategies around product development and promotional campaigns.

The increasing competition of the 1970s and 1980s changed the way retailers approached their customers and research started to see the value for consumers in much more complex dimensions of hedonic consumption (Hirschman & Holbrook, 1982). By the 1990s, researchers had shifted their focus to value creation (Zeithaml, 2000). Electronic mediums have further complicated the value proposition and access to information has taken prominence in hyper-velocity retail markets (Bodkin & Perry, 2004). As we enter a new millennium, value has become value-added. As a dimension of value-added, consumers and retailers are involved in assessment of 'values' (Wood, 2002) based on environmental stances (Kennedy, 2007), trust (Ashworth et al., 2006) and integrity (Mujtaba & Sims, 2006).

To more clearly understand the contemporary perspective of value as a concept, it is important to examine how retail has changed since the 1980s. We have evolved from retail markets in which there were relatively few specialty and deep-discount retailers, to a marketplace dominated by deep discount players and a growing numbers of specialty players. Filser et al., (2001, p. 105) have schematically depicted this evolution (as presented in Figure 4.1). The 1980s saw a dominance of mid-market retailers, most in department store formats. With the entrance of deep discounters such as Wal-Mart and Costco during the 1990s, there began a polarization between deep-discount formats (with strong market penetration) and specialty players (whose value proposition was defined by quality and added services). The side-by-side presentation of the specialty retailers and deep discounters demonstrates the historical evolution of retailers (see Figure 4.1).

With the historical evolution of specialty and deep discounters, value for the customer is important. In its simplest form, value for the consumer is the sum total of benefits (whether tangible or intangible) that enhance not only the core product (Payne, 2006), but also the role and use of the product (Manning et al., 2001). Ultimately, consumers do not buy commodities; they buy the value derived from features and benefits

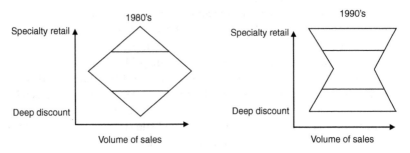

Figure 4.1   Evolution of specialty and deep discount retail
Source: Filser et al., 2001

that help to solve a given problem (i.e., 'its winter, I'm cold, I need a coat to keep me warm'). As consumers choose between deep discount and specialty shopping environments, the consumer's experience and overall value assessment can be viewed as a multi-layer model encompassing various meanings.

Holbrook's customer value

Morris Holbrook (1999, p. 1) believed that customer value plays a crucial role at the heart of all marketing activity and therefore deserves the attention of every researcher. To this end, Holbrook (1999, p. 4) has created a 'Typology of the Consumer' in which he tried to understand a given type of value only by considering its relationship to other types of value (Table 4.1).

> When we say that customer value is an interactive relativistic preference experience, we mean that the relationship of consumers to products (subjects to objects) operates relativistically (depending on relevant comparisons, varying between people, changing among situations) to determine preferences that lie at the heart of the consumption experience. In this sense, prescriptively as well as descriptively, Consumer Value shapes the design of Marketing Strategy. (Holbrook, 1999, p. 9)

Although Holbrook considered both self – and other-oriented dimensions, for the purposes here, only self-oriented dimensions of the model are highlighted and discussed. The consumer interface with technology and

Table 4.1 Holbrook's typology: A framework for analysis and research

		Extrinsic	Intrinsic
Self-Oriented	**Active**	**EFFICIENCY** (O/I Convenience)	**PLAY** (Fun)
	Reactive	**EXCELLENCE** (Quality)	**AESTHETICS** (Beauty)
Other-Oriented	**Active**	**STATUS** (Success, Impression Management)	**ETHICS** (Virtue, Justice, Morality)
	Reactive	**ESTEEM** (Reputation, Materialism, Possessions)	**SPIRITUALITY** (Faith, Ecstasy, Sacredness)

Source: Holbrook, 1999, p. 12

its impact on the consumer's perception of value can best be viewed as self-oriented experience, with both active and reactive responses (that can be examined from both an intrinsic and extrinsic dimensions). Efficiency, play, excellence and aesthetics are all important dimensions of the value expectations consumers have when using multiple electronic touch points and each is discussed in more detail in a contemporary context.

Efficiency

Drawing from earlier works, Holbrook (1999) frames efficiency as an extrinsic value, resulting from an active use of a product that achieves some self-oriented purpose. What is important is Holbrook's perspective that output/input is most commonly seen as convenience divided by time. Today, time has become a most precious commodity for all shopping segments, whether deep discount or true specialty. Even high-involvement purchases require respect for the time constraints placed on busy consumers. Within a selling model, extra time spent in one shopping environment translates into a greater overall saving of time for the consumer. For example, trust built over time by shopping at a specialty menswear store leads to much quicker decisions on the part of the consumer, reducing the need to browse at several retail outlets. The experience for the consumer has a high level of self-oriented efficiency.

Retailers have known historically that there is a relationship between the amount of physical time spent with a customer and the total dollars they spend. Over time, loyal customers will spend more dollars on regular price items and retailers become more profitable. It has also been shown that there is also a positive effect between the customer amenities (or creature comforts like spacious change rooms, atmospherics, flowers, complimentary water and fresh coffee) and the amount of dollars a customer will spend. It is cheaper to keep a loyal customer, than to cultivate a new one (Manning et al., 2001).

Play

'The [web] sites that engage and entertain customers will be winning here in the near future' stated Bob Myers, senior vice president of QVC. com. QVC.com is a large multimedia retailer (founded in 1986 by Joseph Segel), built on technology and guided by the principles of: Quality, value and convenience (Tedeschi, 2007). A shift from 'extrinsic' to 'intrinsic' dimensions of value examine 'play' and 'aesthetics' as a self-oriented elements of value (Holbrook, 1999, p. 18). Note that all the intrinsic forms of value have the greatest potential to create a differentiating value proposition for consumers choosing to use the internet. Play (fun) has been viewed by classic axiologists as an experience pursued as an end in itself (Santayana, 1896, p. 19). In the exchange between customer and sales associate, once a relationship has been established, there is often an element of play (that being in contemporary settings equated to fun). Light conversation and the enthusiasm on the part of the sales associate make for an enjoyable experience for the customer (and customers will report, 'I shop there because I have fun'). Customers, for whom this level of play (or fun) is important in the face-to-face experience, also expect play as a dimension in other channel formats.

Excellence

In defining excellence, Holbrook feels that consumer satisfaction with a product's quality is closely linked to its ability to perform a function that can be measured relative to its performance and the consumer's expectations (Garvin, 1998). Reactively speaking, a customer may appreciate the fact that a winter coat is rated for −40° Celsius weather, without personally wanting to experience such weather conditions to test the rating. Similarly, the comfort of knowing a fabric is water repellent does not require the gale force rains of the tropics to appreciate the technology. Excellence in a product's quality also ties in with aesthetic value.

Aesthetics

For Holbrook, the hallmark of aesthetic value in general or beauty in particular, is that it is enjoyed purely for its own sake (Holbrook, 1999, p. 20). The direct reference to the fashion industry by Holbrook is important:

> As one example of a product associated with aesthetics along with other aspects of consumer value, fashion is often prized for the beauty of its product design – that is, on the grounds of a pleasing appearance – as well as for (say) the ability of clothes to keep us warm (efficiency), the role of self-decoration in conveying the impression of prestige (status), or the rules of decorum that involve covering oneself up for ethical reasons (virtue). (Ibid., p. 20)

One can extend Holbrook's observations to include all value dimensions of the 'Typology of Value', particularly if there is an examination of specialty retail environments. Excellence (quality) is a pillar of the specialty purchases. In addition, the reputation, materialism and value placed on possessions that are part of the esteem-as-value link value relative to dollars spent (and the importance of play has already been noted). As for the ecstasy and magic of spirituality-as-value, one need only envisage the unforgettable moment in time when a bride selects the 'perfect dress' for her 'special day'. For some, shopping has replaced traditional forms of spirituality with 'around the corner' spirituality (Andieu et al., unpublished). With the aforementioned dimensions (efficiency, play, excellence, and aesthetics), both retailers and consumers co-create value.

The roots of contemporary consumer value

The term 'value' has many meanings for the consumer and is in a constant state of change. Value has the following characteristics: quality (Abbott, 1955), hedonic experiences (Holbrook, 1999), relationships, price (Duckler, 2001) and service (Zeithaml, 2000). As long as there is competition and the global economy continues to grow, the term value will continue to not only evolve, but also will become increasingly more complex.

The baby boomers have long been the focus of academic and applied research (Andruss, 2005). The emergence of a new generation of shoppers, Gen-Y and N-Geners (the children of the baby boomers), is changing traditional retail paradigms and has created further interest for researchers (Schneider, 2004). Technology creates a seamless link between work, play and education for the N-Geners. Therefore, there will be interest for researchers in analyzing changing consumer preferences and how the value for retailers will be redefined as firms expand the touch points for this economically powerful demographic group.

The post-war years of the 1950s and 1960s marked a period of accelerated change and innovation in consumer products (Knox, 1969), technology, fashion, music (Campbell & Brody, 2008), art and space travel (Massie, 1966). When marketing was introduced by Fred J. Borch as a business term, researchers not only found new interest in consumer value (Lamont, 1955) but also in marketing channels, (Clewett, 1954) and quality and competition (Abbott, 1955). 'Value' as a term had now become more interesting to marketers and was incorporated into discussions involving the consumer, retailer, and supplier.

During the 1970s and 1980s the relationship between the consumer, retailer, and supplier changed significantly. In an attempt to maximize shopping opportunities, products started to be merchandised in 'shop within a shop' concepts and designers turned to stand-alone locations that were either company owned or had a licensee arrangement (for example, Polo/Ralph Lauren, Tommy Hilfiger, and the GAP). Designers also expanded to non-traditional lifestyle concepts that included clothing, accessories, footwear, small leather goods, kids wear, eyewear, fragrances and home furnishings. Logos were used extensively and 'Young Urban Professionals' sought self-gratification through brand alignment. Perceptions of value were synonymous with the prestige associated with internationally recognized brands. Researchers began looking at value as a complex concept linked to hedonic consumption (Holbrook & Corfman, 1983), service (Zeithaml, 2000), quality (SteenKamp, 1989) and price (Dodds, 1991).

'Valued-added' became the hallmark to describe the relationship between the retailer and the consumer in the 1990s. Researchers turned their focus to how to create increased value for the consumer (Woodruff, 1997). The gap between deep-discount retailers and specialty retailers was growing (Filser et al., 2001), and so too was the gap between consumer perceptions and expectations of value (Zeithaml, 2000). Even the manufacturers were becoming part of the value equation (Sparks and Legault, 1993) as retailers strived to recreate the experiential dimensions of the total customer experience (Badot & Dupuis, 2001). The concept of value for the retailer had grown to become a 'complex set of value-based promises' (Payne, 2006, p. 105), and for the consumer value was what was ultimately bought in addition to the benefits and solutions he or she received from the process (Payne, 2006).

Throughout the later part of the 1990s and into the new millennium, the proliferation of the internet and electronic communication formats created both challenges and opportunities for the retail industry (Levenburg, 2005). Early beliefs that the internet was a selling platform (Liu and Arnett, 2000) were replaced with business models that saw the power of the internet for brokering information and giving the consumer optional methods of communication (Andersen, 2005).

With the .com bust and the collapse of certain global giants (like Enron and WorldCom), 'value' for the consumer and the retailer became an alignment of 'values'. Trust both on- and off-line is an important ingredient in securing customer loyalty (Ribbink et al., 2004). Consumers want to do business with companies that are socially responsible; thus successful companies are able to reinvent value in today's society (Normann & Ramirez, 2000).

Currently, value constructs have seen less emphasis placed on price, quality and service. The new value paradigm recognizes the emerging significance of experiential value (Mathwick et al., 2001) and the experiential perceptions of value (Mathwick & Malhotra, 2002). The 'what's-in-it-for-me' consumer is now looking for, and expecting, high levels of entertainment value. The ultimate experiential value is more often an expression of hedonic value (Holbrook, 1999) allowing consumers to escape into the physical and virtual worlds of experiential retailing.

The touch point theory of value

The relationships (and channels) between consumers and retailers has become steadily more complex since William Petty's (1685) earliest discussions of value. Just as value defined by labour evolved to value in use and value in exchange to value defined as a mathematical expression to value being defined in post-war consumerism by price, quality, service and hedonic pleasures to an obsession with customer-centric value models, so too the modern concept of 'location, location, location' has been replaced by 'available, available, available.' Technology has turned availability into the new 24/7 value reality. Consumers and retailers create value for each other through a myriad of optional communication and shopping touch points allowing for a bilateral customization process for both. Consumers get to choose goods and services on their terms; the memorable and engaging quality of the experience is the

Table 4.2 Potential click-and-mortar touch points between the retailer and consumer

Mortar	Click
Product/selection	Web access /internet
Price/quality	Supplier links (two-way)
Location	Blogs
Staff/service	Wikis
Environment	Brand communities/social networks
Company values	Kiosks
Catalogues	Product-rich information
Promotions	Information-rich site
Community involvement	Online coupons
Supplier relationships	'My Account'
CRM systems	Employee access
RFID (Radio Frequency Identification)	Text messaging/Twitters

gauge by which consumers measure value. The retailer on the other hand has created value for himself because he is perceived as current and savvy and will earn the right have to his customer's loyalty. Touch points of value can be categorized as either 'mortar' and/or 'click' driven and Table 4.2 highlights potential click-and-mortar touch points used between a retailer and a consumer.

Shared value between retailers and consumers

Normann & Ramirez (2000) suggest that retailers and consumers need to devise a strategy that would see them working together to co-create value. Accordingly, value is a term with multiple definitions and implications. The extrinsic needs of the retailer for value, in the form of profitability, can be viewed as contradictory to those of the opportunistic consumers who define value, for example, as being characteristic of deep-discounted prices. However, a long-term view of consumer/retailer relationships will illustrate several common elements of value between them. Multi-channel formats create financial value, loyalty and extended reach for the retailer, while also creating convenience, selection, and one-stop shopping for the consumer. Building strong face-to-face relationships and/or electronic touch points build shared value in the form of trust, for both the retailer and consumer. The consumer trusts the retailer to provide the best solutions for his or her needs and the retailer trusts that the consumer will be a loyal customer. The alignment of values within a brand community binds channel members together in an inter-connected, interdependent bond that builds mutual value over time.

Methodology of consumers in a contemporary Canadian survey

In order to assess the contemporary situation of value, a series of dichotic and open-ended questions were asked of Canadian specialty menswear consumers in order to gather information regarding consumers' perception of value. The target sample set was males between 25 and 55 years of age, with an annual income of more than $50K CAN per annum. Respondents from an independent specialty menswear retailer, a regional specialty menswear retailer and a national specialty menswear retailer were targeted as representative of the menswear specialty industry in Canada. Subjects were recruited from customer databases and through radio solicitation. With consistent findings between these retailers, the sample set is considered generalizable and the exploratory results of the survey are presented here.

Findings of consumers in a contemporary Canadian survey

The results of the contemporary Canadian survey allow investigation of 648 respondents, their demographic characteristics and their perceptions toward value. Table 4.3 identifies specific demographic characteristics of the sample used in this research.

The greatest number of respondents in this research fall between the ages of 31 and 50 and this distribution is appropriate for menswear clothing purchases. Although respondents' income levels were not specifically asked, the higher numbers of university- and graduate-educated customers in the sample suggests the data are consistent with the normative income of consumers of specialty menswear retailers (of $50K+ CAN per annum). Similarly, the majority of the respondents in the sample reported that on a monthly basis they have some contact/communication via internet/email with the specialty menswear retailer. In addition, the majority of respondents report that they are high users of the internet and communicate frequently by email.

The majority of respondents report that it is important for a retailer to have a website and feel that click-and-mortar strategies add more value (see Table 4.4). Traditional forms of communication (newspapers,

Table 4.3   Respondents demographic characteristics

Variables		Values	N	%
AGE	AGE groups in years (N=645)	20–30	112	17.4
		31–40	182	28.2
		41–50	181	28.1
		51–60	129	20.0
		61+	41	6.4
EDUCATION	EDUCATION level (N=641)	High School	39	6.1
		College	74	11.5
		University	264	41.2
		Graduate	264	41.2
CONTACT	monthly CONTACT/communicate via internet/email with the specialty menswear retailer (N=500)	<50/month	346	69.2
		>100/month	4	0.8
		0/month	150	30.0
ACCESS	monthly ACCESS the internet and/or communicate by email (N=497)	<100/month	125	25.2
		>100/month	372	74.8
USER	USER of the internet and email (N=647)	Seldom	10	1.5
		Occasional	19	2.9
		Frequent	618	95.5

Table 4.4   Customers and specialty menswear retailer websites

Variables		Values	N	%
IMPORTANCE	**Importance** for the specialty menswear retailer to have a website (N=644)	Not answered	81	12.6
		Yes	372	57.8
		No	170	26.4
		Not sure	21	3.3
COMBINATION	The **combination** of retail locations and access to a website adds more value (N=564)	No	205	36.3
		Yes	329	58.3
		Maybe	5	0.9
		NA	25	4.4
TRADITIONAL	**Traditional** forms of communication are more important than using the specialty menswear retailer website or being contacted by email (N=575)	No	282	49.0
		Yes	227	39.5
		Maybe	4	0.7
		Not Sure	62	10.8
VALUE	What gives more customer **value** (online/email, face-to-face, both online/email, other, NA/I don't know) (N=578)	Access to Internet	37	6.4
		Face to Face	434	75.1
		Both	82	14.2
		Not sure	25	4.3

catalogues, etc.) are less important than using the specialty menswear retailer website or being contacted by email. The results suggest that the respondents seem to have accepted technology as a preferred form of communication (from the specialty menswear retailer). Overall, the majority of respondents in this research feel that face-to-face interaction gives more customer value than online/email, both online/ email or other interaction forms. The strong response in favour of face-to-face interaction suggests that brick-and-mortar is a stronghold in this retail sector. However, about 14 per cent of respondents feel that both access-to-internet and face-to-face provides more customer value. This suggests that an emerging trend is for customers to find value in a combination of face-to-face and internet interactions. Consumers and retailers in specialty retail environments are migrating from brick-and-mortar formats based on personal relationships (Peppers & Rogers, 2004), memorable experiences (Backstrom & Johansson, 2006; Mathwick & Malhotra, 2002) and value propositions that are historically driven by the perceived quality of products, customer service and/or price proposition. Overall, a large percentage, 58.3 per cent, of respondents feel that the combination of retail locations and access to a website adds more value for the customer.

Table 4.5 Customer loyalty

I am a loyal customer of the menswear retailer because of the...	N=648	%
Brands/style/labels/fashion	39	6.02
Selection	60	9.26
Quality	115	17.75
Service/custom fitting/professionalism/advice	259	39.97
Staff	160	24.69
Location	20	3.09
Relationships	40	6.17
Other	116	17.90
Product	105	16.20
I am not a loyal customer	96	14.81
I work there	1	0.15
I heard the radio ad	8	1.23

When respondents were asked to explain why they were loyal customers of the menswear retailer in an open-ended question the following results were revealed (Table 4.5).

The terms used by respondents to explain why they are loyal to the menswear retailer clearly identify service/custom fitting/professionalism/advice as a top choice.

When respondents were asked to explain why they shop at the menswear retailer, an open-ended question revealed the following results as presented in Table 4.6.

The terms used by respondents to explain why they shop at the menswear retailer demonstrate no consistent value proposition for all retailers, it varies by specific retail format and strategies.

When respondents were asked to explain why they like the menswear retailer website, an open-ended question revealed the following results as presented in Table 4.7.

Table 4.6   Customer shopping behaviours

I shop at the menswear store because of the ...	N=648	%
Reputation	8	1.23
Environment	13	2.01
Convenience	12	1.85
Location	19	2.93
Brands/labels/style/fashion	99	15.28
Selections	112	17.28
Variety	7	1.08
Relationships	31	4.78
Staff	118	18.21
Quality	245	37.81
Product	180	27.78
Service/advice/professionalism/custom fitting	222	34.26
Other	94	14.51
I work there	0	0.00
I heard the radio ad	13	2.01
I do not shop there	57	8.80

Table 4.7 Customer views of retailer website

I like the menswear retailer website because of the...	N=648	%
Look/layout/design/mature/simple/trendy	78	12.04
Colors	7	1.08
NA/don't know what I like about the website/I've never been to it	292	45.06
Information/promos/emails	84	12.96
Ease of use/navigation/interactive/quick loading most	35	5.40
Nothing	25	3.86
Tips	32	4.94
Other	28	4.32

Table 4.8 Customers' wants in a retailer website

What would you like to see added to the menswear website...	N=648	%
Tips (grooming, dressing, etc)	27	4.17
Pictures	84	12.96
Links to specific sales associates	6	0.93
Links to brand websites	11	1.70
Fashion articles	4	0.62
Coupons	6	0.93
Prices	33	5.09
Trends	21	3.24
Online shopping	35	5.40
Product descriptions/information	53	8.18
Other	105	16.20
NA/I don't know	246	37.96
Nothing should be added	26	4.01

For the open-ended question asking respondents to explain why they like the menswear retailer website, each retailer exhibits different descriptives by the customer respondents. The responses regarding website preferences are heavily weighted to informational content in a website that is well-designed visually.

When respondents were asked to explain what they would like to see added to the menswear website, an open-ended question revealed the following results as presented in Table 4.8.

For the open-ended question asking respondents to explain what they would like to see added to the menswear website, the respondents clearly would like to see pictures, online shopping, and product descriptions/information added to the current menswear retailer website(s).

When respondents were asked to explain why they dislike the menswear retailer website, an open-ended question revealed the following results as presented in Table 4.9.

For the open-ended question asking respondents to explain why they dislike the menswear retailer website, each retailer exhibits different descriptives by the customer respondents. The respondents clearly do not like the lack of content, the staticness, and the flash on the menswear retailer website.

Table 4.9 Customers' dislikes of retailers' websites

What is liked least about the menswear website ...	N=648	%
Lack of content	99	15.28
No prices	20	3.09
No online ordering	17	2.62
Website is too basic	16	2.47
Lack of links	5	0.77
Website doesn't work properly	12	1.85
Flash on the website	14	2.16
Not user friendly	14	2.16
Staticness	39	6.02
NA/don't know what I dislike about the retailer's website/I've never been to it	280	43.21
Other	39	6.02
Dislike nothing	95	14.66

Discussion

The survey of contemporary Canadian consumers allows advancement in the field of value research. The customer respondents in the data were all male, which represents the target market for menswear specialty retailers. The respondents were considered mid- to high-income earners, with annual incomes of more than $50K CAD per annum. Retail feedback suggests a large percentage of the respondents earn in excess of $100K CAD per year. The sample exhibits buying preferences for quality, high-end designer products which reflect their lifestyles, acquired wealth and social status. The customers indicate their preferences for service, custom fitting, professionalism and advice from their retailers of choice.

Extrinsically, according to Holbrook, customers value excellence (quality) and efficiency (convenience) (Holbrook, 1999). Both characteristics typify the majority of consumer responses. Intrinsically, this same group (customers) appreciates having a memorable experience (of play and fun) and values both the design integrity of their purchases and the retailer's meticulously detailed shopping environments (aesthetics) (Holbrook, 1999).

Generally, the contemporary data suggest that customers perceive more value with click-and-mortar strategies. Interestingly, respondents who specified that they did not access the company's website also indicate it is important for the retailer to have a website. Overall, customers express strong website preferences for information, web design, and a need for pictures, online shopping and product descriptions.

Conclusion

Contemporary consumer data support the literature that click-and-mortar strategies inherently provide more value for consumers. Similarly, there was moderate support for click-and-mortar strategies providing more value for retailers. The contemporary data also suggest that a click-and-mortar strategy continues to provide more value for consumers (as in the aggregate sample set). Consumers feel that information, pictures and product descriptions are important criteria for the website strategies of the retailers.

With the responses of contemporary consumers, a retail communication strategy needs to include electronic mediums such as: internet access, website, email communication, and (more recently) text messaging. An overwhelming percentage of customers consider themselves asto be 'frequent' users of the internet and websites. Even though the majority still prefers to shop face-to-face, the data suggest consumers derive more value from click-and-mortar strategies, face-to-face or methods that combine both strategies.

Websites are important information tools used by both existing and potential customers. The need for user-friendly sites with ease of navigation that are interactive and quick loading are important. Customers expect to access a variety of information which includes: product information (including prices,) links to designer/supplier sites, fashion articles, trends, links to sales associates, coupons, promotional details and online shopping. To attend to customers expectations, retailers need to invest in state-of-the-art technology and allocate the human resources necessary to maintain websites on a regular basis.

An analysis of the construct value suggests that traditional advertising strategies are losing their impact as more consumers are using the internet to gather information and pre-shop online. Savvy retailers will need to re-think their traditional marketing approaches when focusing on different demographic groups, for example, the N-Geners who are now entering their twenties. Consideration of electronic communication (i.e., emails, text messaging and e-flyers) is also important and these mediums are more cost effective than traditional methods (i.e., inserts, paper catalogues, etc.). Advancements in technology and diverse approaches have become more relevant for generations of individuals who have never known a world without technologically driven communication channels. Value for the millennia must balance the demands of the consumer for experiential constructs with the integration of state-of-the-art technology.

References

Abbott, L. (1955). *Quality and Competition: An Essay in Economic Theory*, New York: Columbia University Press.

Adelaar, T., Bouwman, H. & Steinfield, C. (2004). Enhancing customer value through click-and-mortar e-commerce: implications for geographical market reach and customer type. *Telemaics and Informatics*, 21, 167–182.

Andersen, P. H. (2005). Relationship marketing and brand involvement of professionals through web-enhanced brand communities: the case of Coloplast. *Industrial Marketing Management*, 34, 285–297.

Andieu, F., Badot, O. & Mace, S. (Unpublished manuscript). Le West Edmonton Mall: Un échafaudage sensoriel au service d'une cosmogonie populair?

Andruss, P. (2005). The GOLDEN age, *Marketing News*, 39(6), 21.

Ashworth, C., J., Schmidt, R., A., Pioch, E. A. & Hallsworth, A. (2006). An approach to sustainable 'fashion' e-retail: a five-stage evolutionary strategy for 'Clicks-and-Mortar' and 'Pure-Play' enterprises. *Journal of Retailing and Consumer Services*, 13(4), 289–299.

Backstrom, K. & Johansson, U. (2006). Creating and consuming experiences in retail store environments: comparing retailer and consumer perspectives. *Journal of Retailing and Consumer Services*, 13(6), 417–430.

Badot, O. & Dupuis, M. (2001). Le reénchantment de la ditribution, *Les Echos, L'Art du Management*, 7, 2–3.

Bendoly, E., Blocher, D., Bretthauer, K. & Venkataramanan, M. (2007). Service and cost benefits through click-and-mortar integration: implications for the centralization/decentralization debate. *European Journal of Operational Research*, 180(1), 426–442.

Berry, L. (1996). Retailers with a future: the new value equation. *Chain Store Age*, 72(10), 4D.

Bodkin, C. & Perry, M. (2004). Good retailers and service providers: comparative analysis of web site marketing communications. *Journal of Retailing and Consumer Services*, 11(1), 19–29.

Bonoma, T. (1976). Conflict, cooperation and trust in three power systems. *Behavioral Science*, 21, 499–514.

Campbell, M. & Brody, J. (2008). Rock and Roll: *An Introduction / Michael Campbell with James Brody* (2nd ed.), Belmount, CA: Thomson Schirmer.

Carpenter, J. & Fairhurst, A. (2005). Consumer shopping value, satisfaction, and loyalty for retail apparel brands. *Journal of Fashion Marketing and Management*, 9(3), 256.

Chircu, A. & Mahajan, V. (2006). Managing electronic commerce retail transaction costs for customer value. *Decision Support Systems*, 42(2), 898–914.

Clewett, R. (1954). *Marketing Channels*, Homewood, IL: Richard D. Irwin, Inc.

Denzin, N. (1978). *The Research Act in Sociology* (2nd ed.), New York: McGraw-Hill.

Dodds & B, W. (1991). In search of value: how price and store name information influence buyers' product perceptions. *The Journal of Consumer Marketing*, 8(2), 15.

Duckler, M. (2001). Price, quality only part of value. *Marketing News*, 35(10), 17.

Filser, M., des Garets, V. & Pache, G. (2001). *La distribution: organization et stratégie*, Editions EMS, Paris.

Garvin, D. (1998). Managing Quality: *The Strategic and Competitive Edge*. New York: The Free Press.

Harrison-Walker, L. & Coppett, J. (2003). Building bridges: the company-customer relationship. *Journal of Business to Business Marketing*, 10(4), 49.

Hirschman, E. & Holbrook, M. (1982). Hedonic consumption: emerging concepts, methods and proportions. *Journal of Marketing*, 46, 92–101.

Hoffman, D. & Novak, T. (2000). How to acquire customers on the web. *Harvard Business Review*, 78(3), 179–188.

Holbrook, M. (1999). *Consumer Value*, New York: Routledge.

Holbrook, M. & Corfman, K. (1983). Quality and value in the consumption experience, in *Consumer Perception of Merchandise and Store Quality*, J. Jacoby & J.C. Olson (eds.), Lexington, MA: D.C. Health, 31–57.

Jevons, W. S. (1957). *The Theory of Political Economy*, with preface and notes and an extension of the bibliography of mathematical economic writings by H. Stanley Jevons (5th ed.), New York: Kelley & Millman.

Keynes, J. (1971). *The Collected Writings of John Meynard Keynes,* London: Macmillan, for the Royal Economic Society.

Knox, F. (1969). *Consumers and the Economy,* London: Harper.

Lamont, W. (1955). *The Value Judgement,* Edinburgh: University Press.

Levenburg, N. (2005). Delivering customer value online: an analysis of practices, applications, and performance. *Journal of Retailing and Consumer Services,* 12(5), 319–331.

Levy, M., Grewal, D., Peterson, R. & Connolly, B. (2005). The concept of the 'Big Middle'. *Journal of Retailing,* 81(2), 83.

Levy, M., Weitz, B. & Beattie, S. (2005). *Retailing Management: Canadian Edition* (1st ed.), Toronto: McGraw-Hill Ryerson.

Liu, C. & Arnett, K. P. (2000). Exploring the factors associated with web site success in the context of electronic commerce. *Information and Management,* 38(1), 23–24.

Manning, G., Reece, B. & MacKenzie, H. (2001). *Selling Today: Creating Customer Value* (2nd Canadian ed.), Toronto: Prentice Hall.

Marx, K. (2005). *Value, Price, and Profit* [electronic resource], Palo Alto, CA: Electric Book Co., c2001.

Massie, H. (1966). *Space Travel and Exploration,* London: Taylor and Francis.

Mathwick, C. & Malhotra, N. (2002). The effect of dynamic retail experiences on experiential perceptions of value: An internet and catalogue comparison. *Journal of Retailing,* 78(1), 5–6.

Mathwick, C., Malhotra, N. & Rigdon, E. (2001). Experiential value: conceptualization, measurement and application in the catalog and internet shopping environment. *Journal of Retailing,* 77, 39–56.

Mujtaba, B. & Sims, R. (2006). Socializing retail employees in ethical values: the effectiveness of the formal versus informal methods. *Journal of Business & Psychology,* 21(2), 261–272.

Napolitano, M. (2005). Get ready for RFID, *Logistics Management* (2002), 44(8), 83.

Normann, R. & Ramírez, R. (1993). From value chain to value constellation: Designing interactive strategy. *Harvard Business Review,* 71(4), 65–77.

Parasuraman, A. & Grewal, D. (2000). The impact of technology on the quality-value-loyalty chain: a research agenda. *Journal of the Academy of Marketing Science,* 28(1), 168–74.

Pareto, V. (2007). *Considerations on the Fundamental Principles of Pure Political Economy,* London, New York: Routledge.

Payne, A. (2006). *Handbook of CRM: Achieving Excellence in Customer Management,* London: Elsevier Butterworth-Heinemann.

Peppers, D. & Rogers, M. (2004). *Managing Customer Relationships: A Strategic Framework,* John Wiley & Sons, Hoboken, NJ.

Ribbink, D., Van Riel, A. C., Liljander, V. & Streukens, S. (2004). Comfort your online customer: quality, trust, and loyalty on the internet. *Managing Service Quality,* 14(6), 446–456.

Ricardo, D. (1817). *On the Principles of Political Economy and Taxation* [electronic resource], London: JM.

Rosenbloom, B. (2007). Multi-channel strategy in business-to-business markets: prospects and problems. *Industrial Marketing Management,* 36, 4–9.

Rosenbloom, B. (1973). Conflict and channel efficiency: some conceptual models for the decision maker. *Journal of Marketing*, 37, 26–30.

Saeed, K., Grover, V. & Hwang, Y. (2003). Creating synergy with a clicks and mortar approach. *Communications of the ACM*, 46(12), 206–211.

Santayana, G. (1896). *The Sense of Beauty*, New York: Dover Publications.

Schneider, H. (2004). Grunge marketing. *Mortgage Banking*, 65(2), 106.

Sharma, A. & Mehrotra, A. (2007). Choosing an optimal channel mix in multi-channel environments. *Industrial Marketing Management*, 36(1), 21–28.

Smith, A. (2001). *An Inquiry into the Nature and Causes of the Wealth of Nations*, London: Electric Book Co.

Sparks, E. & Legault, D. (1993). A definition of quality for total customer satisfaction: the bridge between manufacturer and customer, S.A.M. *Advanced Management Journal*, 58(1), 16.

SteenKamp, J. E. M. (1989). Product Quality: *An Investigation into How It Is Perceived by Customers*, Maastricht, The Netherlands: Van Gorcum, Assen.

Stern, L. W., El-Ansari, A. & Coughlan, A. (2006). *Marketing Channels* (7th ed.), Upper Saddle River, NJ: Prentice Hall.

Tedeschi, B. (2007). Awaiting real sales form virtual shoppers.

Tsay, A. A. & Agrawal, N. (2004). Channel conflict and coordination in the ecommerce age. *Production & Operations Management*, 13(1), 93–110

Wood, S. (2002). Future fantasies: a social change perspective of retailing in the 21st century. *Journal of Retailing*, 78, 77–83.

Woodruff, R. B. (1997). Customer value: the next source for competitive advantage. *Academy of Marketing Science Journal*, 25(2), 139.

Zeithaml, V. A. (2000). Service quality, profitability, and the economic worth of customers: what we know and what we need to learn. *Academy of Marketing Science Journal*, 28(1), 67.

5
A Framework of Two Tiers to Enhance Trust in Recommender Systems

Avi Noy and Yuval Dan-Gur

Introduction

Online recommender systems use the information provided by the community, explicitly or implicitly, to generate and present recommendations on various items, locations, organizations and people. These systems use the bidirectional capabilities of the internet to collect opinions and present feedback in multiple techniques. Though the ability to share judgments across a huge community of users is fostered, these systems have their own weaknesses such as a low ratio of participation and a relative inability to elicit truthful, reliable and effective recommendations. Trust is the belief in the reliability, truth, ability or strength of someone or something. The processes of trust building are actually the processes of forming the expectations. Issues of trust, reputation and recommendations have become important topics of research in many fields but especially in electronic commerce where buyers and sellers rarely know each other. The use of reputation and recommendation mechanisms may decrease the uncertainties but sometimes fail to be trusted.

To overcome these limitations, several recommender systems use a multi-tier approach which generates feedback in two or more tiers using diverse mechanisms. Part of these systems employs both implicit and explicit information elicitation and presentation methods so that recommendations are generated both by humans and by software mechanisms.

This chapter discusses trust in recommender systems, the limitations that exists in the current mechanisms and presents a framework of recommender mechanisms arranged in two-tiers that elicit feedback from both humans and software agents to overcome the weaknesses. Finally, we discuss the potential contribution and implications of this approach.

The concept of trust in e-commerce

In numerous situations decision makers solicit other people's opinions prior to making a decision in the hope of improving their own judgment, because of lack of information or when multiple sources of information exist. This task becomes even harder when these sources provide conflicting or even opposite opinions.

This situation exists in online shopping and e-commerce settings. While it is often relatively easy for consumers to get a list of alternatives in an online shopping situation – using a search engine, a consumer opinion site or a price comparison agent – it is not that easy to make a choice between available alternatives, particularly choosing one that is most favourable to the consumer (Sultan et al., 2002). A consumer will typically refer to a trusted source or will get assistance from various online reputation and recommender systems which provided her beneficial truthful feedback in earlier occasions.

There are numerous definitions of the term trust. Trust is defined as '1. firm belief in the reliability, truth, ability, or strength of someone or something. 2. acceptance of the truth of a statement without evidence or investigation. 3. the state of being responsible for someone or something' (Oxford English Dictionary, 2009). Luhmann (1979) uses a similar definition and suggests that trust is the belief by one party about another party that the other party will behave in a predictable manner. Jøsang & Lo Presti (2004) emphasize the concepts of dependency and relative security in their definition. Trust is viewed as both a belief in the trustworthiness of the other party and a behavioural intention to rely on this party in a situation of vulnerability (Doney & Cannon, 1997; Ganesan, 1994; Ganesan & Hess, 1997).

The concept of trust has been approached from different perspectives by many scholars (Yoon, 2002). Trust is considered important in management literature because it is a good predictor of satisfaction (Driscoll, 1978). In studies of buyer-seller relationships, trust in a sales agent evolves over time and is based on a buyer's observation of a sales representative's honesty, reliability, consistency and trustworthiness (Anderson & Narus, 1990; Biong & Selnes, 1996; Doney & Cannon 1997; Ganesan, 1994). Previous academic research has emphasized the significance of trust in internet strategy (Hoffman et al., 1999; Urban et al., 2000).

Komiak et al., (2005) suggested that trust is essential in online shopping and electronic commerce environments due to the lack of institutional guarantees that the electronic vendor or agent will provide reliable and unbiased recommendations. Lee & Turban (2001) suggest that consumer trust in internet shopping is driven by trustworthiness of the internet merchant, trustworthiness of the internet shopping medium and contextual factors and that individual trust propensity moderated each of the relationships between the antecedents of trust and trust

It has been observed that online trust depends on six factors (Cheskin Research, 1999): 1) Seals of approval including security measures indicators; 2) Brand: firm's reputation, past experience, promotions, variety of products; 3) Navigation: the ease of finding what a visitor seeks; 4) Fulfilment: the process a customer follows from the time of purchase until the product is received; 5) Presentation: ways in which the looks of the site communicate meaningful information; 6) Technology: the technical functionality of the site. Online trust is different from offline trust because of the physical distance between buyer and seller, the separation between buyer and products and the absence of salespeople. Websites attempt to close part of these gaps and facilitate consumer trust by providing replacements to the human merchant in the form of virtual advisors, also known as reputations and recommender systems. It has already been shown that that the presence of virtual advisors can enhance trust in a website (Urban et al., 2000).

While virtual advisors are already popular in numerous websites, these mechanisms suffer from a variety of problems and biases. In the next section we discuss virtual advisors on the internet called recommender systems.

Recommender systems

How recommender systems elicits the wisdom of crowds

While information on the web continues to increase, it is important to be able to collect data in one place and filter out unnecessary information, focusing only on recommended items. The term 'wisdom of crowds' was coined by Surowiecki (2004), who discusses how the wisdom of crowds improve decision making. Various mechanisms have emerged as a response to the information overload problem and to facilitate knowledge aggregation. These systems elicit feedback from community members to produce recommendations. This technology include recommender, ranking and reputation systems, and provide users with collaborative knowledge as rankings and opinions, and more proactive and personalized information services (O'Donovan and Smith, 2005; Resnick et al., 2000). Examples of these systems include Google's page ranking system (Page et al., 1998); Amazon's recommendation system (Benkler, 2006); Epinions reputation system (Massa & Avesani, 2005); Slashdot rating systems (Benkler, 2006; Poor, 2005; Ubois, 2003); and eBay's reputation system (Resnik & Zeckhauser, 2002).

According to both theory and empirical results, integrating even a few opinions of a group is beneficial in the decision-making process (Surowiecki, 2004). Research has demonstrated that both mechanical and intuitive methods of combining opinions improve accuracy (Yaniv, 2004). This interior process of opinions' aggregation and processing is imitated on the internet by large scale word-of-mouth networks (Dellarocas, 2003).

Literature uses various names and occasionally distinguishes between the systems. The term recommender systems is used to describe mechanisms which generate recommendation on items which a consumer may like (Resnik & Varian, 1997). Social collaborative filtering is one of the most successful technologies of recommender systems. It filters information according to the similarity between the user and other community members (Sarwar et al., 2000). Another group of technologies are item-based collaborative filtering. It recommends items according to the similarity between items (Sarwar et al., 2001).

The core task of a recommender system is to recommend, in a personalized manner, interesting and valuable items and help users make appropriate choices from a large number of alternatives, without sufficient personal experience or awareness of the items' alternatives (Grasso et al., 2000; Oard & Kim 1998; Resnick & Varian, 1997). The everyday recommendations we receive rely mainly on human-analyzed sources: movie reviews, rumours, word of mouth, surveys, guides, friends and recommendation literature (Resnick & Varian, 1997; Shardanand & Maes, 1995). Filtering processes contribute to recommendations that make parts of the information inaccessible (or invisible) to us, as in newspaper editors' selections (Shardanand & Maes, 1995) and store owners who decide which products to put at the front, at the back or not to carry at all.

Reputation systems are a separate group of mechanisms. They solicit and publish feedback, ratings and opinions (Resnick et al., 2000). This technology has emerged on the internet to foster cooperation and trust among strangers. It harnesses the communication capabilities of the internet to produce large-scale, word-of-mouth networks in which people share and consume ratings, comments and opinions on a wide range of topics (Dellarocas, 2003). The contributors of ratings and consumers of reputation may be traders in online auctions who buy and sell items of unknown quality from one another without prior acquaintance; or consumers who seek advice about a product or another object on which they have limited information, such as a cellular phone, a restaurant or even a college professor. A reputation system elicits, aggregates and distributes feedback about participants' past behaviour or other consumers' opinions. Some reputation systems publish numerical rankings, while other distributes textual reviews and comments. Though only a few producers or consumers of the ratings know one another, reputation systems help people decide whom or what to trust, encourage trustworthy behaviour, deter participation by those who are unskilled or dishonest and assist in making a decision by sharing the collective rating of the item (Dellarocas, 2003; Mellor, 2009; Resnick et al., 2000).

Reputation systems are sometimes called online feedback mechanisms (Dellarocas, 2003), while Benkler (2002, 2006) coined the term peer-production systems to describe a more general concept of production systems that depends on individual action that is self-selected and decentralized, such as Wikipedia or free software projects. To eliminate confusion, we shall use the term *recommender systems* to refer to both types of systems following this paragraph.

While a few years ago people based their decisions on traditional word of mouth, professional advice or advertisements, the explosion of recommender systems is changing people's behaviour. Consumers now increasingly rely on opinions and advice published by these systems to make a variety of decisions ranging from what seller to buy from (Resnik et al., 2000), what movie to watch, to what stocks to invest in (Guernsey, 2000).

Explicit and implicit recommendations

Recommender systems use two fundamental methods to solicit and present recommendations and reputations: explicit and implicit methods. The use of an explicit rating is common in everyday life; ranging from grading students' work to assessing competing consumer goods (Alton-Scheidl et al., 1997; Resnick et al., 2000). Frequently ratings are made on an agreed upon discrete scale (e.g., star ratings for restaurants, buyers/sellers in auctions). Implementations of ratings for computerized systems have largely followed this explicit approach. A central feature of explicit ratings is that the evaluator has to examine the item and assign it a value on the rating scale. This imposes a cognitive cost on the evaluator (Nichols, 1997). The outcome of the recommender system may also be presented explicitly, as averages of item ratings as on the Epinions, Amazon and Toysrus websites; or sums of positive, neutral and negative feedbacks as on the eBay website.

Implicit ratings are automatically inferred from a user's behaviour and automate the process of feedback collection. This method removes the cost to the evaluator of examining and rating and removes the difficulty of a small number of users who tend to explicitly rate items. Examples to this method includes Google's page rank algorithm where a web page is rated based on how many links point to it, and how many links point to the pointing page and so on (Page et al., 1998). In Google's case, there is also an implicit signal of the outcome. The ordering of the results acts as an implicit indicator of reputation (Dellarocas, 2003).

Problems and weaknesses of recommender systems

The challenges recommender system designers face are increasing as these systems spread on the internet and new concerns appear. Several types of problems and weaknesses are associated with this technology. We can align them across the operating phases of the system starting with: 1) data elicitation; 2) information extraction, processing and aggregation; and 3) distribution and presentation.

A first set of problems is related to the data elicitation phase. First, explicit mechanisms are vulnerable, since feedback is voluntarily and only a minority of users provides feedback (Resnick et al., 2000). The process creates strong incentives to free ride. According to Mellor (2009), online sales are affected by the number of reviews posted. As visitors are more reluctant to buy when a product does not attract a reasonable number of reviews, the lack of sufficient feedback may harm online sales. A second problem is ensuring honest feedback. Users may abuse the system with distorted or false data (David & Pinch, 2006). A third problem is avoiding negative feedback (Resnick et al., 2000) or elimination of such feedback by the website (Richards, 2009). A fourth problem is that an honest contributor may be misjudged as a corrupt one or a defector may be mistreated as a countable one (Conte & Paolucci, 2002; Paolucci, 2000). A fifth problem is the cognitive load effort required to assign accurate, explicit ratings, making it difficult to assemble large populations (Oard & Kim, 1998). A sixth limitation is the absence of contextual cues (Dellarocas, 2003) which is common to computer-mediated interactions.

The information extraction, processing and aggregation phase suffers from biases since presumably feedback providers comprise of an unrepresentative sample (Egger, 2000). It may be that dissatisfied consumers will be substantially less likely to give feedback or reviews. Since the majority of the feedback is positive, some crucial information will be lost. A second problem is the ease of changing online identities. A user with a negative reputation can register with another name and effectively erase previous rating (Resnick et al., 2000) or can build a good reputation and then cheat, disappear and reappear under a new identity (Dellarocas, 2003). A third problem is data sparseness when the number of people who have rated the items is relatively small compared to the number of items (Terveen & Hill, 2001) which makes it difficult for a system to produce recommendations based on similarity between users. A third problem is the inability of many mechanisms to differentiate between feedbacks and feedback providers; and the failure to assign an appropriate weight to each. As such, a positive accumulative feedback which is a sum of positive and negative postings for a specific item may distract the focus from the negative feedback (Resnick et al., 2000). On eBay, recommendation consumers don't know if the reputation is based on feedback from low-value transactions. On other sites, consumers don't know who the raters are and what their experiences are.

The distribution and presentation phase suffers from lack of portability across systems (Resnick et al., 2000) and lack of information-sharing capabilities between websites. And finally, systems suffer from a conformity effect. Users can be manipulated by system interfaces to rate items toward the system's presented prediction, whether that prediction is accurate or not (Cosley et al., 2003).

While part of the problems discussed in this section exist in other internet settings, some of them can reduce the trustworthiness of the recommender mechanism. Ample solutions to these deficiencies arose during the last decade. One of them is recommendation formation based on implicit feedback (Dellarocas, 2003; Nichols, 1997). The ability to elicit feedback by automated mechanisms can solves part of the problems but can also introduce new difficulties related to trusting feedback and advice generated by a computer system.

Human-computer interaction and recommender systems

Trust is thought to be one of the important emotional elements that influence human-computer interaction (Lee & See, 2004; Dzindolet et al., 2003). Human-computer interaction is essential to the success of using the system. Users may have a level of trust in a device, but also have a level of trust in the success of cooperation with the device (Muir, 1994;

Muir & Moray 1996). When discussing trust in an automated device we need to question the attitude of humans towards computers.

Attributing human qualities to computers

The attribution of human qualities to computers has been suggested in earlier research. The media equation theory suggests that people interact with computer systems as if they were social actors and that the interaction with computer and other new media is fundamentally social and natural as in real life (Reeves & Nass, 1996).

Users' affective and social reactions to automated tools affect acceptance of and interaction with such systems. A possible implication is that social rules and principles of human-human interaction can also be applied to human-computer interaction (Cramer et al., 2008). Moon (1998) propose that computers are readily recognized by users as being 'similar' or 'dissimilar' to themselves based on minimal, text-based manipulations of the 'computer's personality'. This perceived similarity has major effects on human-computer relationships: users are more 'socially attracted' to similar computers (compared with dissimilar ones) and find the former to be more 'intelligent' and more enjoyable to interact with. Nass & Moon (2000) review a series of experimental studies showing that individuals apply social rules and expectations to computers. These studies indicate that people apply gender stereotypes and behaviours – such as politeness and cognitive commitment – to computers.

It is questionable if trust in a person and trust in a computer agent are fundamentally the same or has different components (Komiak et al., 2005). It is accepted that trust in a person can be conceptualized as trust in the person's competence, benevolence and integrity (McKnight et al., 2002). Some researchers are doubtful whether trust in the benevolence and integrity of a technological artefact exists (Friedman et al., 2000), while others believe that trust in a technological object contains elements of trust in competence, benevolence and integrity (Cassell & Bickmore, 2000; Komiak & Benbasat, 2004; Komiak et al., 2005; Wang & Benbasat, 2003).

Media equation and recommender systems

When studying recommender systems it is important to understand whether people will perceive differently recommendations solicited explicitly from humans or collected and delivered automatically by a computer system, and what methods can potentially amplify trust in the system. Numerous questions arise, such as: How do people respond to advice from a machine? Should the recommendation process be seen as a natural process of advice giving and taking (Gates et al., 1999; Jungermann, 1999; Terveen & Hill, 2001), and if so, how does one assess the usefulness of the advice (Harvey & Harries, 1999)? Do users tend to make attributions of responsibility when interacting with computers and blame them for failed outcomes (Moon & Nass, 1998)? How do users respond to incorrect system advice (Dijkstra 1999) and do they trust it (Lerch & Prietula, 1989)?

A framework of two-tier recommender systems

Recommending in two tiers

An implicit mechanisms can resolve many of the concerns presented above including: lack of voluntary feedback; avoidance of providing negative feedback; classification errors; cognitive load; biases of feedback providers; data sparseness; and conformity. However the questions presented in the previous paragraph are disturbing, since they introduce a new dimension of problems which does not exist while using explicit mechanisms.

The mixture of several mechanisms into a single system seems to provide a superior solution. The notion of a multi-tier approach in recommender systems has already been presented in the literature. Benkler (2002, 2006) discusses the development of peer-production systems which are comprised of multi-layer mechanisms. Chiang (2006) discusses the problem of distorted information and suggests overcoming this problem by using a reputation level of a higher level 'reputation of the information of reputation'. David & Pinch (2006) clarify how the abuse of online reputation systems has led to the implementation of a recommender system structure with six levels. Poor (2005) discusses the use of moderators and a second level of meta-moderators on the Slashdot website. Ubois (2003) interviews Slashdot's creator/director, who suggests using the contributor's posting history, and the subnet posting history as rating moderators or filters.

We depict a framework which combines both human- and computer-generated recommendations in the two tiers and concentrate on current implementations of these mechanisms and future opportunities of this concept. The attribution of human behaviour to computers sheds new light on the analysis of recommender systems. Can human recommendations and rankings, combined with computer-generated recommendations, facilitate trust in these systems?

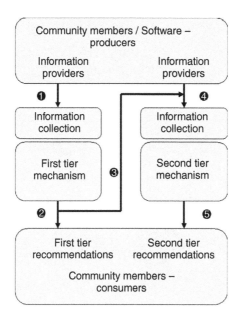

Figure 5.1 A framework of two-tier recommender systems

The framework presented in Figure 5.1 describes a recommender system with two tiers. The producers of the information, community members in the case of explicit ranking, or software agents in the case of implicit collection method, elicit the feedback (1). The system aggregates the data and transforms it into a valuable recommendation by the first-tier mechanism (2) which is distributed to community members. This straightforward process operates in numerous recommender systems which are currently deployed on the web. The differences between the systems are basically their collection and aggregation methods, recommendation algorithms, and information presentation techniques. When applying a second tier, the recommendations are aggregated both from the first tier (3) and filtered by information providers (4) which can again be humans or software agents (4). The second tier usually uses a different type of algorithm or technique to produce second-tier recommendations (5) that are distributed to the community.

The implementation of human-computer generated recommendations

Two potential sources of information providers/information elicitation exist in the domain of recommender systems, humans and software

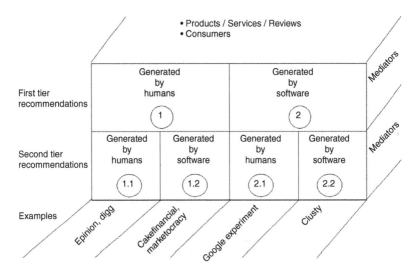

Figure 5.2   A model of two-tier recommender mechanisms

agents. Both can publish opinions, feedback or recommendations in the first- and second-tier mechanisms. The partition into two sources in the first tier leads to four combinations in the second tier as presented in Figure 5.2.

The model illustrates, for example, that a website's first-tier mechanism can collect recommendations from community members and generate first-tier recommendations (1). The second-tier recommendation can also be generated using data assembled from the community (1.1). Figure 5.2 presents several examples of contemporary mechanisms which are deployed on various websites. These technologies are described in Table 5.1. Note that some of the mechanisms go even further by integrating additional tiers.

How a hybrid system facilitates trust

The hybrid mechanisms that were developed to collect both explicit and implicit feedback try to remove part of the weaknesses that exists in a single-tier mechanism. The ability to compare the recommendations of community members and engage users in the process by providing feedback or filtering the automated results grants the hybrid approach additional boost, since explicit recommendations can be compared automatically and implicit feedback can be rated manually.

Table 5.1   Examples of recommender mechanisms which use two tiers

Example (number follows Figure 5.2)	Website	Category	First-tier mechanism	Second-tier mechanism
1.1	Epinions	Products reviews	Users write reviews about products	Members rate the reviews and the reviewers
	digg	Articles and stories	Users post stories	Users rate the postings
1.2	Cakefinancial, marketocracy	Online	Members manage an investment portfolio, others can see their portfolio	The system grades users according to their portfolio performance
2.1	Google voting experiment	Search engine	Google presents relevant search results	Users votes influence the personal search experience by adding, moving and removing search results
2.2	Clusty	Meta search engine	Clusty searches a number of free search engines and directories, not Google or Yahoo	Results accompanied with subject subdivisions based on words in search results, intended to give the major themes. Click on these to search within results on each theme

The model presented in Figure 5.2 is simplified and generalized. It ignores the internal algorithms and additional variables which influence the implementation. The type of feedback used by the system to generate recommendations is not the only part that was omitted. Due to limited space, Figure 5.2 also excludes some of the options that are available for use as collection, aggregation and presentation methods. These options differentiate between the various implementations that exist. Due to this enhanced manipulation in two tiers, the second-tier recommendations may be more accurate, insightful and reliable. The outcome process can highlight crucial information, cluster it or even explain explicitly or implicitly how the system generated the recommendations. These factors are the drivers of trust.

Summary

The research on recommender systems is still in its formation stage. The performance of systems is incomparable due to the lack of standard metrics, standard datasets and standard infrastructure for controlled experiments. The progress made in recent years in developing algorithms to improve accuracy is not sufficient to gain additional users' acceptance and trust.

Previous studies have raised many of the weaknesses and limitations of recommender systems that are inherent in the existing architecture. This includes a wide range of issues related to human-computer interactions: the lack of transparency into the recommendation process (Herlocker et al., 2000); the perceived automated process (Lueg & Landolt 1998); the cognitive load effort to assign ratings (Oard & Kim, 1998); the self-serving bias (Moon & Nass, 1998); and the user's agreement with advice that comes from a system (Dijkstra, 1999). Also, the evidence that recommender system interfaces may affect users' opinions has recently been addressed (Cosley et al., 2003; Herlocker et al., 2000). The multi-tier framework presented in this chapter to overcome some of the limitations is consistent with discussions of several scholars who already suggested that a multi-tier system would perform better than a single tier. The use of a hybrid mechanism which combines data collected from both human and computers takes this approach a step further and may predominate.

This concept has theoretical and practical implications. The use of a two-tier mechanism may eliminate some of the weaknesses inherent in a simple one-tier system. By providing additional layers of filtering, clustering or ordering the system can present accurate and more relevant and even personalized information which reduces risk and may be perceived as more reliable and trustable. A two-tier mechanism which collects information as ratings, opinions and behaviours, from both humans and computers may even increase the perception of trust, since it may strengthen elements in the systems which suffer when using a single source of information. On the contrary, inadvertent design of the system may achieve an opposite goal. Since the complexity of the system increases, a user may find it harder to understand the operation.

Maes in Shneiderman & Maes (1997) claim that it is an important inter-action design challenge to achieve understanding and control in user-agent interaction and in this way achieve users' trust.

If the user understands how a system works and can predict system actions and outcomes, the user can focus on the task he or she is per-forming instead of trying to figure out how the system operates. Cramer et al., (2008) suggest that in the case of user-adaptive recommender sys-tems, it may be even more vital for the users to understand how the sys-tem decides on a recommendation. They find that trust was positively correlated with perceived understanding of the recommender system.

Practical implications include the opportunity of website to incorpor-ate a hybrid mechanism which may facilitate trust in the system. Before adding a second-tier mechanism to an existing system, one should analyze the deficiencies of the existing system and decide on the set-ting of the second tier. For example, if a website is currently using a recommender system which collects and publish explicit ratings and opinions, and finds that users abuse the system, it can improve the system be adding a second tier which filters out these users either by human-generated recommendations in which existing members of the systems rate the previous feedback, or by automatically prohibiting spe-cific users from posting multiple ratings. This filter can be applied for a limited duration, according to users' previous behaviour or according to their seniority.

Supplementary empirical studies are required to examine whether a two-tier mechanism is actually perceived to be more trustable and whether there are differences between the four combinations presented in Figure 5.2. Researchers may also study the specific domains that benefit mostly from the introduction of a specific combination of first and second tiers.

References

Alton-Scheidl, R., Schumutzer, R., Sint, P. P. & Tscherteu, G. (1997). Voting and rating in Web4Groups. In *Voting, Rating, Annotation: Web4Groups and Other Projects: Approaches and First Experiences,* Alton-Scheidl, R., Schumutzer, R., Sint, P. P. & Tscherteu, G. (eds.), Vienna, Austria: Oldenbourg, 13–103.

Anderson, J. & Narus, J. (1990). A model of distributor firm and manufacturer firm working partnerships. *Journal of Marketing*, 54 (April), 42–58.

Benkler, Y. (2002). Coas's Penhuin, or Linux and the nature of the firm. *Yale Law Journal*, 112(3), 369–446. Available at: http://www.benkler.org/CoasesPenguin. html (accessed 28 Mar 2009).

Benkler, Y. (2006). *The Wealth of Networks: How Social Production Transforms Markets and Freedom*. New Haven, CT: Yale University Press.

Biong, H. & Selnes, F. (1996). *The Strategic Role of the Salesperson in Established Buyer Seller Relationships*, Cambridge, MA: Marketing Science Institute.

Cassell, J. & Bickmore, T. (2000). External manifestation of trustworthiness in the interface. *Communications of the ACM*, 43(12), 50–56.

Cheskin Research (1999). eCommerce trust study. *Cheskin Research and Studio Archetype/Sapient*. Available online at: http://www.cheskin.com/cms/files/i/articles//17__report-eComm%20Trust1999.pdf (accessed 28 Mar 2009).

Chiang, Y-S. (2006). To be others' eyes and ears? Trust and the credibility of reputation. Presented at the 1st World Congress on Social Simulation, (Student contest), Kyoto, Japan.

Conte, R. & Paolucci, M. (2002). *Reputation in Artificial Societies. Social Beliefs for Social Order*. Boston: Kluwer.

Cosley, D., Lam, S. K., Albert, I., Konstan, A. J. & Riedl, J. (2003). Is seeing believing? How recommender system interfaces affect users' opinions. In *Proceedings of the SIGCHI Conference on Human Factors in Computing Systems*, Ft. Lauderdale, FL, New York: ACM Press, 5(1), 585–592.

Cramer, H. S. M., Evers, V., Ramlal, S., van Someren, M., Rutledge, L. W., Stash, N., Aroyo, L. M. & Wielinga, B. J. (2008). The effects of transparency on trust in and acceptance of a content-based art recommender. *User Modeling and User-Adapted Interaction*, 18(5), 455–496.

David, S. & Pinch, T. (2006). Six degrees of reputation: The use and abuse of online review and recommendation systems. *First Monday*, 11, Available online at: http://www.firstmonday.org/issues/issue11_3/david/ (accessed 28 Mar 2009).

Dellarocas, C. (2003). The digitization of word of mouth: promise and challenges of online feedback mechanisms. *Management Science*, 49(10), 1407–1424.

Dijkstra, J. J. (1999). User agreement with incorrect expert system advice. *Behaviour and Information Technology*, 18(6), 399–411.

Doney, P. M. & Canon, J. P. (1997). An examination of the nature of trust in buyer–seller relationships. *Journal of Marketing*, 61, 35–51.

Driscoll, J. W. (1978). Trust and participation in organizational decision making as predictors of satisfaction. *Academy of Management Journal*, 21(1), 44–56.

Dzindolet, M., Peterson, S.A., Pomranky, R.A., Pierce, L.G. & Beck, H. P. (2003). The role of trust in automation reliance. *International Journal of Human-Computer Studies*. 58(6), 697–718.

Egger, F. N. (2000). 'Trust me, I'm an online vendor': towards a model of trust for e-commerce system design. Presented at CHI '00 Conference on Human Factors in Computing Systems, The Hague, The Netherlands, 101–102.

Friedman, B., Kahn, P. H., Jr. & Howe, D. C. (2000). Trust online. *Communications of the ACM*, 43(12), 34–40.

Ganesan, S. (1994). Determinants of long-term orientation in buyer–seller relationships. *Journal of Marketing*, 58, 1–19.

Ganesan, S. & Hess, R. (1997). Dimensions and levels of trust: implications for commitment to a relationship. *Marketing Letters*, 8(4), 439–448.

Gates, C. S., Aggarwal, C. C. & Maglio, P. (1999). Recommender systems: knowledge from mining user experiences. *IBM Research*, Technical Report, ibm-rc-21447.

Google Voting Experiment, http://www.google.com/experimental/a840e102.html

Grasso, A., Meunier, J. L. & Thompson, C. (2000). Augmenting recommender systems by embedding interfaces into office practices. In *Proceedings of the Hawaii International Conference on System Sciences*, 247–275.

Guernsey, L. (2000). Suddenly, everybody's an expert on everything. *The New York Times*, February 3, 2000.

Harvey, N. & Harries, C. (1999). Using advice and assessing its usefulness. In *HICSS-32, Proceedings of the Thirty-Second Annual Hawaii International Conference on System Sciences*, Maui, Hawaii: ACM Press, 1059.

Herlocker, J., Konstan, J. & Riedl, J. (2000). Explaining collaborative filtering recommendations. In *Proceedings of the Conference on Computer Supported Cooperative Work*, 241–250.

Hoffman, D., Novak, L. & Peralta, M. (1999). Building consumer trust online. *Communications of the ACM*, 42(4), 80–85.

Jøsang, A. & Lo Presti, S. (2004). Analysing the relationship between risk and trust. *International Conference on Trust Management*, Oxford, UK.

Jungermann, H. (1999). Advice giving and taking. Paper presented at the *HICSS 99'*, Hawaii, 1999.

Komiak, S. Y. X. & Benbasat, I. (2004). Understanding customer trust in agent-mediated electronic commerce, web-mediated electronic commerce, and traditional commerce. *Information Technology and Management*, 5(1&2), 181–207.

Komiak, S. X. Y., Wang, W. & Benbasat, I. (2005). Trust building in virtual salespersons versus in human salespersons: similarities and differences. *e-Service Journal*, 3(3), 49–63.

Lee, J. D. & See, K. A. (2004). Trust in automation: designing for appropriate reliance. *Human Factors*, 42(1), 50–80.

Lee, M. K. O. & Turban, E. (2001). A trust model for consumer internet shopping. *International Journal of Electronic Commerce*, 6(1), 75–91.

Lerch, F. J. & Prietula, M. J. (1989). How do we trust machine advice? In *Designing and Using Human-Computer Interfaces and Knowledge-Based Systems*, G. Salvendy & M. J. Smith (eds.), Amsterdam: Elsevier, 410–419.

Lueg, C. & Landolt, C. (1998). A Java-based approach to active collaborative filtering. In *Summary of the ACM SIGCHI Conference on Human Factors in Computing Systems, (CHI 98)*, Los Angeles, 319–320.

Luhmann, N. (1979). *Trust and Power*, London: Wiley.

Massa, P. & Avesani, P. (2005). Controversial users demand local trust metrics: An experimental study on epinions.com community. In *Proc. of AAAI-05*, 121–126.

McKnight, D. H., Choudhury, V. & Kacmar, C. (2002). Developing and validating trust measures for e-commerce: an integrative typology. *Information Systems Research*, 13(3), 334–359.

Mellor, P. (2009). Fair comment. *The Economist*, Mar 5, 2009. Available online at: http://www.economist.com/science/tq/displaystory.cfm?story_id=13174365 (accessed 28 Mar 2009).

Moon, Y. (1998). The effects of distance in local versus remote human-computer interaction. In *Proceedings of the CHI 98'*, Los Angeles, CA, 103–108.

Moon, Y. & Nass, C. (1998). Are computers scapegoats? Attributions of responsibility in human-computer interaction. *International Journal of Human-Computer Studies*, 49, 79–94.

Muir, B. M. (1994). Trust in automation: part I. Theoretical issues in the study of trust and human intervention in automated systems. *Ergonomics*, 37, 1905–1922.

Muir, B. M. & Moray, N. (1996). Trust in automation. Part II. Experimental studies of trust and human intervention in a process control simulation. *Ergonomics*, 39(3), 429–460.

Nass, C. & Moon, Y. (2000). Machines and mindlessness: Social responses to computers. *Journal of Social Issues*, 60(1), 81–103.

Nichols, D. M. (1997). Implicit rating and filtering. In *Proceedings of the 5th DELOS Workshop on Filtering and Collaborative Filtering*, Budapest, Hungary, 10 –12 November 1997.

Oard, D. W. & Kim, J. (1998). Implicit feedback for recommender systems. Paper presented at the *AAAI Workshop on Recommender Systems*, Madison, WI.

O'Donovan, J. & Smith, B. (2005). Trust in recommender systems. In *Proceedings of the 10th International Conference on Intelligent User Interfaces*, San Diego, CA, 167–174.

Oxford English Dictionary (2009). Available online at: http://www.askoxford.com/ (accessed 28 Mar 2009).

Page, L., Brin, S., Motwani, R. & Winograd, T. (1998). The pagerank citation ranking: bringing order to the web. Technical report, Stanford University.

Paolucci, M. (2000). False reputation in social control. *Advances in Complex Systems*, 3(1–4), 39–51.

Poor, N. (2005). Mechanisms of an online public sphere: the website Slashdot. *Journal of Computer Mediated Communication*, 10(2), article 4. Available online at: http://jcmc.indiana.edu/vol10/issue2/poor.html (accessed 28 Mar 2009).

Reeves, B. & Nass, C. (1996). The media equation: how people treat computers, television, and new media like real people and places. Cambridge, UK: Cambridge University Press.

Resnick, P. & Varian, H. R. (1997). Recommender systems. *Communications of the ACM*, 40(3), 56–58.

Resnick, P. & Zeckhauser, R. (2002). Trust among strangers in internet transactions: empirical analysis of eBay's reputation system. In M. R. Baye (ed.) *The Economics of the Internet and E-Commerce. Advances in Applied Microeconomics*, Vol. 11. Greemwich, CT: JAI Press.

Resnick, P., Zeckhauser, R., Friedman, E. & Kuwabara, K. (2000). Reputation systems. *Communications of the ACM*, 43(12), 45–48.

Richards, K. (2009). Yelp and the business of Extortion 2.0. *East Bay Express*. Available online at: http://www.eastbayexpress.com/gyrobase/yelp_and_the_business_of_extortion_2_0/Content?oid=927491&page=1 (accessed 28 Mar 2009).

Sarwar, B., Karypis, G., Konstan, J. & Riedl, J. (2000). Analysis of recommendation algorithms for e-commerce. *EC'00*, October 17–20, 2000, Minneapolis, Minnesota.

Sarwar, B., Karypis, G., Konstan, J. & Riedl, J. (2001). Item based collaborative filtering recommendation algorithms. *WWW10*, May 15, 2001, Hong Kong.

Shneiderman, B. & Maes, P. (1997). Direct manipulation vs. interface agents. *Interactions*, 4(6), 42–61.

Shardanand, U. & Maes, P. (1995). Social information filtering: algorithms for automating 'word of mouth'. Paper presented at the *ACM SIGCHI '95*, Vancouver, Canada.

Sultan, F., Urban, G. L., Shankar, V. & Bart, I. Y. (2002). Determinants and role of trust in e-business: a large scale empirical study. Working Paper, eBusiness Research Center, Penn-State University.

Surowiecki, J. (2004). *The Wisdom of Crowds: Why the Many Are Smarter than the Few and How Collective Wisdom Shapes Businesses, Economics, Societies and Nations*. New York: Doubleday.

Terveen, L. & Hill, W. (2001). Beyond recommender systems: helping people help each other. In *HCI in the New Millennium*, J. Carroll (ed.), Boston: Addison-Wesley.

Ubois, J. (2003). Online reputation systems. *Esther Dyson's Monthly Report*, 21(9), 23 October 2003.

Urban, G. L., Sultan, F. & Qualls, W. (2000). Placing trust at the center of your internet strategy. *Sloan Management Review*, Fall(1), 39–48.

Wang, W. & Benbasat, I. (2003). An empirical investigation of intelligent agents for e-business customer relationship management: a knowledge management perspective. In *Proceedings of the 11th European Conference on Information Systems*, Naples, Italy, 2003.

Yaniv, I. (2004). The benefit of additional opinions. *Current Directions in Psychological Science*, 13, 76–79.

Yoon, S-J. (2002). The antecedents and consequences of trust in online purchase decisions. *Journal of Interactive Marketing*, 16(2), 47–63.

Part 2

Knowledge Sharing and Electronic Collaboration

6
Barriers to Electronic Clustering
Helen Cripps

Introduction

Within industrialized countries one of the main producers of wealth and prosperity has been 'well coordinated and sustainable systems, capable of converting technological innovation assets into substantial levels of local industrial productivity and global competitiveness', (Scheel, 2002, p. 356). One of the ways of achieving this has been through the establishment of regional clusters. At the time of this research, there was a belief within government circles in Western Australia that collaboration using information communication technology (ICT) would assist regional economic growth. Initial research in a multi-industry regional cluster showed a low level of ICT sophistication, therefore, the research focused on the relationships between the firms in the cluster and the use of collaborative e-commerce. The study was undertaken in a cluster located south of the city of Perth. The cluster had a number of unique elements including the dominance of high-priced and low-volume industrial manufacturing, a number of large multinational firms and the pre-eminence of large defense contractors. The drive behind the government-funded research was to find ways to facilitate greater collaboration using ICT between the firms in the regional cluster. It was perceived that there was a significant gap between the large firms and the lower tiers of middle-sized and small firms. The local governments (municipalities) involved in the research hoped that increased online collaboration would assist the medium-sized and smaller firms to grow, thus improving the economic robustness of the region.

Regional economic development

Globalization and the rise of technology have reduced the role location plays in competitive advantage as knowledge, resources, capital and technology can now be sourced from global markets and it is no longer necessary for firms to locate near the markets they serve. Internet services such as web portals and auction sites have become the enablers of globalized e-business and e-commerce. Businesses are now becoming embedded within 'networks of collaborative relationships that influence the flow of resources among the stakeholders', (Ratnasingam, 2004, p. 382).

Technology and the accompanying globalization diminished the impact of governments on their local economies (Porter, 2000). However, government intervention in regional economies continues with a duel approach focusing on the development of existing natural resources and the provision of incentives to those who relocate into the region being developed (Etzkowitz, 2007). The development or revitalization of regional economies that have suffered an economic downturn has been the focus of programs and policies across Europe, the United States and Australia (Maude, 2004). Even with the rise of technology, economic development from a government policy perspective is often reliant on the provision of infrastructure such as industry parks and business incubators (Drabenstott, 2005).

A review of the literature identified five regional economic development strategies based around: entrepreneurship; networks; innovation systems; triple helix and clusters. The literature also indicated a set of common characteristics associated with regional economic development, these being knowledge creation and sharing, intellectual property, technology transfer, technological innovation, growth and export, collaboration, education and training, use of ICT, infrastructure provisions and a focus on SMEs (Cripps, 2007). Of the regional economic development strategies clustering displayed all the economic development characteristics previously listed including collaboration and the use of ICT which were the main focus of the study.

Clusters

Porter (2000) defined clusters as 'geographic concentrations of interconnected companies, specialized suppliers, service providers, firms in related industries, and associated institutions (e.g., universities, standards agencies, trade associations) in a particular field that compete but also cooperate' (Porter, 2000, p. 15). Boekholt and Thuriaux

(1999, p. 381) defined clusters as 'networks of production of strongly interdependent firms, (including specialized suppliers), knowledge producing agents (universities, research institutes, engineering companies), bridging institutions (brokers, consultants) and customers, linked to each other in a value-adding production chain'. Clusters differ from networks in that membership of a network is often defined whereas a cluster is an informal grouping of firms, (Boekholt & Thuriaux, 1999). The advantages of clustering include the increased supply of specialized inputs; access to new and expert knowledge; access to institutions, public goods and government incentive programs (Porter, 2000).

Though many governments have backed away from direct intervention in cluster development, Lundequist and Power, (2002) suggest that government still has a role as a source of resources for regional development. The provision of meeting places within the cluster can foster trust, collaboration and knowledge exchange. The common strategies for regional cluster development policy include the creation of regional identity through location incentives, recruitment of existing business to the region, the support of business networks and the provision of business development services, the support and expansion of research and development through building university research competencies, creating non-university laboratories and research centres, R&D incentives, subsidies and awards. Also important is the provision of physical infrastructure for business development such as business incubators facilities including laboratory space, buildings and business parks. Other areas include the provision of training and basic education, regulatory assistance and regulatory enforcement, procurement and supply chain development (Feser, 2002; Sölvell et al., 2003; OECD, 2005). For a cluster to be successful there needs to be continual improvement of the government polices and strategies that support the cluster's informal networks, knowledge exchange and targeted education programs (Lundequist & Power, 2002; Boekholt & Thuriaux, 1999).

Clustering as a means of regional economic development has been popular, particularly in Europe, although the Porter model has not received universal acceptance as the answer in every situation (Palazuelos, 2005).

The Australian context of regional economic development

In contrast to the United States and the majority of European countries, Australia can be characterized in economic terms as a small country which is heavily reliant on natural resources rather than high-tech and knowledge-intensive industries (Maude, 2004). Key for government in supporting regional economic development is the use of a top-down strategic approach to furthering Australian industry and the engagement of all economic stakeholders in this process (Department of Transport and Regional Services, 2002). Beneath the overarching government strategy, regions must themselves develop a bottom-up approach based on their regional assets and strengths. In the Australian context, the impediments to regional economic development identified by Department of Transport and Regional Services (2002, p. 197) include: 'difficulty in accessing skills, in particular, difficulties with the recruitment and retention of skilled labour; a lack of awareness of new business opportunities; under-developed business skills; a lack of supportive infrastructure; perceived shortfalls in an area's "lifestyle" and "livability" attributes; a lack of access to capital; and a low take up rates of government business assistance'.

According to a 2004 study conducted by Global Entrepreneurship Monitor, Australia was in the top five countries on their Entrepreneurial Activity Index of the OECD countries (Fitzsimons et al., 2004). In contrast to the level of entrepreneurship, Australia is outside the top 10 of OECD countries in innovation. Australia has a number of strengths including 'a broad scientific base, world class in some areas; success in converting knowledge into patents; and high growth in several areas including biotechnology, pharmaceuticals and office and computing equipment'. It also has some notable weaknesses including 'insufficient attention to the development of human capital, (for example, entrepreneurship); low average company size which may impede ability to compete in new industries and innovate; in international terms, business expenditure on research and development is poor; and many research institutions have poor linkages with potential users of research' (ABF 2005, p. 19). For Australia to become an innovative nation, government policy must address the gap between R&D and commercialization in both the public and private sectors, boosting the capacity at a firm level to create, diffuse and apply knowledge to form a strong innovation system within the country (ABF, 2005).

Small to medium sized firms (SMEs) were the focus of the Federal Government Business Networks Program established in 1995 (Killen et al., 2003). Only 2 per cent of SMEs participated in the program compared to between 10–15 per cent in an equivalent program in Denmark (Fulop, 2000). Fulop (2000) found that none of the participants in the networks studied in the research were committed to business growth in the network. The research found that the use of formal contracts rather than relationship building lead to reduced levels of trust between firms in the networks (Fulop, 2000). However, there were examples of significant levels of integration of networks where the business had high levels of complementarity. Killen et al., (2003) note that the Business Network Program ran only three years compared to similar programs in other countries which ran for considerably longer and were more successful (The Department of Industry, Tourism and Resources, 2004).

Clusters in Australia

Of the regional economic development strategies, clusters seem to have been the most extensively applied in an Australian setting. The creation of industry clusters has been growing in popularity in Australia since the 1990s with particular focus on regions that have suffered economic hardship – much of which rose out of the economic restructuring of the 1980s (Roberts & Enright, 2004). The 1980s were characterized by 'the restructuring of the manufacturing sector; growth in the development of business services, especially financial services; corporatization of many State owned enterprises such as Qantas and the Commonwealth Bank; reform of the public sector under National Competition Policy; improvements in productivity gains; removal of protective tariffs and financial deregulation and Australia mimicking the structure of the US economy' (Roberts & Enright, 2004, p. 102). These changes saw the decline in the old manufacturing industries, with many moving offshore or being acquired by multinationals.

The environment of the 1990s saw two forms of cluster develop in Australia. Firstly, single industry clusters, which usually rise out of old industries that have been restructured. Secondly, groupings of industries regionally based and connected through networks. These clusters are often facilitated by public policy support directed at industry innovation and collaboration between firms to build the cluster (Roberts & Enright, 2004). These clusters tend to be weaker as they lack the strength of a national industry. For clusters to succeed they require 'substantial capacity building to support regional strategic infrastructure ... to turn a local or regional network of firms and industries into a cluster' this often requires significant long term commitment from government sources (Roberts & Enright, 2004, p. 117).

Of the clustering programs initiated over the 1990s many failed due to a lack of resources, experience or expertise in regional development and failure to create linkages with international markets. Though originally driven at a federal level, the majority of the support and funding for cluster programs came from state governments (Roberts & Enright, 2004; Department of Industry, Tourism and Resources, 2004). Often these programs were based around technology parks or innovation centres. In the Australian context, the key factors to be considered when developing a cluster are: organic growth in response to changing circumstances, maximization of the creative conditions and facilitation of spin off and growth opportunities (Department of Industry, Tourism and Resources, 2004).

According to Blandy (2004), the development of clusters over time stemmed from a region's economic foundations including existing companies and local demands for products and services. Clusters emerge from the local community to become economic champions for the region's progress. There is an ongoing cycle between the cluster's development and its original foundations and this interplay assists in the stimulation of the industry cluster. Blandy (2004) suggested that the interest in the development of local economies through government policy seems to have a universal appeal.

Generally, the clusters in Australia are not well developed compared with those of the US and Europe due to the small size of the domestic economy, lack of critical mass within industries, lack of suitable local partners, multinationals conducting R&D offshore, the strength of the export-focused resources industry over other industries and the lack of regional specialization which reduces the opportunity of cluster building (Maude, 2004). There has been little evidence of regional industry specialization, co-located firms or clusters in Australia. Many of the government-facilitated clusters reviewed by the Department of Industry, Tourism and Resources (2004) had failed.

Three critical issues hamper the development of clusters in Australia 'insufficient critical mass, lack of focus and distinctiveness and political and administrative difficulties' (Roberts & Enright, 2004, p. 116). According to Roberts & Enright (2004) there has been a lack of cohesive policy and action between all three levels of government in Australia and a lack of buy-in from industry means that Australia has yet to fully reap the benefits of clusters that have been experienced by other OECD countries. A lack of knowledge, expertise and commitment among those agencies that are to facilitate the process has hampered effective cluster development. Further research is required into the effective building of clusters within the Australian context as they will assist Australian industry to compete in the global market place (Roberts & Enright, 2004). Clustering has only had minor acceptance in urban

Australia where, it is argued by Roberts & Enright (2004), it would be most effective.

It has been recognized that 'Cluster development on its own is not a panacea for economic development, but rather, depending on the sustainability and effectiveness of the cluster model, a powerful tool for growth' (The Department of Industry, Tourism and Resources, 2004). There has been a move away from direct intervention by government towards the facilitation of collaboration between firms within the cluster and between public and private organizations (Innovation Lab Australia, 2002). Regional development agencies, large industry associations, corporations and industry alliances can assist in the development of clusters by attracting high-level functions and services that are critical to the needs of firms in the cluster (Roberts & Enright, 2004).

The physical proximity within clusters supports communication, the development of social networks, collaboration and competition which are enhanced by knowledge exchange and market flows (Innovation Lab Australia, 2002). Clusters provide a means for SMEs to overcome the disadvantages of their size and their lack of access to knowledge, thus enhancing their ability to innovate both in local and international markets (Innovation Lab Australia, 2002). Multinational firms are attracted to clusters where there is innovation, technology and market intelligence. Clusters are likely to be successful if there is a commitment to the process of building trust, respect and collaboration to reach a common goal (Roberts & Enright, 2004).

According to the Department of Industry, Tourism and Resources (2004, p. 5), 'Australia should now generate its own clustering traditions, taking account of its own unique geographical, cultural and historical factors ... establishing a benchmark for a sustainable cluster in its own right, rather than be shackled to past 'truisms' that may, (or may not) apply to the Australian environment'.

Research methodology

Prior to this research, data was gathered from the literature, overseas experts, a pilot study and a pilot case study. This information was used to design a research instrument which was administered to firms in the marine, defense and resources cluster located in the Henderson/ Rockingham region located south of Perth, Western Australia. Interviews were conducted with a representative senior executive from companies located in the cluster as well as external organizations such as education institutions, government departments and industry peak bodies. In total 35 interviews were conducted in 35 companies. All the interviews were taped with the interviewee's permission and then transcribed and analyzed accordingly. Nvivo 7 software was employed for qualitative data analysis in order to thematize the material (Miles & Huberman, 1994). The results and their discussion are outlined below.

Expert interviews

Prior to the main study a number of unstructured interviews were undertaken as part of an international study tour. Locations and experts selected for interview were identified from the literature. The interviews provided a cross-section of information on the defense and marine industries and case studies on industry and regional cluster development. From the interviews and the pilot case study the following expert insights for practitioners were compiled in relation to cluster development (Table 6.1).

Though collaboration as part of cluster development was addressed, there was no direct reference to the collaborative use of ICT or systems for knowledge sharing. The collaborative use of ICT was also absent within the research finding which are outlined below.

Table 6.1 Cluster development

Factors to Be Considered in Cluster Development

- Is there a sustainable market for the products and industries?
- Will the presence of an external facilitator such as the government lead to leadership problems and conflict of interests?
- What are the agreed targets identified for the cluster?
- Are any of the following drivers for the establishment of clusters present?
  - joint production through purchasing
  - logistics and supply chain development
  - firm formation through incubation
  - spin off and business service
  - joint sales through joint product or regional branding and foreign market promotion
  - joint R&D
  - intelligence on the market or innovations
  - lobbying government policy, regulations and for the provision of infrastructure and human resource upgrading – technical, managerial training and education system interface

Continued

Table 6.1 Continued

Precipitating Factors in the Region

- The presence of a dominant firm or a cluster champion.
- Inter-regional collaboration to gain larger markets and a wider mix of competencies.
- An existing culture of collaboration and participation.
- An existing exports focus.
- Clusters need a combination of different companies.
- History or advantage for a region or industry.
- Government and peak industry bodies in support.
- The creation of supply chains and the development of complementary providers.

Specific Facilitation Activities

Mapping the Cluster

- Identify and map the common and rare capabilities within the cluster and identify related industries to counter the instability in the market by providing firms with alternative markets for their competencies should the dominant market suffer a downturn.
- Creating a database of companies' capabilities in the region in order to identify capabilities that link to certain industries so that companies can have flexibility to switch industries in the case of a downturn.
- Mapping industries in the region to identify linkages/supply chains between industries both direct and indirect.
- Use the database to aid local contracting by firms and to develop consortiums to tender for contracts using the search capability.

Collaboration

- Encouragement of projects involving collaboration between companies and the academic sector.
- Facilitate collaboration between competitors.
- Find a champion to lead collaboration.
- Collaboration around a common goal.

Firm-Level Support

- Encourage existing companies to relocate into the area using economic, environmental and lifestyle factors and incentives.
- Provide service including business mentoring, business incubators, market research and listings of suppliers and potential buyers.
- Develop flexibility within the firms in the region so as to enable them to ride out fluctuations in the market conditions in order to ensure the continuing survival of the cluster.
- Seek ideas and expertise from around the world and modify it to work in the specific region.
- Remember no cluster is complete, there is always room for improvement.

Results and discussion

One of the reasons this study was undertaken was to gather examples of the use of ICT to assist firms to work collaboratively and grow their markets. Unfortunately this was not possible due to the low level of ICT use within the cluster both by the individual firms and within a collaborative context. This finding was unexpected in light of the previous literature which suggested that the adoption of ICT would benefit collaborative relationships (Ratnasingam, 2004). Although ICT is designed to facilitate the sharing of information and assist collaboration, the characteristics of high security, secretiveness and the high level of competition in the region made the development of trust and the willingness to share information difficult. These factors have impeded the adoption of collaborative ICT in the Henderson/Rockingham cluster (Ryssel et al., 2004; Perry et al., 2002).

The respondents did identify benefits using ICT within the cluster that were consistent with the literature, however the drawbacks were significant as detailed in Table 6.2.

Although there were a number of collaborative relationships represented within this study, the majority of business relationships were of a subcontractor nature with a significant power asymmetry. It has been suggested that smaller firms are more likely to adopt ICT if pressured by a larger more powerful collaborator (Morris et al., 2003). The lack of evidence in the study supporting this concept may be due to the overall low level of ICT use, particularly by smaller firms.

The literature suggested that the presence of a prior relationship, which builds trust, might facilitate the use of collaborative ICT (Vlosky et al., 1997; Ratnasingam, 2004). If this is the case the relationships contained within this study were often fraught with significant difficulties which may have inhibited the adoption of collaborative ICT. If firms require a level of ICT adoption as suggested by the diagram on the left side of Figure 6.1, then only four of the firms interviewed would be in a position to move on to collaborative commerce.

Within the study there were two possible examples of what could be termed the collaborative use of ICT, the first being the alliance developed to manufacture and upgrade the ANZAC class frigates where there was a limited use of common ICT. The second example was a firm with a spreadsheet-based workflow management system. The interviewee from this firm had previous experience in ICT as he came from a systems management background as opposed to a Navy or trades background and this prior experience may have encouraged him to create and implement the system (Chau, 2004; Martin & Matlay, 2001).

Table 6.2   Benefits and drawbacks of ICT adoption

Benefits

Results	Literature
• Convenience in the transfer of information and collation of data on the progress of projects.	• 24-hour trading and information exchange and management.
• Overcoming distances particularly working in export markets.	• Expanded marketplaces. • Access to new customers and trading partners.
• Increased efficiency and reduced costs.	• Productivity improvements.
• Provision of long-term data on workflows which allows better scheduling.	• Potential cost reductions. • Customization of products and services.
• Improved communication and the reduction of confusion.	• Cost savings in communications and marketing.
• Allowing the dissemination of information across organizations to obtain a uniform understanding on a collaborative project.	• Greater business exposure. (du Plessis & Boon, 2004; McIvor & Humphreys, 2004; Raisinghani et al., 2005; Chau, 2004)
• Greater access to classified material which assists with scheduling of projects.	

Drawbacks

• The leaking of intellectual property.	• Concerns over privacy and security.
• The general lack of technology literacy among firms in the industry.	• Lack of technological skill and experience.
• The need for cultural change within the collaborating organizations.	• Applicability to the organization's business model.
• Technical problems such as network failure.	• Lack of awareness. • Skill shortages.
• The double handling of information and the lack of coordination between collaborating firms and their IT systems.	• The high cost of entry. • Lack of financial resources. • Insufficient return on investment.
• Lack of compatibility between systems in the large firms and their collaborators.	• Lack of support from management. • Telecommunications infrastructure, customer demand for online services. • The size of the organization. (Lawton et al., 2003; Zhu et al., 2003; Wu, et al., 2003; OECD, 2004; OECD, 2001; Lee et al., 2003)

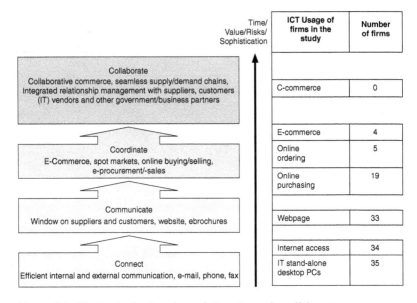

Figure 6.1 Electronic business's evolution towards collaborative commerce (ARC Grant Application, 2004)

Insights for government and practitioners

One of the outcomes of the research project was to provide insights into collaborative relationships and the use of ICT to inform the development of government policy in the region. The research findings suggest that to facilitate the economic growth of the cluster at Henderson/Rockingham the following factors for successful cluster development need to be addressed:

- Building on pre-existing relationships within the cluster.
- The engagement of key decision makers.
- The identification of a cluster champion or champions.
- Identifying and working with those willing to embrace change.
- Mapping the cluster to identify common and rare capabilities.
- The exploitation of regional strength and history.
- The willingness to provide a united identity within the marketplace.
- The development and implementation of consistent policies across all levels of government.

When attempting to develop policy to facilitate collaborative relationships at the industry and firm level there are a number of characteristics identified in the study that require consideration including:

- The low usage of ICT within this cluster due to its characteristics of high security, competition and low-volume/high-cost projects.
- The hierarchal nature of the relationships within the cluster with the dominance of less than ten national or international firms.
- The unwillingness of the small firms in the region to grow beyond a certain size.
- Lack of collaboration between firms, especially the smaller ones, to access export markets.
- The lack of cross collaboration between industries in the region and the lack of information exchange and local innovation.
- The low level use of collaborative ICT as an impediment to opportunities for growth and in reducing the competitiveness of the industries in a global marketplace.

These factors mean that any form of strategy considered by government agencies to facilitate economic growth, collaboration and the use of ICT would require significant resources and a cultural shift within the cluster.

Conclusion

The study was exploratory in nature and as such the findings cannot be generalized. The absence of collaborative e-commerce in the cluster studied may be cultural, as participants in the study often commented on the dominance of competition rather than collaboration in the local the business environment. The presence of heavy manufacturing that dominated the cluster may also be a contributing factor to the low level of collaborative ICT (Salo & Cripps, 2007). The research does highlight the differences between clusters in Europe and Australia and the fact that one size does not fit all. From the Australian perspective the findings are concerning because low levels of collaboration and ICT use do not aid the local or international competitiveness of the industries represented in the cluster. Despite Australia's physical isolation it must compete in a globalized electronic economy.

References

Australian Business Foundation (ABF). (2005). National innovation systems: Finland, Sweden & Australia compared. Learnings for Australia, http://www.abfoundation.com.au/pdf/NISRoosShortPaper22Nov05.pdf. (accessed 15 March 2006).

Australian Research Council. (2004). Collaborative SME commerce in regional knowledge ketworks Australian Research Council grant application, Edith Cowan University, Perth, Australia.

Blandy, R. (2004). Industry clusters program: a review. http:/www.business.unisa.edu.au/cid/publications/blandy/ BV2010_clusters_review.pdf. (accessed 11 November 2006).

Boekholt, P. & Thuriaux, B. (1999). Public policies to facilitate clusters: background, rationale and policy practices in international perspective. In OECD (ed.), *Boosting Innovation: The Cluster Approach*, Paris: OECD, 381–412.

Chau, S. (2004). The use of e-commerce amongst 34 Australian SMEs: an experiment or a strategic business tool. *Journal of Systems and Information Technology*, 7(1), 49–66.

Cripps, H. (2007). Collaborative business relationships and the use of ICT: the case of the marine, defence and resources cluster, Western Australia. Phd Thesis, Edith Cowan University, Perth Australia.

Department of Industry, Tourism and Resources. (2004). AEEMA–Enhancing national economic benefits through a new cluster paradigm, final report. Prepared under the Innovation Access Program, http://www.aeema.asn.au/ArticleDocuments/61/Final(%)20Cluster(%)20Report(%)20-(%)20Jan(%)2004.pdf. (accessed 15 February 2007).

Department of Transport and Regional Services. (2002). *Regional Business Development Literature Review*, Melbourne: SGS Economics and Planning.

Drabenstott, M. (2005). A review of the federal role in regional economic development, www.kansascityfed.org (accessed 23 January 2007).

du Plessis, M. & Boon, J. A. (2004). Knowledge management in ebusiness and customer relationship management: South African case study findings. *International Journal of Information Management*, 24, 73–86.

Etzkowitz, Henry. (2007). Strategic business nets – their type and management triple-helix relations among 'technology, organization, and territory. *Research Policy*, (forthcoming).

Feser E. (2002). The relevance of clusters for innovation policy in Latin America and the Caribbean. Background paper prepared for the World Bank, LAC Group. Chapel Hill: University of North Carolina.

Fitzsimons, P., O'Gorman, C. & Murray, S. (2004). How entrepreneurial was Ireland in 2004? The Irish Annual Report. Dublin: Global Entrepreneurship Monitor, Cahill Printers.

Fulop, L. (2000). A study of government-funded small business networks in Australia. *Journal of Small Business Management*, 38(4), 87–91.

Innovation Lab Australia. (2002). Innovation Lab Australia as an ICT cluster. Mimeo, Canberra.

Killen, C., Hunt, R., Ayres, B. & Janssen, C. (2003). Strategic alliances for world competitiveness: the case of GPC electronics. http://www.mgsm.edu.au/download.cfm? DownloadFile=E4E5ACEA-C18F-4D5F-9FF9CF58EC539D4A. (accessed 20 August 2006).

Lawton-Smith, H. & Dickson, K. (2003). Critical factors in inter-firm collaboration. *National Journal of Technology Management*, 25(1/2), 34.

Lee, W. B., Cheung, C. F., Lau H. C. & Choy, K. L. (2003). Development of a web-based enterprise collaborative platform for networked enterprises. *Business Process Management Journal*, 9(1), 46–59.

Lundequist, P. & Power, D. (2002). Putting Porterinto practice? Practices of regional cluster building: evidence from Sweden. *European Planning Studies*, 10(6), 209–228.

Martin, L. M. & Matlay, H. (2001). Blanket approaches to promoting ICT in small firms: some lessons from the DTI ladder adoption model in the UK. *Internet Research: Electronic Networking Applications and Policy*, 11(5), 399–410.

Maude, A. (2004). Regional development processes and policies in Australia: a review of research 1990–2002. *European Planning Studies*, 12(1), pp. 3–26.

McIvor, R. & Humphreys, P. (2004). The implications of electronic B2B intermediaries for the buyer-supplier interface. *International Journal of Operations & Production Management*, 24(3), 241–269.

Miles, M. B. & Huberman, A. M. (1994). *Qualitative Data Analysis* (2nd ed.), Thousand Oaks, CA.

Morris, D. Tasliyan, M. & Wood, G. (2003). The social and organizational consequences of the implementation of electronic data interchange systems: reinforcing existing power relations or a contested domain? *Organization Studies*, 24(4), 557–574.

OECD. (2001). The internet and business performance. Business and Industry Policy Forum Series, Reports and Proceedings, Paris: France.

OECD. (2004). ICT, e-business and SMEs. Working Party on the Information Economy, Organisation for Economic Co-Operation and Development, Paris: France.

OECD. (2005). Business clusters: promoting enterprise in Central and Eastern Europe. Organisation for Economic Co-Operation and Development, Paris: France.

Palazuelos, M. (2005). Clusters: myth or realistic ambition for policy-makers? *Local Economy*, 20(2), 131–140.

Perry, C., Cavaye, A. & Coote, L. (2002). Technical and social bonds within business-to-business relationships. *Journal of Business & Industrial Marketing*, 17(1), 75–88.

Porter, M. E. (2000). Location, competition, and economic development: local clusters in a global economy. *Economic Development Quarterly*, 14(1), 15–34.

Raisinghani, M. S., Melemez, T., Zhou, L., Paslowski, C., Kikvidze, I., Taha, S. & Simons, K., (2005). E-business models in B2B: process based categorization and analysis of B2B models. *International Journal of E-Business Research*, 1(1), 16–36.

Ratnasingam. P. (2004). The impact of collaborative commerce and trust in web services. *Journal of Enterprise Information Management: An International Journal*, 17(5), 382–387.

Roberts, B. H. & Enright, M. J. (2004). Industry clusters in Australia: recent trends and prospects. *European Planning Studies*, 12(1), 99–121.

Ryssel, R., Ritter, T. & Gemünden, H.G. (2004). The impact of information technology deployment on trust, commitment and value creation in business relationships. *Journal of Business & Industrial Marketing*, 19(3), 197–207.

Salo, J. & Cripps, H. (2007). Impediments to IT adoption in business relationships: evidence from Australia and Finland. Paper presented at the 2007 IMP Conference, Manchester, August 2007.

Scheel, C. (2002). Knowledge clusters of technological innovation systems. *Journal of Knowledge Management*, 6(4), 356–367.

Sölvell, O. Lindqvist, G. & Ketels, C. (2003). The cluster initiative greenbook. Presentation at the TCI Global Conference, Gothenburg: Germany.

Vlosky, R. P., Wilson, D. T. & Vlosky, R. B. (1997). Closing the interorganizational information systems relationship satisfaction gap. *Journal of Marketing Practice*, 3(2), 75–86.

Wu, F., Mahajan, V. & Balasubramanian, S. (2003). An analysis of e-business adoption and its impact on business performance. *Academy of Marketing Science Journal*, 31(4), 425–447.

Zhu, K., Kraemer, K. L. & Xu, S. (2003). Electronic business adoption by European firms: a cross-country assessment of the facilitators and inhibitors. *European Journal of Information Systems*, 12, 251–268.

7
Assessing the Value of Knowledge: A Knowledge Market Perspective

Amir Parssian and Craig Standing

Introduction

Electronic collaboration involves considerable knowledge sharing. This can take place within firms and between firms and can often result in new knowledge being created. In essence, many digital environments provide a marketplace for knowledge exchange and creation. Although only a portion of all knowledge exchange results in a financial transaction, digital knowledge environments exhibit many of the characteristics of more formal electronic marketplace structures where knowledge is created, exchanged and sold.

Despite the wealth of research on knowledge management, none of the existing studies address the issue of knowledge quality, its assessment and impact on business performance. Nonaka (1998) links knowledge quality to 'the extent to which the knowledge created within the organization is truly worthwhile for the organization and society' and argues that 'judging knowledge quality is qualitative in nature'. However, his work does not elaborate on the mechanism of such judgment. In this work, we propose a framework to assess the quality of knowledge and its depreciation over time. Such assessment could provide companies with invaluable insights to manage their corporate knowledge more effectively. Disposing of low quality or outdated knowledge could reduce the risk of decisions being made based on those knowledge elements.

The framework we propose departs from the traditional knowledge types of tacit and explicit. We feel that a finer categorization of knowledge types leads to more appropriate quality metrics. For this, we redefine knowledge types into five distinct categories. Further, our framework links knowledge quality to information quality, decision-maker quality, and temporal effects of knowledge depreciation.

We argue that there are still fundamental questions that need to be answered in relation to knowledge management. In particular, issues related to knowledge quality and its value need to be more clearly defined so that organizations can focus on the creation, sharing and storage of knowledge that has a greater potential to make a strategic impact. In addition, organizations need to be aware of how knowledge appreciates and depreciates in value through time so as to maximize the returns they obtain for knowledge exchange.

Knowledge types and their value

An assessment of the value of knowledge and its depreciation needs to consider the type of knowledge being assessed. Taxonomies of knowledge have been referred to in a number of leading knowledge management contributions.

The most common knowledge typology cited in the literature is the tacit and explicit classification proposed by Nonaka (1998). Nonaka drew upon the Polanyi's argument that 'we know more than we can tell' (Polanyi, 1966, p. 4). Explicit knowledge is codified in books, manuals, corporate documents and information technology systems and can be more readily transmitted between people. Tacit knowledge is personal, developed through experience and related to action and involvement. This makes it difficult to formalize, codify, and communicate to others. The two dimensions of tacit knowledge are technical and cognitive. The former relates to personal skills and is often referred to as 'know how'. The latter relates to beliefs, ideals, values and mental models that create our perception of our environment.

The notion of tacit knowledge has been used in a confused and contradictory manner in much of the knowledge management literature (Hedesstrom & Whitley, 2000). According to their literature analysis, Hedesstrom & Whitley (2000) state that authors either view tacit knowledge as something that is difficult to articulate or that all knowledge is tacit until it is made explicit. Further they identify that the knowledge management literature does not align with Polanyi's philosophical position that tacit knowledge is an indispensable part of all knowledge. They argue that it is conceptually inappropriate to make clear distinctions between tacit and explicit knowledge.

A further distinction of knowledge types by Nonaka (1998) is the individual/collectivist definition. Individual knowledge is created and used by the individual but the collectivist or social knowledge is created within groups. This is elaborated in a later work (Nonaka & Konno, 1998) which discusses shared spaces for emerging relationships or ba. Such a space can be physical (e.g., buildings), virtual (e.g., email) or cognitive (e.g., ideas) or a combination. Knowledge is embedded in *'ba'* (shared spaces) and exists on many levels such as individual, team or project, organization and market environment.

Zack (1999) attempted a conceptual classification of knowledge in relation to its use which included declarative (knowledge about), procedural (know-how), causal (know-why), conditional (know when), and relational (know with). He further refined the knowledge types in a strategic context and proposed Core, Advanced, and Innovative knowledge types where core knowledge enables a firm to just stay in business, advanced knowledge allows the firm to be a viable competitor and innovative knowledge enables a firm to be a market leader.

A pragmatic approach to knowledge management classifies knowledge according to organizational uses, such as knowledge on customers, products, processes, best practices and so on (Alavi & Leidner, 2001). The benefit of the pragmatic approach is that that the knowledge types are clear and easy to communicate within an organizational context. The problem with the pragmatic classification is that it is weak on grouping knowledge types together and could lead to a seemingly endless list of knowledge types to manage.

We propose a knowledge type classification that is pragmatic, consistent with Polany's understanding of tacit and explicit knowledge, considers Nonaka's individual/social knowledge concepts, and incorporates the knowledge spaces explained by Nonaka and Konno (1998). The five knowledge types are explained below and summarized in Table 7.1. Knowledge types vary in their depreciation rates. There are some that depreciate quickly such as project specific knowledge and those that depreciate more slowly such as industry sector knowledge (Figure 7.1). The value of knowledge is related to its scarcity and capability to add business value.

Project knowledge

Knowledge specifically related to a project is project knowledge. This includes knowledge about the aims and objectives of the project, the resources available, the expertise available, capabilities of individuals and teams and how these are interrelated and required to achieve outcomes. This is knowledge and not just information as it relies on experience in the project, even if this is just a few weeks or months. It enables project managers, for example, to achieve outcomes by drawing on resources and expertise. Someone new to a project would not have this specific project knowledge and would therefore be less effective.

Table 7.1   Knowledge classification

Type of Knowledge	Appreciation	Depreciation	Relative Value Related to Scarcity and Its Contribution to Business Value
Project Knowledge	Increases over project	No depreciation until project completed, then rapid	High – but depends on complexity of project
Domain Knowledge	Increases through formal courses and training	Depreciation depends upon rate of change in domain	High because it is complex and takes years to acquire – but depends upon domain and supply/demand for workers.
Organizational Knowledge	Increases with interactions within the organization	Depreciates as organization changes structures, policies and procedures	Low/medium value – as all employees have access to this knowledge as it is often made explicit.
Industry Knowledge	Increases with interactions within industry sector and reading of industry-related material	Slow depreciation rate as industry trends are slow to develop and decline	Low value as many people have access to it.
Economic Environment	Increases with interactions within economy sector and reading of industry-related material	Slow depreciation rate as industry trends are slow to develop and decline	Low value as many people have access to it.

Project knowledge may appreciate in value during the project but rapidly depreciates after the conclusion of the project. It can be fast to acquire, but it also has little value after the project has been completed, unless the same people and context are replicated within another project.

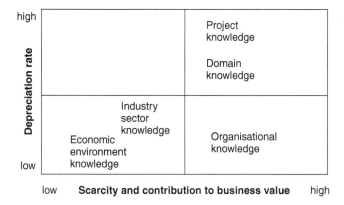

Figure 7.1 The value of knowledge types

Domain knowledge

Domain knowledge is related to a specific application area, for example, database design, software development, defining requirements, hardware capabilities and information technology implementation. It is formed from a combination of experience, formal learning from courses and knowledge from books. It relies not just on information but also on the knowledge of how to apply the information to solve problems or develop creative solutions.

The rate of depreciation of domain knowledge is related to the rate of change in knowledge and information within the specific domain. Generally, knowledge in the IT field changes more rapidly than accounting or management practices. Even within the IT field some domain knowledge changes more rapidly. For example, information on hardware capabilities changes more rapidly than database design principles and the rate of information obsolescence impacts on related knowledge value.

Organizational knowledge

Projects are completed within an organizational framework. Knowledge of organizational processes and how to get things done in an organization are important. Organizational knowledge relies on information of organizational processes, job roles, policies and procedures, organizational aims and objectives and organizational culture and history. When this information is used in an effective way to achieve ends, it can be considered to be organizational knowledge. The depreciation rate of organizational knowledge depends upon the rate of change within the organization but generally it can be considered as slow to depreciate.

Industry sector knowledge

Organizations and projects operate within an industry sector environment. Knowledge about trends and effective methods within an industry sector can provide a competitive advantage to an organization. The emergence of new trends, new strategic relationship developments and changes to industry structures can be important sources of information that when used to achieve outcomes and deliver additional business value can be considered knowledge. An example would be the change in the structure of the travel industry due to the emergence of the internet and the rapid growth of direct online travel purchasing by consumers.

Depreciation of industry sector knowledge is related to its scarcity. When the structures and trends are well established and commonly known then they have less competitive value.

Knowledge of the economic environment

Knowledge about trends and effective methods in the wider environment can be useful. These are the same as industry sector knowledge. An example would be the increasing sophistication of consumers and the desire to be in control of purchasing decisions and the need for access to information to make informed purchasing decisions.

Knowledge quality assessment framework

All the knowledge types we have defined are formed by an information conversion mechanism where the quality of information would directly impact the initial knowledge quality. Holtham (2004) presented a corporate memory model shown in Figure 7.2, which describes the relationships among elements of data, information and knowledge but does not elaborate on conversion mechanisms from one to another. Neither does

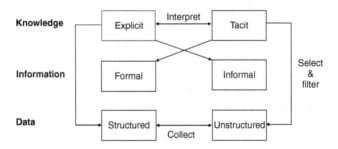

Figure 7.2 Corporate memory (Holtham, 2004)

it include the quality aspects of each element and their impact on the conversion process.

The conversion process from information to knowledge is usually complex and context dependent. Further, decision makers do not process and apply information to build knowledge in the same manner. Therefore, the quality of knowledge built depends on both information quality and the decision maker's ability to process the information at hand into useful knowledge. These elements are shown in Figure 7.3.

The combination of low ability (skill) of the decision maker in information synthesis and knowledge building with either high or low information quality would lead to low-quality knowledge. In these cases, the knowledge builder is not able to process and utilize the information in an optimal manner to reach the desired decision outcome. The quality of knowledge will also be low when the decision maker has high ability to build knowledge but is provided with low-quality information. High-quality knowledge can be obtained with a combination of high-quality information and high-quality decision maker.

The information-knowledge conversion grid can be further developed to incorporate knowledge types and their general knowledge value (Figure 7.4). This diagram highlights the fact that high-value knowledge is very much the exception rather than being pervasive in organizations.

The quality of a knowledge element could erode over time. This holds that the knowledge element loses its value and applicability over time and thus its value depreciates. For example, when consultants who utilize knowledge about specific projects find that over time the techniques offered by a particular knowledge element have become obsolete and, therefore, less useful for new projects that demand newer techniques. That particular knowledge element has depreciated in value

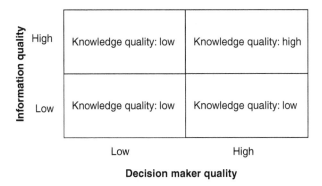

Figure 7.3   Information-knowledge conversion grid

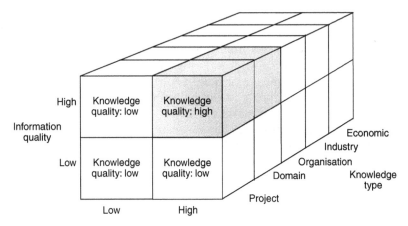

Figure 7.4 Information-knowledge-value grid

with the passage of time. Combining these knowledge quality factors, we present our conceptual knowledge quality framework that maps the relationships among these factors in Figure 7.5.

The framework implies that data stored in the corporate data repositories are extracted by means of processes to produce information products. The quality of produced information depends on the quality of data and processes involved. Poor-quality data, such as inaccurate or incomplete data, will lead to low-quality information. For instance, inaccurate sales data would result in inaccurate aggregate quarterly reports used by business managers to monitor business performance. Quality of processing data would directly affect data quality. Poorly designed and low-performance systems would not be able to process large volumes of data in a timely manner, which leads to obsolete information especially for time-sensitive decisions. The decision maker utilizes the information in a decision-making process to build knowledge.

The quality of built knowledge (K_Q) is a nonlinear function of information quality (I_Q), decision-maker quality (D_Q), and knowledge age (T_K) (i.e., the time units through which knowledge has been applied). Furthermore, the quality of a desired output (O_Q) would be used to assess and measure the applied knowledge. This can be formulated as:

$$K_Q = \frac{I_Q \, D_Q \, O_Q}{\beta \, T_K}$$

where $0 < \beta \leq 1$ is a knowledge-type specific depreciation parameter. Higher β indicate faster temporal depreciation of the knowledge

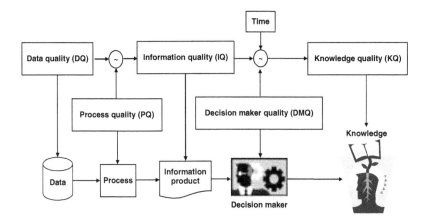

Figure 7.5 The knowledge quality framework

element. This formula can be used for tagging knowledge elements within knowledge bases. The quantitative nature of this tagging could help the users of a knowledge base to determine the usefulness of a particular element. The following example demonstrates the tagging mechanism.

Knowledge tagging example: financial derivatives

An experienced financial analyst obtains a set of financial information from a corporate repository and designs a financial derivative to be sold to interested customers. The sales prove to be successful during a six-month period and the analyst records the design process along with the sales outcome in the knowledge base to be shared with other interested parties. We assume the following parameters:

IQ=0.90 (on a scale of 0 – where 1 indicates perfect information)
DQ=4 (on a scale of 1–5 where 5 indicates highest decision-maker quality)
OQ=0.8 (on a scale of 0–1 where 1 indicates most desirable outcome)
TK=6 (time units measured on number of months)
β=0.8 (assuming high depreciation rates for financial-related knowledge)

These lead to K_Q=0.60 indicating the value of this knowledge element at the time of its contribution to the knowledge base. After 12 months,

K_Q reduces to 0.30 reflecting its quality erosion over time due to volatile financial markets. As the tag value for this knowledge element changes, prospective knowledge users can determine the usefulness of this particular element to design similar derivatives.

This quantitative quality tagging mechanism also allows for a periodic knowledge auditing and removal of outdated elements, which leads to a higher performance for knowledge search engines and a more desirable application of knowledge.

Conclusion

The value of knowledge within organizations is determined by the quality of information and the knowledge type. In this chapter, we have proposed a model that identifies the value of knowledge through time and recommends an approach to incorporate this knowledge into a database. Through the application of this knowledge, organizations can start to focus on the areas of knowledge that are most valuable and through improved awareness and management of the resource seek to gain a competitive advantage.

References

Alavi, M. & Leidner, D. E. (2001). Review: Knowledge management and knowledge management systems: conceptual foundations and research issues. *MIS Quarterly*, 25(1), 107–136.

Hedesstrom, T. & Whitley, E. A. (2000) What is meant by tacit knowledge: towards a better understanding of the shape of actions. Proceedings of the *8th European Conference on Information Systems*, 46–51, Vienna.

Holtham, C. (2004). Converting the knowledge of a distributed workforce into a competitive weapon. London: City Business University School, EMG. In *Knowledge Orientation in Organizations* by E. Truch published by Ashgate publishing, Ltd.

Nonaka, I. & Konno, N. (1998). The concept of 'Ba' building a foundation for knowledge creation. *California Management Review*, 40 (3), 40–54.

Nonaka, I. (1998). A dynamic theory of organisational knowledge creation. *Organization Science*, 5(1), 14–37.

Polanyi, M. (1966). *The Tacit Dimension*, Gloucester, MA: Peter Smith.

Zack, M. (1999). Developing a knowledge strategy. *California Management Review*, 41(3), 125–145.

Part 3

Electronic Marketplaces and Portals

8
The Relationship Between Electronic Marketplace Strategy and Structure

Craig Standing and Susan Standing

Introduction

The number of business-to-business electronic marketplaces (B2B e-marketplaces) reached a peak in 2000 after which a period of consolidation took place (Day et al., 2003). The significance of e-marketplaces has not diminished since those that remain offer a more viable and sustainable business model for organizations to participate in. Although, researchers have given some attention to the antecedents of successful e-marketplace participation by organizations, there has been relatively little attention given to the e-marketplaces themselves. In particular, the literature on e-marketplaces has not explicitly addressed the strategic implications embedded within e-marketplace structures. The structural implications of e-marketplaces go beyond the perception of bias and neutrality mentioned in the literature (Brunn et al., 2002).

The purpose of this chapter is to examine the relationship between e-marketplace strategy and e-marketplace structure. A classification of e-marketplace strategies is presented. The benefits and issues related to each structural form are examined through an extensive literature analysis and a number of examples. The resulting framework of structural implications can be used by e-marketplace developers to decide on an e-marketplace structure to match their strategy and by potential participants to inform their e-marketplace selection and assess associated risks.

Electronic marketplaces

A plethora of e-marketplace models exist and terms such as exchanges, hubs, auctions and catalogue aggregators have been used to describe them (Grewal et al., 2001). In its simplest form a B2B e-marketplaces can be defined as 'an inter-organizational information system that allows the participating buyers and sellers in some market to exchange information about prices and product offerings' (Bakos, 1997). In addition, they can be either vertical or horizontal, although this is no longer a clear-cut separation. Some larger vertical marketplaces have moved towards a more 'complete solution' to procurement needs and horizontal marketplaces enable the purchase of industry specific goods. Indeed, e-marketplace structures are complex and vary considerably according to the market maker's business strategy. The identifiable ownership and governance structures are:

- *Private marketplaces* (hierarchies) – operated by individual companies to connect directly to their buyers/suppliers (e.g., Volkswagen);
- *Public or intermediary marketplaces* – independently owned and may be horizontal operations (e.g., Ariba) or operate within a specific industry (e.g., ChemConnect);
- *Consortia marketplaces* – owned by normally competitive organizations within one industry (e.g.; Covisint); and
- *Community or cooperative e-marketplaces* – ownership and management is spread over a large number of participants and in some cases all members (e.g., regional e-marketplaces).

Ownership and governance structures have only been given a brief treatment in the e-marketplace literature. A general assumption is that ownership structures can affect the level of bias found in a marketplace (Kaplan & Sawhney, 2000). Private marketplaces are often thought to be biased in favour of the owner, but consortia and intermediary marketplaces are thought to project a neutral stance. The benefits of a neutral marketplace are perceived to outweigh other models due to increased transparency, better exploitation of market and supply chain efficiencies and higher levels of trust between trading parties (Brunn et al., 2002; Cousins & Robey, 2005).

The establishment of trust is an important consideration in the development of an e-marketplace. Trust reduces frictions in commerce and enables belief in the other party to fulfil obligations (Kambil & van Heck, 2002). These obligations are seen differently by buyers and sellers, where the former view focuses on trust and associated terms of reliability and performance, while the sellers view buyers as motivated by performance on product attributes, price and product availability. In the electronic environment trust has added dimensions that need to be overcome if business is to flourish and protect firms from opportunistic behaviour (Bakos, 1998). This view is supported by Ba & Pavlou (2002) who highlight the differences in transaction-specific risks both on- and off-line. They examine the use of feedback mechanisms and analyze the effect of such mechanisms on trust in e-markets. Interestingly, they have found that credibility trust (a belief that the other party is honest, reliable and competent) can exist without prior interactions.

To establish trust and reduce risk, market makers are turning to a number of initiatives, including digital signatures, legal frameworks, insurance schemes and comprehensive security systems. The use of third parties, such as escrow services, risk-management companies, certificating authorities and credit agencies are important elements in the establishment of trust (Bakos, 1998; Timmers, 1999; Friedman et al., 2000; Jones et al., 2000; Schoder & Yin, 2000; Saeed & Leitch, 2003; Verhagen et al., 2006).

The literature pertaining to e-marketplace ownership has been over-simplified. E-marketplaces can employ a variety of tactics and mechanisms to achieve their objectives. These tactics and mechanisms include defining and implementing the e-marketplace structure. The implications of structure and ownership are manifold and impacts on the overall success of the e-marketplace from both owner and participant perspectives.

Kaplan and Sawhney's (2000) proposed model focuses on the procurement aspects of e-marketplaces. It differentiates purchases into manufacturing and operating inputs then further distinguishes the method of purchasing into spot and systematic sourcing. The dynamism of the market makers, seeking to survive in an overcrowded environment, has led to a blurring of these categories and marketplaces can now offer trading mechanisms to support one or more of the categories in the model.

Kaplan and Sawhney also make the important distinction between aggregation and matching mechanisms. The former is static in nature with fixed prices and either pre-negotiated contracts or meta-catalogues. This is in contrast to the matching mechanism where prices are dynamic and buyers and sellers are fluid. Matching is a complex mechanism, but the development of software and the increasing experience of market makers are contributing to greater accessibility.

Several further classifications have been developed addressing different aspects of e-marketplaces. Sculley & Woods (2001) have added to an earlier model by Forrester Research. These models are firmly based on the type of transaction mechanism and do not differentiate between what and how businesses buy. As e-marketplaces develop more complex, multiple offerings, the transaction mechanism model becomes less valid.

Piccinelli et al., (2001) takes a different approach and their proposed four categories of e-marketplaces are based on the level of automation and the impact of pricing models. By using the level of automation as a criterion, it is possible to distinguish the complexity of the different types of marketplaces, which is a useful guide when technological capabilities are important. Their model also recognizes that other services offered by e-marketplaces beyond those of buying and selling have an impact on pricing and sales. This will have an influence on the selection of an e-marketplace by a prospective buyer who is seeking more than a trading mechanism.

Choudhury et al., (1998) confine their differentiation of marketplaces to the level of service required by the buyer. From a transaction perspective there are three levels of activity: identification of a buyer/supplier, selection of a buyer/supplier and facilitation of the execution of a purchase (Choudhury et al., 1998). In addition, e-marketplaces now offer a range of information functions or value-added facilities tailored to their market. These include a diverse range from industry news, complex online collaboration resources and full community style sites. The additional services are intended to enhance the marketplace's *value proposition* and attract higher levels of activity from marketplace participants (Brunn et al., 2002). This distinction has the advantage of clarity, but it does not take into account the benefits that may be found in the value-added facilities which are a particular feature of the community portals described by Piccinelli et al., (2001).

The above classifications each have their own perspective and the relevance of the classification feature used depends upon the view of the primary objective of the marketplace. However, none of the models described address the strategic intent and motivations of the market makers as a central concept to the development of e-marketplace structures.

A classification of e-marketplace strategies and motivations

The strategic intents and motivations for developing and participating in e-marketplaces have been developed from an extensive literature review. The motivations for e-marketplace development and participation are classified according to whether they produce economic, relational, service or community benefits. We include discussion of Porter's Five Competitive Forces as a parallel framework to show how our classification builds on and develops existing theories of competition. E-marketplaces are primarily viewed in the literature as economic entities (Choudhury et al., 1998). However, this perspective is an oversimplification of the strategies and benefits associated with e-marketplace participation. The four key drivers or motivations for e-marketplace development and participation are presented in this section as a group of complimentary, and on occasions competing, e-marketplace drivers.

Assessing competition within an industry is considered an important part of strategy development. The strategies and motivations associated with e-marketplace development and participation can be understood within a competitive analysis framework such as Porter's Five Competitive Forces (Porter, 1980; Porter, 2001) and the three key strategies of cost reduction, differentiation and focus. Porter's early work (1980) was further developed to consider the impact of the internet on industry competition (Porter, 2001). He argues that although the internet has had a major impact on aspects of conducting business the five competitive forces have not basically changed in significance. Figure 8.1 applies the Five Forces Framework to B2B E-marketplaces. According to Porter, the most important determinant of a marketplace's profit potential is the intrinsic power of the buyers and suppliers in the product area (Porter, 2001). If buyers or sellers are in the minority or possess differentiated products, they will gain power and profit. Most of the treatment of e-marketplaces by Porter refers to intermediaries but he does note that if it is easy for buyers to transact directly with suppliers then they are less likely to use intermediary e-marketplaces and instead develop their own private e-marketplaces (Porter, 2001). The ease with which e-marketplaces can be developed is clearly a problem for profitability and even industry associations that take over the management of digital exchanges to provide a 'public good' may fail to provide ongoing benefits.

The three strategies identified by Porter can be applied to e-marketplace participation. E-marketplaces can be used as a method to drive down the costs of procurement (cost strategy), as a method to offer superior value-added services (differentiation) or as a method of streamlining procurement channels (focus). However, e-marketplace benefits are wide ranging and extend beyond economic benefits for a company. E-marketplaces have the potential to alter industry sector dynamics,

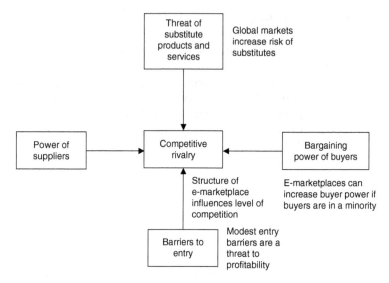

Figure 8.1   Five forces model applied to B2B E-marketplaces
Source: Adapted from Porter, 2001

especially when the major industry sector players cooperate in consortia. We argue that a multi-dimensional perspective of e-marketplace structures should take into account a wide range of economic, relational, service and community benefits. This classification both supports and extends Porter's Competitive Forces Model as it is not limited to a purely economic perspective.

Economic

Major drivers for the development of inter-organizational information systems (IS) are economic (Table 8.1) and involve three potential benefits for participants: cost reductions, productivity improvements and product/market strategy (Barrett & Konsynski, 1982). According to Porter (2001), the main economic benefits of e-marketplace participation for buyers are low transactions costs and sometimes the ability to pool markets and in the case of sellers, lower transaction costs and access to wider markets. E-markets are likely to improve the bargaining power of either buyers or sellers if one of them is in a minority (Porter, 2001).

The two mechanisms for conducting business activity are hierarchies (fixed relationships with suppliers handled within the firm) and markets (Williamson, 1975). Markets are seen as being more efficient from

Table 8.1 Economic implications of e-marketplace development and participation

Economic Category	Specific Item	Source
Cost Reductions	Efficient price search	Bakos, 1997; Bakos, 1998; Choudhury et al., 1998; Malone et al., 1987
	Price competition	Modahl, 2000
	Increased margins	[Bakos, 1997; Mahadevan, 2000]
	Transaction cost savings	Bakos, 1997; Bakos, 1998; Clemons et al., 1993; Malone et al., 1987; Tumolo, 2001
	Lower prices	Tractinsky & Jarvenpaa, 1995
	Productivity improvements through value-add facilities	Brunn, et al., 2002; Bakos, 1998
	Reduces inventory levels	Choudhury et al., 1998; Lin & Hsieh, 2000
	Speed and efficiency of transaction	Lin & Hsieh, 2000; Timmers, 1999; Williamson, 1975
Markets	Wider access to markets	Modahl, 2000; Tumolo, 2001
	Pool markets	Porter, 2001
Higher prices	Higher price premiums	Daripa & Kapur, 2001; Mahadevan, 2000
High costs of participation	High transaction commission	Yoo et al., 2003; Kambil & van Heck, 2002
	High subscription fees	Federal Trade Commission, 2000
Lack of value proposition	Lacks critical mass and competition	Brunn et al., 2002; Tumolo, 2001; Yoo et al., 2003
	Lack of demand	Gartner, 2001
	Lack of value added information	Bakos, 1998; Grewal et al., 2001

a transaction cost perspective. Transaction costs are the costs associated with finding someone with whom to do business, reaching an agreement about the price and other aspects of the exchange, and ensuring that the terms of the agreement are fulfilled (Williamson, 1975). E-markets have the potential to streamline and manage these activities and reduce some of the transaction costs associated with conducting business compared with hierarchies where a company has to manage its suppliers and procurement processes (Malone et al., 1987). However, market efficiencies may be related to certain types of non-recurrent transactions (Williamson, 1975) and some organizations develop closer relationships with their suppliers to obtain supply chain efficiencies as a form of competitive advantage (Clemons et al., 1993).

The impact of e-markets on the price of goods bought and sold is a contentious issue. In some cases, e-markets enable buyers to obtain a better price but may also allow suppliers to obtain a higher price premium when they have information on availability of products (Choudhury et al., 1998). This line of reasoning can be extended to a range of e-marketplace issues since both consumers and suppliers can leverage information technology (IT) to their advantage within the e-marketplace environment (Grover & Ramanlal, 1999; Soh et al., 2006). Even within e-marketplaces it has been found that the benefits derived from participation are not automatic or evenly distributed among participants (Grewal et al., 2001). In an e-marketplace some members may be passive in that they conduct few or no transactions and so derive few benefits from membership (Grewal et al., 2001).

The flexibility and accessibility of the internet enables e-marketplaces to choose the extent of their target market area, ostensibly restricted only by language and 'distance related problems' (Tractinsky & Jarvenpaa, 1995). Many e-marketplaces, for example, advertise their 'global reach' and allow participants the opportunity to trade worldwide, frequently offering a selection of language options. The development of third-party logistic organizations and the proliferation of freight marketplaces offering a range of value-added services including customs, currency exchange and cargo tracking have alleviated many of the distance-related problems, though costs remain significant (Richardson, 2000). Organizations seeking to extend their markets internationally have to address the development of strategies for managing globally. Despite the accessibility of the internet, IT does not operate to global standards (Tractinsky & Jarvenpaa, 1995). This leads to variations in operating environments and operating costs. Systems tend to reflect the dominant nationality of an organization's headquarters highlighting cultural differences in such areas as administration, design and production processes (Tractinsky & Jarvenpaa, 1995). Furthermore, elements of cultural difference are evident in holidays, time management, business practices and payment methods while complex differences in legislation (privacy, data protection and import/export laws) apply across national and trading block boundaries. All these differences impact on the ability to establish relationships with physically dispersed suppliers (Kraut et al., 1998) and build up trust (Ganzaroli, 2000) thereby inhibiting the development of a global supplier base. From both the market maker and supplier perspectives, these differences also inhibit the ability to address differing customer expectations of care and support at a time when electronic commerce has led to greater expectations of individualization (Sculley & Woods, 2001).

Relational view

A relational view of e-marketplaces focuses on the social and political intent within a relationship (Table 8.2). Specifically, the term relationalism has been used to cover implicit open-ended relational contracts (Grover et al., 2002), but here we use it also to cover more formal explicit contracts that have various levels of relational embeddedness. In other words, the social factors that are part of a relationship or alliance, although they have economic implications, may be an important strategic objective in developing an e-marketplace.

An e-marketplace can be understood as a type of inter-organizational relationship (Oliver, 1990), network or alliance (Koch, 2002). Oliver (1990) proposes six generalizable determinants of inter-organizational

Table 8.2 Relational implications of e-marketplace development and participation

Relational Category	Specific Item	Source
Strategic dependence	Less dependence on a small number of suppliers	Malone et al., 1987; Bakos, 1997; Tumolo, 2001
Power	Exert influence others to join (compulsion)	Grover & Ramanlal, 1999
	Power asymmetry	Grover & Ramanlal, 1999
	IT lock-in	Williamson, 1975
Legitimacy	Fear of being left out	Grewal et al., 2001
	Reputation, image, prestige	Grewal et al., 2001
Reciprocity	Cooperative, collaborative approach to exchange information	Bakos, 1998; Tractinsky & Jarvenpaa, 1995; Brunn et al., 2002; Malhotra et al., 2005

relationships, which are relevant to e-marketplaces:

1. *Necessity* – to fulfil legal or regulatory requirements. For example, some private and government procurement systems are based on e-marketplaces. If companies wish to tender for contracts it must be done through the e-marketplace.

2. *Asymmetry* – potential to exert power over other organizations. Electronic marketplace consortia can be formed by major players in a market to exert influence over other organizations to participate (Grover & Ramanlal, 1999). Consortia members are in a position to define the policies and structure of the e-marketplace. When suppliers have to adopt specialized information and technology systems to participate in the e-marketplace then the supplier may feel 'locked-in'. Porter (2001) argues that the open nature of the internet is less likely to result in lock-in. Although, this may be true for business-to-consumer e-commerce it unlikely to apply to the same extent to B2B e-commerce since these systems require specialized software, training and experience. Williamson (1975) argues that lock-in is symmetrical since the buyer cannot easily or quickly change suppliers. While this may act as a barrier in fixed supply chains the buyer may have considerable choice within the supplier participant base in an e-marketplace.

3. *Reciprocity* – desire to cooperate, collaborate and coordinate. Hierarchical e-marketplaces require the organizations in their supply chain to cooperate and collaborate by transacting and exchanging information (Malhotra et al., 2005).

4. *Efficiency* – internally focused efficiencies. E-marketplace participation may be seen as a way to reduce the cost of procurement.

5. *Stability* – in response to environmental uncertainty. A company may decide to enter an e-marketplace so it can become less dependent on a small number of suppliers.

6. *Legitimacy* – related to reputation, image, prestige, or congruence with prevailing norms in the environment. This has been shown to be an ineffective rationale for e-marketplace participation as companies that emphasize this as their reason for e-marketplace participation are more likely to be passive members (Grewal et al., 2001).

E-marketplace owners and participants may be motivated by some of the above determinants. For example, a major purchaser may be able to use its power and influence as a consequence of being both the owner and the major purchaser to exert influence on suppliers to join or to engineer favourable market conditions (Grover & Ramanlal, 1999).

Service motive

Strategic objectives driving e-marketplace development can be related to service and quality improvement. These may include such things as continuity of supply (Gartner, 2001; Federal Trade Commission, 2000), convenience and speed of processing (Lin & Hsieh, 2000) and greater choice for buyers. Improved service can also be delivered by offering a greater range of services in a one-stop-shop environment providing value-added information and delivery logistics services (Choudhury et al., 1998; Brunn et al., 2002). Along with a greater range of offerings are the capabilities to customize and personalize offerings through the digital medium (Bakos, 1998). According to Porter (2001) a destructive aspect of the internet is the reduction of competition to price alone. Forgotten in this, Porter argues, is the ability of the internet to support improved service through convenience, standardization, specialization and customization.

The service motive is closely aligned to the economic motive, but it has been included as a separate factor as some organizations may be more interested in improving the level of service than reducing costs (Table 8.3). Higher service typically comes at a cost but an organization may choose to deliver higher levels of service despite the extra cost to gain a competitive advantage. There are five dimensions by which consumers evaluate service quality (Berry & Parasuraman, 1991; Bebko, 2000) and these are explained in relation to e-marketplaces:

1. *Tangibles* – The appearance of physical facilities, equipment, personnel and communications materials.

Table 8.3 Service implications of e-marketplace development and participation

Service Category	Specific Item	Source
Improved efficiency	Speed and efficiency of transaction	Lin & Hsieh, 2000; Yoo et al., 2003; Mahadevan, 2000; Timmers, 1999
Specialized service	Personalization Customization	Bakos, 1998; Weill and Vitale, 2001 Bakos, 1998; Tumolo, 2001
Greater range of services	Value-added information	Choudhury et al., 1998; Brunn et al., 2002
Continuity of demand	Continuous demand for products	Gartner, 2001; Federal Trade Commission, 2000

An obstacle for the online environment is making the service tangible. One method of making the service more tangible is to provide consulting support to the organizations to help them effectively use the e-marketplace. Value adding services bundled together provide the image of a one-stop shop for procurement needs.

2. *Reliability* – The ability to perform the promised service dependably and accurately.

The participants need to trust that the e-marketplace will work effectively. The reputation of the e-marketplace is important in this respect. Participation in the e-marketplace may build up an expectation of continuity of demand for suppliers.

3. *Responsiveness* – Providing a prompt service and the desire to help customers.

A major driver for participation is the speed and efficiency with which the transactions are conducted. An e-marketplace can provide a range of value-added services to participants.

4. *Assurance* – The knowledge and courtesy of employees and their ability to convey trust and confidence.

The governance structure of the e-marketplace plays an important role in building trust between parties.

5. *Empathy* – The caring, individualized attention the firm provides its customers.

The e-marketplace can personalize and customize services for participants.

Improvements in service are likely to be a major driver for government agencies developing e-marketplaces to interact more effectively with suppliers. Consortia and private e-marketplaces would also be concerned about using e-marketplaces to deliver better levels of service. Intermediary e-marketplaces need to consider the range and quality of service they provide in order to attract participants and maintain participant numbers.

Community motive

Some e-marketplaces are created with a community emphasis. This is usually done through stimulating economic activity working on the premise that if local/regional business flourishes then so will the communities they are part of (Dans & Freire, 2002). The market maker, usually local or state government, provides encouragement to adopt e-marketplace trading and in doing so raise the level of general e-business knowledge, skills and technologies within the business community (Table 8.4). The e-marketplace itself can be viewed as an online business community. However, the ultimate aim underlying such a strategy is to further develop at least one of the following:

- *Business in a region or locality.* There are several examples of regional e-marketplaces sponsored by governments in Australia at the state and local levels (Standing et al., 2003; Dans & Freire, 2002; Brunn et al., 2002).
- *Industry sector within a country or region.* A specific industry sector, possibly through a business association, may consider a community approach in order to achieve critical mass for buying and selling (Porter, 2001). The wine industry in Australia, for example, could take a community perspective. Participants would typically be small producers that would not have the resources or bargaining power to operate independently. Working together in a cooperative style venture has the potential to impact on the viability of an industry sector as a whole. This type of arrangement has significant overlap with relational motivation. However, a distinguishing feature is that all or at least a large number of participants have a sense of ownership in the marketplace.

Online communities that focus on resource sharing or act as learning networks are known as soft networks and could also fall in to this category (Sherer, 2003). However, instead of concentrating on the buying and selling and products and services the emphasis is on the sharing of information and knowledge that can be used to improve products and services or create new products or services (Malhotra et al., 2005).

Table 8.4 Community implications of e-marketplace development and participation

Community Category	Specific Item	Source
Community benefits	Impact on region or locality Impact on industry sector	Dans & Freire, 2002 Sherer, 2003
Resource sharing	Set up and running costs shared	Sherer, 2003
Collaborative network	Emphasis on collaborative networks for information sharing and innovation	Yoo et al., 2003; Brunn et al., 2002

Strategic implications of e-marketplace structures

E-marketplace strategies have implications for the structural form of the e-marketplace. It is argued that the choice of e-marketplace structure is strategic in nature. Four e-marketplace structures are identified: Intermediary, Hierarchy, Consortium, and Large Group.

Intermediary e-marketplace

While disintermediation has been posed as a real threat for businesses that have acted as intermediaries, some suggest that the internet has increased the number of intermediaries to the extent that there is a transformation of intermediation taking place. In the e-marketplace arena there has been a very high failure rate in public e-marketplaces, although the potential of the model is still recognized (Gartner, 2001). In the e-marketplace arena, 'neutral' intermediaries have set up to match buyers with sellers. To avoid bias, it is suggested that buyers and sellers be treated equally (Sculley & Woods, 2001). However, the whole concept of bias and neutrality in e-marketplaces has probably been oversimplified since intermediaries have the scope to provide certain participants with extra information, to allow some entry to the e-marketplace and refuse others entry.

Intermediary e-marketplaces must make a profit to be sustainable. Both buyers and sellers therefore should view the market maker as any other business partner or provider and consider issues such as cost of membership, transaction costs as well as level of service provided (Table 8.5). When viewing the e-marketplace from a network or relational perspective a company should assess the quality and number of members. It should also consider whether some participants are being favoured in terms of preferential market information. A prospective participant should not assume the market place is unbiased and is totally transparent. From a service perspective the range of value-added facilities and support could be assessed in addition to continuity of supply.

Hierarchy e-marketplace

Hierarchy e-marketplaces are frequently referred to as private e-marketplaces. The e-marketplace owner typically has both a strong quality or service motive and economic motive in setting up the e-marketplace. The owner/buyer may put in place policies to stimulate competition between suppliers by promoting higher levels of participation and by transaction mechanisms such as reverse auctions. The power and influence is vested in one entity. Sellers should be aware of

Table 8.5 Benefits and problems associated with intermediary e-marketplaces

Intermediary	Economic Implications	Relational Implications	Service Implications	Community Implications
Strategy: To realize supply chain efficiencies and improved service	High cost of participation	Attempt at transparency	Professional e-marketplace – technical, administrative support	Perceived as favouring a wider geographical market
	Ongoing maintenance of marketplace responsibility of intermediary	Reluctance to share information due to security and privacy issues	Value-added market information usually available	
	Existing marketplace – no set up costs	More likely to be perceived as unbiased	Access to e-marketplace advice and expertise	
	May lack critical mass and competition/ demand			

the potentially increased power of the buyer and that the buyer could also have a monopoly on the information created on marketplace transactions. There would appear to be little impetus to provide high levels of value-added service in a hierarchy since that may improve the bargaining power of the supplier. Certain types of information may be made available to suppliers to improve the quality of products and services supplied. Although there can be a community objective in the development of the marketplace, it could be argued this is the owner exerting its influence and applying pressure to reduce transaction costs.

The Western Australian government has created and manages an e-marketplace in the form of a hierarchy where it is the sole buyer and has many sellers. The state Government Electronic Market (GEM) (http://www.gem.wa.gov.au/Gem) is Australia's first comprehensive online government buying service. GEM services cover a wide range of government buying. GEM was created with the aim of reducing costs through the introduction of more efficient procurement practices for government. In addition to cost reduction, GEM also has a number of other objectives that are aimed at improving the service to suppliers (taken from the GEM website):

- Increasing the accountability and transparency of government purchasing.
- Increasing the levels of compliance with state supply.
- Commission procurement and purchasing policy (including Buy Local and Common Use Contract policies).
- Demonstrating leadership in the implementation of the Australian Procurement Construction Council (APCC) guidelines and standards for electronic procurement.
- Assisting West Australian industry to enter the world of e-commerce in a safe and secure government environment.

The e-marketplace involved considerable set up costs and was aimed at improving supply chain efficiencies. The state government also emphasized improvements in supply chain service as a major driver. The development of a private e-marketplace by the government was less likely to create security issues compared with adopting an intermediary. GEM has struggled to obtain a critical mass of transactions with many small and medium enterprises being suspicious of the government's motives for developing the e-marketplace. The perception from some SMEs is that the motive is mainly to increase competition between suppliers and as a result drive down costs. SMEs are sensitive to the power asymmetry with the government and that government's access to additional market information through GEM will exacerbate the issue. The government of Western Australia is a major purchaser in the region and it is important for many companies to be awarded contracts. According to the GEM developers the set-up and ongoing maintenance of the system has been expensive but it has improved communication with suppliers in terms of contract requirements and communication of opportunities. Some suppliers felt they were disadvantaged by the e-marketplace since they lacked the IT sophistication to effectively use it.

Overall, the developers of GEM found that the e-marketplace reduced transaction costs related to procurement and therefore this coupled with the increased competitive pressure on suppliers provided economic benefits. The benefits and problems associated with GEM are summarized in Table 8.6.

Consortia e-marketplace

Shared ownership by a small group of organizations takes on the form of a consortium where power is vested across the group, unless one of the group members takes a leading role. In this respect, one of the group members may take on the role of the quality leader. From an economic

Table 8.6 Benefits and problems associated with hierarchy e-marketplaces

Hierarchy	Economic Implications	Relational Implications	Service Implications	Community Implications
Strategy: To realize supply chain efficiencies and improved service	Set up according to buyer needs	Security risk less in private e-marketplace	Security risk less in private e-marketplace	More likely to focus on the industry sector of developers (buyers)
	Set up costs	May lack market transparency	Improved communication with buyer	
	Ongoing maintenance of marketplace	Locked into buyer technology	Lack of IT/e–business sophistication in suppliers	
	Increased competition between suppliers	More likely to be perceived as biased		
		Conditions may favour buyer		

perspective the group can share the expense of managing the e-marketplace. An advantage of group ownership is that critical mass of participants should be easier to achieve which in turn should reduce the cost of goods and services by raising competition between suppliers. The strongest argument for group ownership is the relational motive since organizations which once viewed one another as competition can collaborate in an industry network which can lead to a decision support and knowledge sharing environment. Such an industry network, however, can form a power block to protect the group's interests and work to exclude competition. The service motive depends upon the ethos of the owners and the level of competition in attracting participants.

Quadrem is an example of a consortium e-marketplace owned by a number of major mining corporations. Quadrem was developed in 2000 by 14 of the world's largest mining, minerals and metals companies as a one-stop solution to specifically meet the eProcurement needs of the mining industry. The e-marketplace now has 20 shareholders and thousands of sellers and hundreds of buying locations, located across the globe. Quadrem has involved considerable investment from the major players and there are high ongoing maintenance costs. The emphasis of Quadrem has been on industry-based supply chain efficiencies and high-quality professional service through a sophisticated technology platform (http://www.quadrem.com). The dominance of the mining companies that set up Quadrem has led some companies to believe that there is a power asymmetry which pressures companies to join. In addition, some felt that the system was not fully transparent as some features may be designed to favour the major buyers. However, both suppliers and buyers acknowledge the improved level of communication, the continuity of demand that major mining companies create, the reliability of the software system and the highly integrated and sophisticated nature of the e-marketplace. The high level of funding for the development of Quadrem and the critical mass of buyers allowed the development of value-added services and information. Security was not mentioned as an issue by the suppliers interviewed. Quadrem has stressed the importance of developing the network of participants and alliances with other e-marketplaces and in this respect emphasizes the relational benefits of e-marketplace involvement as much as the economic benefits. The benefits and problems identified with Quadrem are summarized in Table 8.7.

Large group ownership e-marketplace

Shared ownership by a large group diminishes the power of any individual owner member (Table 8.8). The e-marketplace forms a weak network arrangement although stronger alliances may develop within the network. The owners would typically be buyers and/or sellers within the marketplace and the broader ownership base would help in gaining a critical mass of participation. Such e-marketplaces can be used to stimulate economic development and the community but may need a champion which is often the government.

A key benefit of this type of e-marketplace structure is that the costs of setting up the marketplace and the running costs are shared broadly amongst the participant owners. In addition the broad ownership structure, if managed effectively, is likely to overcome perceptions of bias. A potential problem associated with a large group e-marketplace structure (cooperative) is designing an effective decision-making and management model. If all participants are involved in the decision making the process may be protracted. The e-marketplace may suffer due to having a 'cooperative' style image which lacks professionalism. Those companies with expertise and experience in e-marketplaces may decide to go it alone and hence those companies that band together in a cooperative arrangement may have very little expertise in the e-marketplace arena.

Table 8.7 Benefits and problems associated with consortia e-marketplaces

Consortia	Economic Implications	Relational Implications	Service Implications	Community Implications
Strategy: To develop a major purchasing entity: to make broad supply chain efficiencies	High set up costs	Dominance of group can persuade suppliers to join	Improved communication with buyers	More likely to focus on the same industry sector of consortia developers (buyers)
	Increased competition between suppliers	Security risk less in private e-marketplace	Group provide continuity of demand	
	Ongoing maintenance of marketplace	Perceived as a power block	Solid ability to execute	
	Improved collaboration with suppliers	Conditions may favour buyers	Usually highly customized and integrated	
		Lack of alternatives for suppliers		
		May lack market transparency		

Table 8.8 Benefits and problems associated with large group ownership (community) e-marketplaces

Large Group	Economic Implications	Relational Implications	Service Implications	Community Implications
Strategy: To develop an online community e-marketplace	Set up costs shared and so reduces costs of participation	More likely to be perceived as unbiased	May lack leadership and management	Government initiatives tend to have a local emphasis
	Lack of funding can create start up challenges	May lack professional image due to lack of funding	May lack expertise in e-marketplace management	Ownership and management responsibilities are shared
	Difficult to communicate value Proposition			

Table 8.9   A summary of the strategic emphasises in e-marketplace structures from the four structures

Strategic Emphasis	Factors	Intermediary	Hierarchy	Consortia	Large Group
Economic	Price reduction through increased competition	High	High	High	Medium
	Emphasis on transaction cost reduction	High	High	Medium	Medium
Relational	High level of power asymmetry	Low	High	High	Low
	Improve collaboration	Low	Low	High	Low
Service	High levels of service	High	Medium	High	Low
	High continuity of demand	High	Medium	High	Medium
Community	Industry sector focus	Low	High	High	Low
	Local focus	Low	Medium	Low	High
Pre-e-marketplace	Industry structure pre-e-marketplace	Local focus with close relationships with a few suppliers	Fragmented procurement system with strong relationships with key suppliers	Independent procurement systems for each company	Fragmented market dependent on procurement practices of individual firms
Post-e-marketplace	Industry structure changes as a result of e-marketplace	Global market with less dependence on a few suppliers	More competitive for suppliers and less fragmented procurement system	More cooperation and industry sector collaboration. More competition between suppliers	Increased choice in buyers and suppliers
Main Benefits		Economic and service	Some economic benefits for buyer and service improvements for buyers and sellers	Relational benefits for buyers and sellers	Some economic benefits
Success or Failure		Success	Mainly a success but some benefits not delivered	Success	Eventual failure due to lack critical mass

Table 8.9 compares the findings from the four structures. The e-marketplaces have a significant impact on the relationships between buyers and sellers. Less dependence on key suppliers and greater competition between suppliers meant that buyers/developers seemed to gain more power and control from the introduction in intermediary and hierarchy e-marketplaces. The four e-marketplaces demonstrate the full range of benefits being obtained.

Discussion

The structure of e-marketplaces has many implications for developers and members or participants. In this section we identify the key implications of e-marketplace structures for developers and participants. The implications are determined from the analysis of the literature and the examples. In the literature, the strategic intent of market makers to establish e-marketplaces has focused mostly on the economic objectives. There is an assumption that the motivations remain purely economic (Grover et al., 2002), but this view does not account for the development of the different market structures that are evident.

The earlier market makers were predominantly intermediaries and established marketplaces for economic motives. The opportunities for lowering transaction costs and reducing procurement spending were identified before the widespread use of the internet (Malone et al., 1987). The uptake of the internet as a trading platform for e-marketplaces has enhanced the cost savings and extended access to new markets. Secondary motives, beyond the economic, are identifiable in intermediary-owned marketplaces, but they are complementary to the main driver. For suppliers, there are some economic benefits but the increased competition offsets the transaction cost savings.

In contrast, hierarchies, or private marketplaces, provide economic savings for buyers but the structure is also suited to delivering service improvements. Such marketplaces draw their supplier base into a closer relationship and enhance the ability of the supplier to interact with the buyer. By offering reliability and responsiveness with the assurance of trust and confidence, the market maker can attract suppliers and reduce the need for extensive searches. This in turn can reduce costs to the end customer and justify the expense of the private marketplace. The advantages of the private marketplace may be offset by suppliers' fears of power asymmetry between the buyer-owner and the suppliers.

Consortia e-marketplaces have relational benefits associated with the cooperative network of key developers. Consortium members have considerable power through their joint ownership and can bring their supplier bases to the marketplace establishing critical mass. Their ability to create an industry network and high levels of service quality are formidable and such networks can move outside the vertical chain.

The community motive is strongly associated with government initiatives in e-commerce. However, many government-sponsored e-marketplaces have not succeeded due to their failure to address community-building tactics early in the e-marketplace life-cycle (Gengatharen et al., 2005). Nevertheless the authors predict the development of large group ownership structures emerging as the ability of e-marketplaces to contribute to community development becomes recognized. The large group, or cooperative, structure may deliver economic and relational benefits in the later stages of the life cycle, but the overall focus in the early phases of development is concerned with community creation. This may take the form of an industry cluster or business in a geographic region.

The introduction of the e-marketplaces had significant impacts on altering the dynamics of the industry sector. Changes at an industry-sector level emphasize the relational (or network) perspective and confirm the importance of examining alternative benefits of e-marketplace participation.

According to Porter (1980), companies can only compete with one primary strategy. A failing perhaps of the e-marketplace developers and participants is that they had several motivations for participation including economic benefits, service benefits, relational benefits and community benefits. The findings from the e-marketplace analysis can be partly interpreted through Porter's Five Forces of Competition such as improved buyer power, increased rivalry and hence pressure on suppliers to reduce prices and barriers to entry. However, the cooperative approach shown by the mining companies in the consortium Quadrem is not fully accounted for in Porter's industry sector perspective.

In examining the implications of e-marketplace structures the primary motivation for establishment by the different ownership models can be identified, although there can be no definitive alignment between them. Many of the early expectations of the internet in relation to low entry barriers, decreased roles for intermediaries, and lower transactions have not been realized. The barriers to effective entry remain high since substantial capital is needed to gain market share. As has already been mentioned, intermediaries, albeit many new ones, have actually flourished on the internet. Rather than the Adam Smith ideal of a perfect market, the internet uses methods and technologies to create its own friction. These take the form of switching costs, either through standards or particular implementations. Porter (2001) has suggested that switching costs are low on the web. While this may be true in the business-to-consumer (B2C) world this is not necessarily the case for B2B activities within electronic marketplaces.

At a conceptual level traditional markets and e-marketplaces are both dependent on architectural considerations. It could be argued that little of significance has changed in the move to e-markets from traditional sourcing of materials and services. However, when business is done electronically all the details related to the market can be recorded digitally. The market maker therefore has information that the other participants do not have access to and this can be used to quickly adapt the marketplace to increase or maintain margins, to develop e-marketplace loyalty, to create barriers to participants dropping out of the marketplace and so on. In addition, some of the information can also be sold to participants as a value-adding service. Indeed, the key business advantage for the market maker is owning the information and not the marketplace. In the pre-digital era, the marketplace itself or access to it in a physical sense was the key advantage.

E-marketplaces can be set up to have a global reach and so the tyranny of distance, at least from a communication perspective is mitigated. The delivery of physical goods from overseas can still be a problem if speed is of the essence but the sourcing of suppliers and the transaction process can be done in real time on a global basis. Business conducted internationally brings along with it its own problems such as working across time zones and linguistic and cultural differences. When the geographical scope of the marketplace increases there is likely to be an increase in the number of potential suppliers, and as a result, this could have the impact of driving prices down. Digitally conducted business processes can reduce delays in the transaction process and also automate much of the transaction process thereby reducing overall transaction costs for the owner. However, these savings may not necessarily be passed on to other participants.

Features of the e-marketplace architecture can be changed relatively quickly, for example, creating additional functionality to gain a competitive advantage of other e-marketplaces or even creating barriers to switching. E-marketplaces are software systems and although software development is a complex process working on a modular basis can improve the capability to quickly change form.

Conclusion

This chapter has classified e-marketplace strategies and related these to e-marketplace structures. There are three main points that can be drawn from this analysis for research and practice. Firstly, the structure of e-marketplaces has a number of implications that are likely to impact on the perception of the success of the e-marketplace. It has been argued that the definition in the literature of neutral and biased e-marketplaces is an oversimplification. Each structure has implications in terms of bias that need to be addressed. Improving the levels of transparency in the e-marketplace so that it is clear which participants have access to certain types of information is one method of reducing perceptions of bias. Prospective participants may be wary that the market structure has been set up and is managed to further the goals of the developer or buyer. E-marketplace owners clearly need desirable outcomes to offset the investment but it likely that the best way to do this is to develop high levels of trust.

Secondly, the discussion has shown that there is a range of strategies that could be important when developing an e-marketplace structure. The literature has emphasized the importance of economic benefits of e-marketplace participation but an e-marketplace can be viewed as a relational entity that delivers relational benefits, a vehicle for improving service and as an online trading community. Although relational, service and community strategies are likely to have economic implications viewing e-marketplaces as purely economic entities is again an oversimplification of their purpose.

Thirdly, different e-marketplace structures are likely to require certain technical features. When a strategy emphasizes economic savings then systems that streamline processes and integrate with back-end systems may be required. Community focused e-marketplaces however may emphasize low-end technology platforms to achieve high levels of participation. A service strategy is likely to offer access to valuable information on the market and provide high levels of technical and administrative support.

References

Ba, S. & Pavlou, P. (2002). Evidence of the effect of trust building technology in electronic marketplace markets: Price premiums and buyer behaviour. *MIS Quarterly*, 26(3), 243–268.

Bakos, J. Y. (1997). Reducing buyer search costs: implications for electronic marketplaces. *Management Science*, 43(12), 1676–1692.

Bakos, J. Y. (1998). The emerging role of electronic marketplaces on the internet. *Communications of the ACM*, 41(8), 35–42.

Barrett, S. & Konsynski, B. R. (1982). Inter-organization information sharing systems. *MIS Quarterly, Special Issue*, 93–105.

Bebko, C. (2000). Service intangibility and its impact on consumer expectations of service quality. *Journal of Services Marketing*, 14(1), 9–26.

Berry, L. & Parasuraman, A. (1991). *Marketing Services: Competing Through Quality*. New York: The Free Press.

Brunn, R., Jensen, M. & Skovgaard, J. (2002). E-marketplaces: crafting a winning strategy. *European Management Journal*, 20(3), 286–298.

Choudhury, V., Hartzel, K. S. & Konsyriski, B. R. (1998). Uses and consequences of electronic markets: An empirical investigation in the aircraft parts industry. *MIS Quarterly*, 22(4), 471–507.

Clemons, E. K., Reddi, S. Y.& Row, M. C. (1993). The impact of information technology on the organization of economic activity: The move to the middle hypothesis. *Journal of Management Information Systems* 10(2), 9–36.

Cousins, K. C. & Robey, D. (2005) The social shaping of electronic metals exchanges: an institutional theory perspective. *Information Technology & People*, 18(3), 212–229.

Dans, E. & Freire, J. (2002). IT as an agent of social change: Lonxanet and the case of the Galician artisanal fisheries. *Proceedings of the Twenty-Third International Conference on Information Systems*, 769–777. Association for Information Systems.

Daripa, A. & Kapur, S. (2001). Pricing on the internet. *Oxford Review of Economic Policy*, 17(2), 202–216.

Day, G. S., Fein, A. J. & Ruppersberger, G. (2003). Shakeouts in digital markets: lessons from B2B exchanges. *California Management Review*, 45(2), 131–150.

Federal Trade Commission. (2000). Entering the 21st century: competition policy in the world of B2B electronic marketplaces. *The Federal Trade Commission B2B Public Workshop Report*.

Friedman, B., Kahn, P. H. J. & Howe, D. C. (2000). Trust on-line. *Communications of the ACM*, 43(12), 34–40.

Ganzaroli, A. (2000). Glocalizing trust: The role of IT in a de-coupling industrial district. *Proceedings of the 8th European Conference on Information Systems*, Vienna.

Gartner. (2001). *Private Marketplaces: What Is the Value Proposition?* Gartner Consulting.

Gengatharen, D., Standing, C. & Burn, J. (2005). Government-supported community portal regional emarketplaces for SMEs: evidence to support a staged approach. *Journal of Electronic Markets*, 15(4), 405–417.

Grewal, R., Comer, J. M. & Mehta, R. (2001). An investigation into the antecedents of organizational participation in business-to-business electronic markets. *Journal of Marketing*, 65(3), 17–33.

Grover, V. & Ramanlal, P. (1999). Six myths of information and markets: information technology networks, electronic commerce and the battle for consumer surplus. *MIS Quarterly*, 23(4), 465–495.

Grover, V., Teng, LT. C. & Fiedler, K. D. (2002). Investigating the role of information technology in building buyer-supplier relationships. *Journal of the Association for Information Systems* (3), 217–245.

Jones, S., Wilikens, M., Morris, P. & Pasera, M. (2000). Trust requirements in e-business. *Communications of the ACM*, 43(12), 80–87.

Kambil, A. & van Heck, E. (2002). *Making Markets. How Firms Can Design and Profit from On-line Auctions and Exchanges*, Boston: Harvard Business School Press.

Kaplan, S. & Sawhney, M. (2000). E-hubs: the new B2B marketplaces. *Harvard Business Review*, May-June, 78(3), 97–103.

Koch, H. (2002). Business to business electronic commerce marketplaces: The alliance process. *Journal of Electronic Commerce Research*, 3(2), 67–76.

Kraut, R., Steinfield, C., Chan, A., Butler, B. & Lloag, A. (1998). Coordination and virtualisation: the role of electronic networks and personal relationships. *JCMC*, 14.

Lin, B. & Hsieh, C (2000). Online procurement: implementation and managerial implications. *Human Systems Management*, 19(2), 105–110.

Mahadevan, B. (2000). Business models for internet-based e-commerce: an anatomy. *California Management Review*, 42(4), 55–69.

Malhotra, A., Gosain, S. & Sawy, O. A. (2005). Absorptive capacity configurations in supply chains: gearing for partner-enabled market knowledge creation. *MISQ*, 29(1), 145–187.

Malone, T. W., Yates, J. & Benjamin, R.I. (1987). Electronic markets and electronic hierarchies. *Communications of the ACM* 30(6), 484–497.

Modahl, M. (2000). Now or Never. *How Companies Must Change Today to Win the Battle for the Internet Consumer*. London: Orion.

Oliver, C. (1990). Determinants of interorganizational relationships: integration and future directions. *Academy of Management Review*, 15(2), 241–265.

Piccinelli, G., Di Vitantonio, G. & Mokrushin, L. (2001). Dynamic service aggregation in electronic marketplaces. *Computer Networks*, 37, 95–109.

Porter, M. E. (1980). *Competitive Strategy: Techniques for Analysing Industries and Competitors*, New York: Macmillan, Free Press.

Porter, M. E. (2001, March). Strategy and the internet. *Harvard Business Review*, 63–78.

Richardson, H. L. (2000). Going global? Master distribution first. *Transportation and Distribution*, 41(10), 43–48.

Saeed, K. A. & Leitch, R. A. (2003). Controlling sourcing risk in electronic marketplaces. *Electronic Markets*, 13(2), 163–172.

Schoder, D. & Yin, P. L. (2000). Building firm trust on-line. *Communications of the ACM*, 43(12), 73–79.

Sculley, A. B. & Woods, W. A. (2001). B2B exchanges. The killer application in the business-to-business Internet revolution. New York: HarperCollins.

Sherer, S. (2003). Critical success factors for manufacturing networks as perceived by network coordinators. *Journal of Small Business Management*, 41(4), 325–345.

Soh, C., Markus, L. M. & Goh, K. H. (2006). Electronic marketplaces and price transparency; strategy, information technology, and success. *MIS Quarterly*, 30(3), 705–723

Standing, C, Sims, I., Stockdale, R. & Wassenaar, A. (2003). Can e-marketplaces bridge the digital divide. *Proceedings of the IFIP Conference on Organisational Information Systems in the Context of Globalisation*, Athens, 339–353.

Timmers, P. (1999). *Electronic Commerce*. Chichester: John Wiley.

Tractinsky, N. & Jarvenpaa, S. L. (1995). Information systems design decisions in a global versus domestic context. MIS *Quarterly* 19(4), 507–529.

Tumolo, M. (2001). Business-to-business exchanges. *Information Systems Management, Spring*, 54–62.

Verhagen, T., Meents, S. & Tan, Y., (2006). Perceived risk and trust associated with purchasing at electronic marketplaces. *European Journal of Information Systems*, 15(6), 542–555.

Weill, P. & Vitale, M. (2001). *Place to Space. Migrating to eBusiness Models*. Boston: Harvard Business School Press.

Williamson, O. E., (1975). Transaction-cost economics: the governance of contractual relations. *Journal of Law and Economics*, 22(2), 233–261.

Yoo, B., Choudhary, V. & Mukhopadhyay, T. (2003). A model of neutral B2B intermediaries. *Journal of Management Information Systems*, 19(3), 43–68.

9
The Use and Perception of E-marketplaces: An Institutional Perspective

Craig Standing, Ian Sims and Susan Standing

Introduction

Institutional structures are recognized as being important in influencing decision making within organizations. Legitimating forces create institutional pressure to conform even in cases where there is little evidence to suggest it will improve efficiency. This chapter examines the reasons behind conformity and non-conformity to information technology decisions from an institutional perspective. In particular, it examines how the rise and fall of e-marketplaces was shaped by institutional forces and provides insights into how new technological initiatives are impacted by organizing visions which draw strongly from institutional theory.

A strong institutional legitimating culture is the key factor in obtaining organizational conformity. For an IT innovation, internal structuring actions such as top management championship, adequate system support, a strategic rationale and external legitimation support institutional conformity. Non-conformity is likely to increase over time when there is negative external legitimation in the environment supporting non-compliance. Delays in realizing cost savings and system and support problems are moderating influences on organizational compliance. In effect, external legitimation is a key factor impacting on institutional non-conformity and overrides internal structures of legitimation when the sentiment has turned against a technology in the wider environment. In addition, we highlight the danger of top management technology champions overselling a new system.

This chapter explains the concepts of institutional theory and organizing visions, and then examines the various ways that institutional theory impacts upon the adoption of technology. In particular, we use the rise and fall of electronic marketplaces to illustrate these impacts and discuss the implications for the notion of IT maturity models.

Institutional theory and technology adoption

The decisions made in organizations are significantly influenced by the norms, values and culture that coalesce to form what researchers in the area term institutional structures. In some organizations, the institutional structures develop over time to increase levels of conformity and this may be seen as an effective approach to obtain compliance with organizational initiatives. Although the reasons for organizational compliance to IT initiatives are becoming understood through research on institutional structures, less is known about the conditions that lead to resistance or non-conformity to decisions on IT implementations, especially where there are strong institutional pressures.

Institutional theory (DiMaggio & Powell, 1983; Meyer & Rowan, 1977) is concerned with how organizations respond to their institutional environments (Bowring, 2000) through the organizational structures that influence decision making and action. In particular, it focuses on the forces of habit, convention and social behaviour that exist in organizations rather than on the rational efficiency-centred decision making that is characteristic of resource-based theory (Oliver, 1991). In institutional theory, legitimacy is the determining factor for organizational structure and practices. Legitimating forces mean that organizations are likely to conform to institutional pressures even though there is little evidence to suggest they will improve organizational efficiency (Yiu & Makino, 2002). Mimetic behaviour leading to isomorphism has been argued to be inefficient but when viewed within the context of risk aversion it may lead to optimal organizational performance (Powell, 1991; Kondra, 1998).

Institutional theory is relevant to studies of the adoption of information technology, e-commerce and other organizational innovations since it takes the perspective that organizations construct an institutional environment that constrains their ability to change in the future due to conformity to institutional expectations (DiMaggio & Powell, 1983). Organizations may fail to realize significant benefits from their IT innovations because they have been adopted for legitimating purposes rather than efficiency motives (Meyer & Rowan, 1977).

Strategic responses to institutional pressures have been proposed by Oliver (1991). These range from passive conformity to active resistance and non-conformity: acquiescence, compromise, avoidance, defiance and manipulation (Table 9.1). Acquiescence can take three forms: habit, imitation and compliance. Habit refers to an unconscious adherence to rules or values. Organizations may imitate other organizations and their technology decisions and such mimetic actions contribute to organizational isomorphism. Acquiescence is more likely to occur where legitimacy and efficiency are pressures for conformity. Compliance is a conscious decision to comply with organizational requests. Complete acquiescence may be undesirable in some situations as there may be conflicting demands upon a unit. As a result, a unit or organization may make compromises by balancing, pacifying or bargaining with external constituents. Organizations can avoid compliance by concealing their actions, buffering or escaping from institutional rules and expectations. Defiance is a stronger form of resistance that can take on the form of dismissing rules, openly challenging rules, and finally aggressively attacking the rules. Manipulation is a method to control or influence institutional pressures (Oliver, 1991).

Table 9.1   Strategic responses to institutional forces (Oliver, 1991)

Strategies	Tactics	Examples
Acquiescence	Habit	Following invisible, taken-for-granted norms
	Imitate	Mimicking institutional models
	Comply	Obeying rules and accepting norms
Compromise	Balance	Balancing the expectations of multiple constituents
	Pacify	Placating and accommodating institutional elements
	Bargain	Negotiating with institutional stakeholders
Avoid	Conceal	Disguising nonconformity
	Buffer	Loosening institutional attachments
	Escape	Changing goals, activities, or domains
Defy	Dismiss	Ignoring explicit norms and values
	Challenge	Contesting rules and requirements
	Attack	Assaulting the sources of institutional pressure
Manipulate	Co-opt	Importing influential constituents
	Influence	Shaping values and criteria
	Control	Dominating institutional constituents and processes

We argue the complementarity of institutional theory and structuration theory (Giddens, 1979, 1984). The latter is concerned with the process of change in structures through time (Schultze & Orlikowski, 2004) while institutional theory examines the implications of the structures. Structuration theory has been used to examine technology adoption and assimilation since organizational structures shape the context and reactions of individuals to proposed changes. Chatterjee et al., (2002) used structuration theory to examine the adoption of web technologies. In their work, top management support, strategic investment rationale and extent of coordination were seen as metastructuring actions against a backdrop of the institutional structures of signification, legitimization and domination (Orlikowski, 1992). Institutional structures of signification provide meaning for people and provide a framework of behaviour. Institutional structures legitimize actions which are aligned to the goals and values of an organization while structures of domination act in a regulatory capacity so that conformity to organizational rules is maintained (Orlikowski, 1992; Chatterjee et al., 2002).

Organizing visions

Institutional theory is closely related to the concept of organizational visions for IT (Swanson & Ramiller, 1997). According to Swanson & Ramiller (2004), an organizing vision 'is a construction in discourse that emerges from a heterogeneous collective consisting of such parties as technology vendors, consultants, industry pundits, prospective adopters, business and trade journalists, and academics'. An organizing vision is a sense-making process that an organization establishes to enable it to not only make adoption decisions on specific systems but to determine their role and organizational contribution. In particular, it can be argued that organizing visions determine the contribution an IT system can make and therefore can determine their success or failure.

Strategic institutional responses

The strategic responses to institutional forces proposed by Oliver (1991) provide a framework for analyzing the actions of organizations. A legitimacy culture typically exists because of resource dependency or because it is seen as the most appropriate way to organize (DiMaggio & Powell, 1983; Meyer & Rowan, 1977). Institutional theory's emphasis on legitimacy as a driving motive for action explains why the norms and values in an organization would tend to lead to acquiescence as a response (Dacin, 1997; Oliver, 1991). Oliver (1991) suggests that studies of 'organizational resistance in institutional environments may be important for substantiating or refining the basic premises of institutional theory'. The research we have conducted over the years in this area highlights a number of issues that suggest that this framework can be further developed.

Changes in strategic response

We argue that an extension in complexity to the notion of strategic responses is required since agencies and organizations actually often change their strategic response over time. Although some organizations adhere to a particular strategy, others change their response and in some cases change it several times. Much of our work has taken place in local and state government. Due to the strength of legitimating structures in government, the prevailing common initial response to new initiatives is acquiescence. In some cases, the perceived problems associated with using a system lead to compromises being made; in other cases disillusionment with a system leads to avoidance.

We propose the notion of *'paths'* of resistance to radical IT adoption within a context of legitimating structures that takes these changes of strategy into account. Our work in government agencies has identified these paths and changes through time and they are highlighted in Table 9.2 for illustrative purposes. Acquiescence is a typical initial response because of the norms within an institutionally conservative environment that encourage conformity. However, when the perception of the technology radically changes in the wider business environment, as was the case with the rapid consolidation of e-marketplaces, it is likely to serve as a catalyst for non-conformity, especially when this is supported by delayed benefits realization, technical problems and recognition of overselling the system.

Overlapping responses

The strategic responses identified by Oliver (1991) show manipulation to be an extreme response to institutional structures. Our work highlights that a response can involve manipulation (influence) within a general strategy of acquiescence. For example, one department (shown in Table 9.2) acquiesced but then attempted to influence (manipulate) the system to support its own ends. To do this it had to be part of the system or to play the 'game'. Hence, the third unit of analysis went through acquiescence, manipulation (influence) and then compromise. Oliver's

Table 9.2 Strategic-response 'paths' to institutional forces (taken from our research cases)

Government Agency 1	Acquiesce (Comply)	Manipulate (Influence)	Avoid (escape)
Government Agency 2	Acquiesce (Comply)	Compromise (Bargain)	Manipulate (Control)
Government Agency 3	Acquiesce (Comply)	Manipulate (Influence)	Compromise (Pacify)
Government Agency 4	Defy (Dismiss)		
Government Agency 5	Acquiesce (Comply)	Compromise (Pacify)	
Government Agency 6	Acquiesce (Comply)	Compromise (Bargain)	Avoid (escape)

classification of strategic responses is presented as mutually exclusive responses and does not account for more sophisticated strategies or overlapping responses. Manipulation is a rather subversive tactic that depends upon a perception of involvement. It is generally not possible to avoid or defy being part of a system and at the same time influence the system by manipulating it. Compromise is a more open and less devious response but one that still assumes involvement in the system.

The idea of multiple layers of legitimacy is consistent with a broader view of institutional theory. Different schools of thought within institutional theory support different but complimentary perspectives of what constitutes an institution and institutionalization (Scott, 2003). Indeed, it is accepted that institutions operate at a variety of levels (Scott, 1995).

Multiple layers of legitimacy

Sociologists such as Selznick (1957) and Zucker (1977) viewed institutions primarily as normative structures where beliefs and norms operate at the organizational level to form a distinctive culture. They emphasize that institutional processes operate at both macro (environmental) and micro (organizational and interpersonal) levels. More recent views of institutionalism emphasize the role of cultural-cognitive processes that highlight shared cognitive transorganizational frameworks and understandings that operate at a macro-level (Powell and DiMaggio, 1991). For example, the role and influence of professional groups are perceived as being largely socially constructed but nonetheless still influential. According to Meyer and Rowan (1977) these types of institutions are likely to take the form of 'rationalized myths'. Institutional analysts emphasizing the regulative features of institutions view them as systems of rules or governance systems which also operate on a macro scale and include legal and economic systems (North, 1990; Williamson, 1979).

These three different perspectives of institutions allow us to uncover multiple layers of legitimation that impact on technology decisions (Table 9.3). This more encompassing view of institutionalism has recently been considered in information systems studies in relation to reconceptualizing users as social actors (Lamb and Kling, 2003) and IS outsourcing decisions (Miranda & Kim, 2006). Rather than assuming that institutional forces only apply to the organization from the external institutional environment we can draw upon the instantiation of institutionalization at various levels within an organization including global, local, organizational, personal and system (Table 9.3).

In terms of e-markets, legitimating forces at different levels can be seen. The pressures to globalize in procurement are a force but the sentiments surrounding e-marketplaces for procurement are also a factor. These can be moderated or even overridden by local (national) perspectives. Legitimation can also be created at the organizational level and personal level, with technology champions for example.

We add 'technology' or 'information system' at the normative and organizational level drawing upon the notion of its duality (Orlikowski, 1992):

> it is also the case that once developed and deployed, technology tends to become reified and institutionalized, losing its connection with human agents that constructed it or gave it meaning, and it appears to be part of the objective, structural properties of the organization. (1992, p. 406)

Table 9.3 Layers of institutional legitimation

Scope of Influence	Type of Legitimation	Level of Influence
Global	Regulative	External
Global	Cultural-Cognitive	External
Local	Cultural-Cognitive	External
Organizational	Normative	Internal
Personal	Normative	Internal
System	Normative	Internal

Technology champion

Technology champions are people in organizations who champion the adoption of a technology (Beath, 1991). A champion is often an informal expert who garners support and organizational resources for a technology (Scheepers, 2003) and aims to draw the attention of senior management. Indeed, the notion of a champion is not restricted solely to the technology domain; in fact any type of organizational innovation can be championed (Markham, 2000). Champions form part of the legitimating environment. They contribute to organizational forces for adoption. Our research has found that an e-marketplace often requires a champion for it to be adopted. Such is the paradigm shift, from hierarchies to markets, an e-marketplace requires a charismatic champion to sell the idea. However there are dangers in overselling a technology. A champion is usually supported by general support for a technology in the marketplace and the two forces can form powerful legitimating structures.

Legitimation is a critical factor in technology adoption

Table 9.4 summarizes the reasons garnered from our years of research for initial conformity and then non-conformity to e-marketplace initiatives organized under the areas of system issues, support issues, strategic

Table 9.4 Reasons for conformity and non-conformity in use of the e-marketplace

Factors Contributing to Conformity/ Non-conformity	System Issues	Support Issues	Strategic rationale	Top Management Support	External Legitimacy
Conformity	Workable system with some technical issues	Support teams put in place	Economic, social and political (image) drivers	Charismatic technology champion Political network of support	Strong legitimating support in environment
Non-conformity	Usability and integration issues increase frustration Evolution of system creates state of flux which provides opportunity for negotiation	Support does not resolve usability and integration issues	Difficulties in realizing substantial cost savings Social and political agenda not a strong driver	Realization of overselling of system leads to expectation/ reality gap by managers Suspicion of the motives of the technology champion by managers	Lack of external legitimating support in environment

rationale, top management support and external legitimacy. Chatterjee et al., (2002) organized the factors influencing web technology assimilation in terms of the structuring actions of strategic investment rationale, extent of coordination (support issues) and top management championship. A strong institutional culture of conformity is the key factor leading to acquiescence, while structuring actions and external legitimacy are supporting factors (Figure 9.1).

We argue from our research that the change in attitude towards e-marketplaces in the wider environment was the key factor that explained increasing non-conformity. The negative sentiment towards e-marketplaces that prevailed at the time of the rapid shakeout in the number of operating exchanges worked as a catalyst for non-compliance and magnified the problems. The delayed cost savings and technical and support issues were magnified at this time by the change in external sentiment towards e-marketplaces which provided legitimating support for non-conformity (Figure 9.1). In terms of non-conformity to institutional forces, negative external legitimation is likely to override the internal institutional pressures.

Organizing visions

The organizational contribution of an information technology is shaped by its organizational vision which as a concept is itself based on legitimation (Swanson & Ramiller, 1997). This organizing vision will determine if the technology has an operational, tactical or strategic contribution. An information system may have strategic potential but if the organizing vision is of a tactical nature then its contribution is

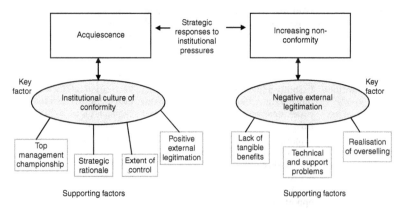

Figure 9.1 Key factors in institutional conformity and non-conformity to IT decisions

defined. In this respect, it is not the technology but the organizing vision for it that is critical to its perceived organizational value. The choice of using the reverse auction, or not, is perceived as a tactical decision. Reverse auctions can be used as a tactical response to sourcing initiatives such as cost savings and increased process efficiencies, and demonstrate the transparency of purchasing decisions. These tactical decisions are mostly concerned with reducing transaction costs and obtaining lower unit prices. The impact of the reverse auction on the supply base results from the strategic sourcing decisions of the organization. It is possible to expand the supply base to identify more potential suppliers or to use the auctions to consolidate the supplier base. The ability for organizations to source goods and services from international suppliers via the auction potentially increases the supplier base. A strategic decision to consolidate the supply base could be implemented through the use of the reverse auction mechanism and provide additional advantages of volume expenditure. However, in some industry sectors such as energy, mining or food, certain contracts can become a template for repetitive or routine purchases. The use of reverse auctions in this way becomes more of a programmed decision rather than a strategic initiative. This seems to emphasize lowest unit cost and undervalue the non-contractible elements of supply. However, shorter-term contracts are not as susceptible to changing market conditions and would require less reevaluation on renewal, allowing the use of reverse auctions to become a more programmed response. We contribute further to Swanson & Ramiller's (1997) organizing vision concept by explaining that although visions can be used to facilitate adoption, they can also constrain or limit the use of a technology.

Conclusions and recommendations

Non-conformity to information technology innovations is heavily influenced by the perception of the technology in the broader environment. The level of popularity of a technology serves as an external legitimating structure that supports internal decisions when adopting technology. The rise of e-marketplaces provided a level of external validation for their adoption. The subsequent rapid consolidation in e-marketplace numbers had a negative impact on the perception of their validity as a procurement approach. The change in sentiment towards e-marketplaces in the business world provided an external legitimating structure to support criticisms of e-marketplaces and increased levels of non-conformity. Practitioners should be aware of the criticisms that are like to ensue when the tide changes against a technology in the environment, even for a temporary period.

Non-conformity to an organizational initiative is likely to increase when entities cannot clearly identify with the purported benefits of the initiative. Proposed efficiency improvements must be significant enough to motivate those in a position of responsibility for adopting the technology to invest considerable time, effort and money in the project. Social ideals such as improving e-commerce adoption by companies are a weak motivator and any resistance from the supplier community is likely to increase the level of non-conformity.

Technical problems with systems and poor usability of systems are reasons for resistance to an initiative. The frustration that arises from poorly designed systems presents a real barrier to their adoption. Design problems associated with e-marketplaces can include poor response times, cryptic instructions, errors in the system, lack of integration with back-end systems and difficult navigation mechanisms. It is incumbent on developers to develop highly usable systems that take into account that many smaller companies will lack IT expertise. When the emphasis is on improving efficiency then attention must be given to the effective integration of systems.

Potential participants may see a government-owned e-marketplace as biased since the market maker is also the buyer. Ownership and governance structures have only been given a brief treatment in the e-marketplace literature. A general assumption is that ownership structures can affect the level of bias found in a marketplace (Brunn et al., 2002). Private marketplaces are often thought to be biased in favour of the owner, but consortia and intermediary marketplaces are thought to project a neutral stance. The benefits of a neutral marketplace are perceived to outweigh other models due to increased transparency, better exploitation of market and supply-chain efficiencies and higher levels of trust between trading parties (Kaplan & Sawhney, 2000). Government agencies adopting e-marketplaces should consider separating the management and buying functions by contracting out the creation and management of the e-marketplace to a third-party provider.

Organizations should be wary of overselling the benefits associated with e-business initiatives as this may create suspicion from potential participants. This suspicion may stem from a perception of government trying to gain 'kudos' from the introduction of a system rather than the benefits that are to be realized by users. Overselling the ideas and the use of charismatic champions may result in the belief of hidden agendas, such as securing identities or increases in power even though strong top management support for IT initiatives are recognized as important. Technology decisions may also meet resistance if strong efficiency gains are not evident (Abrahamson & Rosenkopf, 1993; Fichman, 2004) and the level of resistance is likely to be magnified if the system has been oversold at the outset.

Levels of conformity and non-conformity to IT related decisions are not easy to predict. Our work has shown that initial acquiescence to a decision can give way to non-conformity when positive legitimating external forces are not present. Many of the contributing factors symptomatic of increasing non-conformity to IT system decisions, including lack of costs savings may in the medium term be addressable but without widespread support for the technology in the environment, internal support for the system is likely to diminish. When a technology loses popularity in the environment, and this is coupled with a perception of overselling the system internally, the institutional non-conformity is likely to intensify.

The adoption of technology and legitimation are inexorably linked (Cousins & Robey, 2005). Indeed, the duality of organizing visions where they are informed by environmental forces and then create perceptions which in turn reaffirm the vision means that once a technology is seen as tactical, rather than strategic, it is unlikely to change. A technology's organizational contribution may be relatively immutable due to the forces of legitimation, even in the face of increased familiarity and experience with the technology. This latter point suggests that increasing organizational maturity in terms of IT adoption and usage is unlikely to happen in an incremental manner. This brings into question the notion of IT maturity models that imply that the transitions between stages are a matter of incremental improvement.

Institutional theory has many impacts on the adoption and use of technology in organizations. Electronic markets are heavily influenced by legitimation and there is evidence to suggest that these are moderated by national and regional cultures. A key issue for organizations is to understand legitimating forces and break free of these where they are counterproductive to their future.

References

Abrahamson, E. L. Rosenkopf. (1993). Institutional and competitive bandwagons: Using mathematical modelling as a tool to explore innovation diffusion. *Academy Management Review*, 18(3), 487–517.

Beath, C. (1991). Supporting the information technology champion. *MIS Quarterly*, 15(3), 355–372.

Bowring, M. A. (2000). De/constructing theory: a look at the institutional theory that positivism built. *Journal of Management Enquiry, 9*(3), 258–270.

Brunn, R., Jensen, M. & Skovgaard, J. (2002). E-marketplaces: crafting a winning strategy. *European Management Journal,* 20(3), 286–298.

Chatterjee, D., Grewal, R. & Sambamurthy, V. (2002). Shaping up for e-commerce: institutional enablers of the organizational assimilation of web technologies. *MIS Quarterly,* 26(2), 65–89.

Cousins, K. C. & Robey. D. (2005). The social shaping of electronic metals exchanges: An institutional perspective. *Information Technology & People,* 18(3), 212–229.

Dacin, M. T. (1997). Isomorphism in context: the power and prescription of institutional norms. *Academy of Management Journal,* 40, 46–81.

DiMaggio, P. J. & Powell, W. W. (1983). The iron cage revisited: institutional isomorphism and collective rationality in organisational fields. *American Sociological Review,* 48, 147–160.

Fichman, R. G. (2004). Real options and IT platform adoption: implications for theory and practice. *Information Systems Research,* 15(2), 132–154.

Giddens, A. (1979). *Central Problems in Social Theory,* Basingstoke, UK: Macmillan.

Giddens, A. (1984). *The Constitution of Society,* Polity Press, Cambridge, UK.

Kaplan, S., and & Sawhney, M. (2000). E-hubs: the new B2B Marketplaces. *Harvard Business Review,* May–June.

Kondra, A. Z. & Hinings, C. R. 1998. Organizational diversity and change in institutional theory. *Organization Studies,* 19(5), 743–767.

Lamb, R. & Kling. R. (2003). Reconceptualizing users as social actors in information systems research. *MIS Quarterly,* 27(2), 197–236.

Markham, S. K. (2000). Corporate championing and antagonism as forms of political behavior: an R&D perspective. *Organization Science,* 11(4), 429–447.

Meyer, J. W. & Rowan, B. (1977). Institutional organisations: formal structure as myth and ceremony. *American Journal of Sociology,* 80, 340–363.

Miranda, S. M. & Kim. Y. (2006). Professional versus political contexts: Institutional mitigation and the Transaction cost heuristic in information systems outsourcing. *MIS Quarterly,* 30(3), 725–754.

North, D. (1990). *Institutions, Institutional Change and Economic Performance,* Cambridge: Cambridge University Press.

Oliver, C. (1991). Strategic responses to institutional processes. *Academy of Management Review,* 16(1), 145–179.

Orlikowski, W. (1992). The duality of technology: rethinking the concept of technology in organisations. *Organization Science,* 3(2), 398–427.

Powell, W. (1991). Expanding the scope of institutional analysis. In *The New Insitutionalism in Organisational Analysis,* Walter Powell & Paul DiMaggio (eds.), Chicago: University of Chicago Press, 183–203.

Scheepers, R. (2003). Key roles in intranet implementation: the conquest and aftermath. *Journal of Information Technology,* 18, 103–119.

Schultze, U. & Orlikowski, W. (2004). A practice perspective on technology-mediated network relations: the use of internet based self-service technologies. *Information Systems Research,* 15(1), 87–106.

Scott, W, R. (1995). *Institutions and Organizations,* Thousand Oaks, CA: Sage.

Scott, W. R. (2003). *Organizations: Rational, Natural, and Open Systems.* New Jersey, Pearson Hall.

Selznick, P. (1957). *Leadership in Administration*. New York: Harper & Row.

Swanson, E. B. & N. C. Ramiller, N. C. (1997). The organizing vision of information systems innovation. *Organization Science*, 8(5), 458–474.

Swanson, E. B. & Ramiller, N. C. (2004). Innovating mindfully with information Technology. *MIS Quarterly*, 28(4), 553–584.

Williamson, O. E. (1979). Transaction cost economics: the governance of contractual relations. *Journal of Law and Economics*, 22(2), 233–261.

Yiu, D. & Makino, S. (2002). The choice between venture and wholly owned subsidiary: an institutional perspective. *Organization Science*, 13(6), 667–683.

Zucker, L. (1977). The role of institutionalization in cultural persistence. *American Sociological Review*, 42, 726–743.

10
Designing Community into an E-Marketplace

Rosemary Stockdale

Introduction

An enterprise of the future is predicted to be one that has an understanding of the need to create and transfer value within and across social networks (Murray & Greenes, 2006). Hagel & Armstrong (1997) were early advocates of including a community element into online businesses and the development of social networks has been an ongoing facet of the growth of the internet and the development of e-business. Building social capital through the development of an online community within a business context is seen as a wise strategic move by influential bodies such as McKinsey Consulting (Bughin & Hagel, 2000). Business benefits are held to be in the areas of market research, relationship building and branding, while customers gain rather more intangible benefits such as community esteem through knowledge, reciprocal exchange of information and a sense of belonging (Stockdale & Borovicka, 2006).

McMillan (2002) considers markets to be social constructions, designed as exchange mechanisms to generate gains from trade. Marketplaces exist because the act of buying and selling is of common interest to the community and serve a purpose within it. Therefore the building of social networks or community within an electronic marketplace would appear to offer opportunities to create and transfer value between the marketplace providers and the marketplace members.

This study explores the idea of designing community into the online marketplace to support the development of social networks that transcend recognized relationship types to build a strong vibrant social marketplace that benefits all stakeholders. TradeMe, a horizontal intermediary e-marketplace based in New Zealand, is used as an illustrative case study to identify the constructs and benefits of building marketplace communities. The study examines the development of relationships and then discusses the issue of generalizing these constructs to other types of e-marketplaces.

E-marketplaces

McMillan (2002) argues that improving the way that marketplaces work increases the gains to all stakeholders. Market design can influence the success of a marketplace by improving the flow of information thereby reducing friction and enabling buyers and sellers to function more efficiently. Technology has proved to be a great facilitator by broadening the reach of markets and supporting increased efficiencies in information exchange. Earlier examples of technologies that have influenced market change include postal services, railroads, telephone, and TV. More recently, the internet and the growth of electronic marketplaces have had a major influence on the way businesses trade.

Bakos (1997) defines an e-marketplace as an inter-organizational information system that allows the participating buyers and sellers in some market to exchange information about prices and product offerings. Choudhury et al., (1998) add that the e-marketplace should enable potential buyers and sellers to be identified and for a transaction to take place. Online marketplaces also support greatly improved information flow that in conventional markets was largely one way using devices such as advertising, yellow pages, word of mouth, branding and intermediaries (McMillan, 2002). The increase in information availability and exchange has alleviated asymmetries in the balance of power within buyer/seller relationships as both buyers and sellers have more transparency and greater choice in identifying trading partners.

This increased ability for buyers and sellers to interact, with accompanying benefits such as transaction cost savings, speed and global reach, has encouraged widespread use of both vertical and horizontal marketplaces. The identification of e-marketplaces as being business to business or consumer orientated (B2B, B2C or C2C) has blurred in recent years, although Standing et al., (2008) acknowledge that the B2B arena is more complex than the B2C. Following the consolidation of marketplaces after the dot.com crash in 2000/2001, a number of industry specific e-marketplaces have been established. At the same time, the growth and accessibility of horizontal consumer marketplaces has been notably swift and eBay has played a major role in this since its inception in 1995. This 'high tech flea market' (McMillan, 2002, p. 19) has moved from being a C2C marketplace to hosting many smaller businesses and supporting a range of transactions that transcend categorization within the normal ranges of business to business or to consumer interaction. Such changes are evident in other marketplaces such as Alibaba where an increasing number of small to micro businesses find a market and spill over into Alibaba's C2C arm, TaoBao (Ou & Davison, 2009).

The interaction between buyers and sellers in the online environment has been a focus of much research including the examination of the growth of embedded relationships supported by information technology (Shultze & Orlikowski, 2004), identification of a hybrid relationship model (Standing et al., 2007) and consideration of the loosely connected one-off transactions that require little in the way of relationship building (Powell, 1990).

Embedded relationships, with their emphasis on recurring interactions and social capital, are highly dependent on goodwill and social/ personal interaction (Schultze & Orlikowski, 2004). They require commitment from both buyers and sellers who gain benefits from a deeply connected, long-standing relationship. In Standing et al., (2007) hybrid model, commitment to social interaction mirrors that of the embedded relationship but the more formal market mechanisms of the arms-length type of relationship are also evident. This hybrid approach enables organizations to achieve competitive market prices while maintaining a visible degree of corporate social responsibility and good relationships with their local suppliers. In contrast to these more social types of relationships, arms-length relationships are more formal and impersonal without assumptions of recurring interaction or interdependence.

The structure of intermediary e-marketplaces implies that arms-length relationships will form (Schultze & Orlikowski, 2004) as buyers and sellers come together through the actions of an independent market provider. However, Driedonks et al., (2005) found that social and political factors and the loss of social capital were influential in determining levels of adoption and sustainability in this type of e-marketplace participation. They also found that dysfunction in the communications channels was a factor, emphasizing the importance of information flow within a marketplace environment.

The role of social networks

The concept of sociability as a beneficial influence in online business is emerging as a topic of considerable interest in the business press. The push for integrating community aspects into e-business practice to gain benefits from sociability has been increasing since Hagel (1999) advocated the need in the late 1990s. Firms are now building on the techniques of targeted marketing to maximize benefits from customer interaction (Miller et al., 2009).

Much of the push towards online communities as a method of building social capital in businesses arises from developments in the open source communities. Consumers have contributed to the collective creative forces, inspiring development (Kozinets et al., 2008) and adding value to the products (Jeppesen & Frederiksen, 2006). Kozinets et al., (2008) see the intersection of creativity and consumption to be at the heart of a new social form of informational innovation. At a more prosaic level, Paterson (2009) raises awareness of the role of non-sanctioned communities, which may result from lack of action on the part of firms who ignore opportunities to build social interaction. The consequences of consumers taking non-sanctioned action may result in a loss of control and missed opportunities to build bonds, create customer loyalty and increase customer satisfaction.

Such studies raise the question of how organizations can take better advantage of the new directions into social computing that IT is facilitating. Arameswaran & Whinston (2007) highlight many questions in their examination of issues in social computing including whether social interactions can be designed to promote benefits and what form these benefits may take. Perhaps more importantly in the context of online communities within a business context is where social capital resides in the relationship. This is a question of altruism versus individualism – does the individual gain from the social interaction for their own ends or as a contribution to the community? And when does the network of individuals become the network as customer? Standing et al.,'s (2007) example of the organization building hybrid relationships to mitigate global market pressures and maintain local community adds relevance to the idea that corporate IT has a role to play in community building to enhance information exchange and link buyer and seller in an environment of multiple interactions (Arameswaran & Whinston, 2007).

The benefits to firms from developing online communities have been identified as the fostering of relationships between customers, reinforcement of brand recognition, use of customer feedback to develop products and services more effectively, accumulate customer information, improve pre- and post-transaction services and the testing of new products (McWilliam, 2000; Williams & Cothrel, 2000; Preece & Maloney-Kritchmar, 2003; Walden, 2000).

Customers are held to contribute to business-sponsored communities to gain information and to interact with others with a similar interest.

They are seen to have an underlying motivation to contribute for reasons of status and prestige or reputation-based rewards (Wasko & Faraj, 2005). To these customer benefits, Wiertz & de Ruyter (2007) add the idea of citizen behaviour or sportsmanship and Dholakia et al., (2004) add social enhancement and entertainment. This aligns with Molesworth & Denegri-Knott's (2008) concept of consumers attaining value not for rational or utilitarian reasons, but for 'desires, thrills, competitiveness, change and meaningful identities' (p. 370). The concept of playfulness within the online consumer society is identified in a study of eBay (Molesworth & Denegri-Knott, 2008), which discusses the concept of play and examines its value to the business world.

While the focus of these latter studies is more on the consumer rather than a business environment, the long tradition of marketplaces serving many purposes within a community (for example the ancient agora or the souk provided facilities for meeting, socializing, buying and selling) may have relevance to the online environment. E-marketplaces in the B2B environment have perhaps overlooked this need for socializing which is characterized in their embedded relationships with established trading partners. Horizontal marketplaces for business and consumer participants tend to fulfil the needs for short-term relationships with no perceived need for social ties.

Concepts of marketplaces and communities

The literature on e-marketplace relationships and on online communities reflects several similarities of constructs. This is to be expected given that both topics are based on social networks and interaction between individuals. This section identifies the key constructs, which are then used to inform the analysis of the case study.

Boundedness

The concept of boundedness in online communities most commonly refers to the physical or geographic location of the community (Preece, 2000). Despite the 'virtualness' of online communities they often reflect a geographic emphasis in that they have a dominant membership from a specific region such as OZMS, an online community for Australians with multiple sclerosis. Membership may also be constrained by language. For example Taobao.com in aimed at Chinese speakers (although a forum has developed to attempt to open access to English speakers). Communities may also be bound by registration or membership conditions and this reflects similar bounds on e-marketplaces where buyers and sellers are required to register with the marketplace provider.

Trust

Trust is held to be a key concept in all forms of e-business and 'when there is trust among people, relationships flourish; without it they wither' (Preece, 2000, p. 191). Acceptable levels of opportunism and cooperation are determined by the stakeholders (Grover et al., 2002) and continued trust is based on past experiences and expectations that future interactions will remain a positive experience (Preece, 2000). The higher the level of risk in the transaction the higher the levels of trust that must be maintained and be recognizable to all stakeholders in the virtual environment (Stockdale & Borovicka, 2006). The rise of social networking and the use of online communities by businesses emphasizes a new direction for trust where some element of control must be ceded to the customer. Peer-to-peer interaction is a common facet of online communities but is not always a welcome concept in many industries where it can be seen as a potential threat to managerial control (Walden, 2000).

Reciprocity

Grover et al., (2002) discuss the social component that is required in inter-organizational relationships as 'relationalism'. This refers to the idea of an implicit contract (rather than a legal statement) that has expectations of reciprocity. This is further identified by Standing et al., (2007) who examine the interdependence of embedded relationships where suppliers will commit to extra work at short notice in return for a higher level of input in the procurement process. Formalization of processes identified in the study resulted in lack of trust and the withdrawal of reciprocity. The concept of reciprocity is identified in online communities where members repay back to the community for benefits they perceive they have gained (Jeppesen & Frederiksen, 2006). This identification with the group appears strong even in situations of weak ties (Preece, 2000), although Schultze & Orlikowski (2004) found that arms-length relationships display more evidence of opportunism and self-interest, and little evidence of reciprocity. This may signal a difference between behaviour in socially orientated online communities and e-marketplace relationships.

Governance

Markets flourish in an environment where it pays to remain honest within the market transactions and require mechanisms to invoke sanctions where these are required (McMillan, 2002). These sanctions may be stipulated by laws or come within the province of the market providers. Nevertheless, they are recognized by the marketplace. Online communities are often less formalized and reputation is often the reward for honest behaviour. Governance in such communities is often by convention and is more attributable to social norms than to contractual agreements (Arameswaran & Whinston, 2007). These opposing views to governance reflect the need for more control in the commercial sphere, whether from legal or financial or managerial reasons. Businesses sponsored online communities use higher levels of oversight and social norms are replaced or complemented by paid moderators and formalized 'terms and conditions' (Stockdale & Borovicka, 2006).

Information flow

The ability to exchange information is a key element of market design. While information flow is never frictionless, the ability of sellers and buyers to more easily identify potential trading partners has a significant impact on search costs (McMillan, 2002). E-marketplaces offer many opportunities for participants to reduce costs related to locating partners and product information (Bakos, 1997). Similarly, in online communities, access to information and exchange of information are seen as primary reasons for joining the community (Hagel & Armstrong, 1997). This is particularly true in online communities related to information-rich sectors such as health and travel (Stockdale, 2008; Wang & Fesenmaier, 2004).

Sportsmanship

There are several terms that encompass the recognition of hedonic needs in the market. These include social enhancement and entertainment from participation (Dholakia et al., 2004) and sportsmanship, which includes the devotion to certain modes of behaviour within commercial online communities (Wiertz & de Ruyter, 2007). Wang & Fesenmeier (2004) identify fun, amusement and enjoyment as needs related to the travel market and Molesworth & Denegri-Knott (2008) examine playful consumption in terms of the business as the game maker such as FaceBook, Second Life and eBay. The term sportsmanship is adopted here to reflect the range of hedonic activities derived from online social communications.

The constructs identified above appear to bear relevance to an examination of the effect of moving sociability into the field of e-business and the online market environment. These constructs are used as a basis for examining the community found within the e-marketplace, TradeMe, and discussed in the following sections.

The case study

This study uses TradeMe, an online New Zealand marketplace, as a case study to examine the constructs of community within the marketplace. A participative role has been taken by the researcher and data are supported by a wide range of literature from both academic and business sources. Data analysis used the constructs identified from the literature and adhered to the hermeneutic principles of interpretive field studies as defined by Klein & Myers (1999).

TradeMe provides an interesting case in this study context as it has established a strong community identity while operating as a commercial entity since its beginnings in 1999. The e-marketplace is similar to the eBay consumer-to-consumer model, offering an auction facility for the general public to list goods for sale. The founder, Sam Morgan, had a background of visiting auction rooms and sales as a child and was familiar with the community spirit that existed among traders (Ross & Holland, 2007). He replicates this sense of community from the beginnings of the early TradeMe site, recognizing that the 'Internet is a community' where people hang out and do stuff (p. 183). He combined his experience of traders with his view of the internet as a community to form a place where 'New Zealanders wanted to hang out, grab a bargain and connect with other Kiwis' (p. 184). An interesting aspect of TradeMe's development has been its low-key approach to marketing. Although the reluctance to advertise began for financial reasons in the start-up period, the e-marketplace does not advertise and relies on word of mouth. Morgan believes that the 'brand was defined by the community' (Ross & Holland, 2007) and this perception remains with the current CEO who maintains that the quality of the e-marketplace encourages extensive blogging about the site by the general public that keeps the brand visible. He argues that once a successful community is established, it will succeed by the 'dynamic of viral uptake' and 'if you build a great site people won't be shy about blogging about it for you' (Kepes, 2008).

Morgan sold the company to Fairfax Media in 2006 for NZ$700 million. In the ten years of its existence TradeMe has expanded its range of services and facilities, which began with the idea of classified advertisements but soon moved into online auctions. There is a strong focus on community elements such as FindSomeone (dating), FlatMate and OldFriends. Profits were in excess of $40 million in 2006 and TradeMe accounts for nearly 70 per cent of all website traffic in New Zealand (MacManus, 2006).

The TradeMe marketplace

The website offers both auction and classified advertisements although the former is by far the most popular. There are over a million items for sale in more than 25 categories from antiques to pottery, glass and toys. In addition, there are property pages, cars and jobs pages. There are also business categories and a thriving livestock and equipment trade between farmers that one might normally associate with more conventionally B2B marketplaces. Additional links to other services include finding a flatmate, a NZ news site, postings for lost pets and a travel site. The link to the community services displays newsletters, discussion forums and site statistics that indicate what sells and the best timing for setting auctions. There is even a webcam of the company offices.

TradeMe is very easy to use and sign-on requires a $10 deposit to set up an account that enables members to begin offering items for auction. There are multiple methods of payment and extensive instructions, fee scales and guidance on buying and selling. There are also TradeMe books (e.g., Saarinen, 2005) that break down the different processes into easy to understand language. Users of TradeMe vary from individuals to small- and medium-sized traders and in the case of property all the real estate agents in New Zealand.

Community within the TradeMe marketplace

Over the decade of building up the marketplace a number of community features were incorporated into TradeMe. These are discussed according to the constructs identified in the literature.

Boundedness

The community is limited to residents of NZ (or Australia if they have a NZ bank account). This boundary was put in place in 2005 and removed a number of members from the marketplace. The reason given at the time was for security, but a key outcome has been an intensifying of the strong cultural identity of the site. This is enhanced by its use of a cartoon kiwi bird as the trademark. Traders are required to register and pay a $10 deposit to open an account but, beyond the geographical boundary, there are few other elements of boundedness or restrictions visible to membership (Preece, 2002).

Trust

Trust is indicated by the market maker through a perception of protection of personal information. TradeMe retains a high reputation within NZ with only a few adverse comments appearing in the press. Trust indicators for members are through a rating and feedback system that is taken very seriously by buyers and sellers. Failure to rate by either party in a transaction can result in acerbic email reminders and a bad rating can escalate discussions to outside blogs and forums. Anyone can elect to blacklist a member, which bars that member from bidding on auctions run by the former. This gives a level of control to those running an auction that enhances trust that auctions will run well. Buyers and sellers have access to previous feedback ratings during a current transaction process. Other forms of trust building include address verification and a star rating system indicating multiple successful trades. Although there are indications that the market maker does monitor the site closely, the generation of trust on the marketplace is strongly attributable to the activities of the members. This reflects more closely with the type of activity visible on socially constructed online communities rather than business-sponsored sites (Stockdale, 2008).

Reciprocity

The nature of relationships in an e-marketplace such as TradeMe is of an arms-length model. There is no requirement for long-term relationships to develop in the buying or selling of items within such a marketplace. However, the identification of Schultze & Orlikowski's (2004) features of embedded relationships such as assumption of recurring interaction, norms of trust and goodwill and high expectations of interdependence and reciprocity are evident in the relationships of members with other members and with the marketplace. In the former case, buyer and sellers that trade items are known to continue communicating and sharing feedback on the success of a purchase. In the latter members of the marketplace appear to transfer the identification of relational partner to the marketplace and there are few overt examples of opportunistic or self-interested behaviour. As to whether this identification with the marketplace is a result of community influences and a sense of social belonging is not clear, but such behaviour is often seen within socially constructed online communities (Stockdale, 2008).

Governance

As noted by Stockdale & Borovicka (2006) in their study of Lonely Planet publications, uncovering the way an online community is managed by its business owner is not an easy exercise. TradeMe is subject to NZ law and has advice areas online to explain what cannot be sold through the marketplace. Beyond this, there are similarities in the appearance of governance through social convention familiar to online communities (Arameswaran & Whinston, 2007). The message boards are not overtly moderated and buyer/seller feedback can be robust at times with little evidence of censorship. This apparent low level of oversight gives the marketplace a greater sense of community than might otherwise be the case as members trade with little apparent input from the market maker.

Information flow

TradeMe offers information on over a million items for sale online at any one time. They offer ease of access and purchase for virtually everything that can be legally sold in New Zealand, from cows to houses, baby toys and antiques. This ability to identify goods and services is a major benefit in New Zealand which has a small, relatively isolated agricultural population that has a high dependence on imported manufactured goods.

The email mechanism for completing transactions is another feature that encourages information exchange. On joining the marketplace, participants link an email account to their membership. Queries on purchases appear on a member's MyTradeMe link on the website but are also sent to the member's email address. On completion of an auction, buyer and seller emails are automatically sent to the other party to enable the transaction to take place between them.

Further information exchange is encouraged by the message board where discussions on a range of subjects not related to buying and selling are conducted in a manner more familiar to online communities than commercial marketplaces.

Sportsmanship

There is an intangible feeling of playfulness and sportsmanship evident in the site and between members of the community. People get great pleasure from perusing the site and indeed access is banned in a number of businesses during working hours and the popularity of major sporting and political events are measurable in the slow down of auction trade (Saarinen, 2005). There is a flavour of the hobby about TradeMe, searching for goods to list, browsing the items for sale, emailing questions and 'joining in' around the discussion boards or commenting on buyers or sellers from recent transactions. As mentioned by the original owner, the site is a place for Kiwis 'to hang out, grab a bargain and connect with other Kiwis' (Ross & Holland, 2007, p. 184). This is an important feature of TradeMe and there have been concerns that the 'flavour' of the site will change with the acquisition of the marketplace by an international company (Dye, 2006) although to date the e-marketplace continues to maintain its membership levels.

There is perhaps a danger that should the site be developed into a more commercial entity that the 'retail mall' will overtake the play element and the site will lose its community appeal. There are early indications that this could happen in TradeMe as information flows from the community members back to the management are no longer easily available. Contact with the market provider is through an expensive phone link or an online form. This lack of ease in communication has the potential to damage the community as evidenced by the experiences of eBay. Molesworth & Denegri-Knott's (2008) study into eBay found that changes that were seen to favour larger sellers, pressure to use PayPal and other non-community friendly moves were having an adverse effect amongst their members. They report that eBay is moving from a 'community of likeminded users' to more closely resemble a retail mall (p. 372). The change towards a retail marketplace environment appears to affect the community adversely and raises the question of whether successful marketplaces can maintain a high level of social interaction over the longer term.

Discussion and conclusion

TradeMe has a vibrant and active online community embedded in its e-marketplace. The value of the community has been identified from the beginning of the company's existence and it has always acknowledged that social activity is an inherent part of its trading. Successful social interaction has enabled TradeMe to establish critical mass, with over two million people (half of the country's population) reputedly listed as active members and five million visits to the site per month (trademe.com). The established customer base offers great loyalty to the marketplace, which has attained iconic status across New Zealand. In return the value proposition to the members includes a high level of enjoyment and the ability to buy and sell with greater facility in a remote, largely rural country. Payment and delivery mechanisms are selected between the buyer and seller in each transaction and not complicated by overseas shipping and payment requirements. Additionally the strong community profile supports social interaction not directly related to transactions and creates a sense of belonging and of being part of a 'kiwi icon'. For buyers and sellers there is access to information about types of purchases and an indication of market price as well as the ability to locate hard to find or replacement goods.

TradeMe sets a geographical boundary to the marketplace that contributes strongly to the community identity that it has built. Culture is not identified as an element of boundedness, but in this case it has a significant influence on members' identification with the marketplace. Further support for considering cultural preferences in the boundedness of a community is indicated in the success of the TaoBao marketplace in China which has ousted eBay from the Chinese market by identifying and providing facilities that were highly valued by their customer base (Ou & Davison, 2009). However, further research is required into the effect of boundedness and social capital within global e-marketplaces to determine a more generalizable relevance.

The social features of trading with a horizontal marketplace such as TradeMe has a strong influence on the relationships of its participants. Community was designed into the original marketplace and has therefore grown with the membership and formed the identity of the business. The mechanisms of the e-marketplace are socially orientated and the constructs of trust and governance reflect this. The features of the former are more closely aligned with the way trust is developed and nurtured in socially constructed online communities in that participants have a measure of input to trust mechanisms, contributing to the ratings of both buyers and sellers. The discussion board also displays little evidence of moderation by the market provider and there are some robust exchanges between members. Moderation is less formalized that in more established communities such as Slashdot, and TradeMe does not have paid moderators as those found on other commercial communities such as Lonely Planet (Stockdale & Borovicka, 2006). Control of finalizing the transaction is ceded to the buyer and seller when an auction is concluded and email addresses are released by the auction mechanism. This inclusive environment works well within the bounds of this horizontal marketplace and promotes the concept of sportsmanship or enjoyment from trading. It is not possible to determine what proportion of the members on TradeMe is small- or medium-sized firms, but there is no identifiable change in the sense of hedonic gains from the different types of members.

TradeMe's success as a horizontal, intermediary marketplace in New Zealand has come from designing and establishing community within its marketplace. It has set the bounds for participation and recognized members' needs and wants in both terms of commerce and social interaction. It has taken opportunities to benefit from social capital within its largely C2C market sector, although there are many evidences of business to business and to consumer involvement. The outcomes for TradeMe are in establishing long-term loyalty in an area traditionally characterized by weak ties and arms-length relationships. This study finds this to be an example of hybrid relationships characterized by social interaction within a market setting. The question now arises as to how applicable this model is to other e-marketplaces?

Further research is required to investigate the viability of the community model beyond the case illustrated in this study. However, the TradeMe example illustrates that information flow, which is so important to market design (McMillan, 2002), is more fluid when e-marketplace participants have an interest in maintaining membership of a marketplace. There are opportunities to develop trust through policies and social protocols developed in socially constructed online communities that encourage participant interaction, information exchange and reciprocity (Stockdale, 2008). This in turn may promote enjoyment and emphasizes the need for more consideration of the role of playfulness in a business model (Molesworth & Denegri-Knott, 2008).

Social capital is seen as important in adoption and use of e-marketplaces (Driedonks et al., 2005). At the same time moves towards more hybrid relationships to balance the needs for corporate responsibilities to local communities while gaining global market price increases the demand for more flexibility in the market. Recognizing the value of sociability in e-marketplaces as a valid and important concept that influences and informs governance and allows for information to flow more freely would support the need for more flexibility. The use of online communities to encourage information flow, reciprocity and trust works well for TradeMe and elements of the design could well be advantageous to other e-marketplaces.

References

Arameswaran, M. & Whinston, A. B. (2007). Research issues in social computing. *Journal of the Association for Information Systems*, 8(6), 336–350.

Bakos, J. (1997). Reducing buyer search costs: implications for electronic marketplaces. *Management Science*, 43(12), 1676–1692.

Bughin, J. & Hagel, J. I. (2000). The operational performance of virtual communities – towards a successful business model? *Electronic Markets*, 10(4), 237–243.

Choudhury, V., Hartzel, K. S. & Kosynski, B. (1998). Uses and consequences of electronic markets: an empirical investigation in the aircraft parts industry. *MIS Quarterly*, 22(4), 471–507.

Dholakia, U. M., Bagozzi, R. P. & Pearo, L K. (2004). A social influence model of consumer participation in network and small-group based virtual communities. *Journal of Research in Marketing*, 21, 241–263.

Driedonks, C., Gregor, S., Wassenaar, A. & van Heck E., (2005). Economics and social analysis of the adoption of B2B electronic marketplaces: a case study in the Australian beef industry. *International Journal of Electronic Commerce*, 9(3), 49–72.

Dye, D. (2006). TradeMe fans fear worst. *New Zealand Herald*. Available online at: www.NZherald.co.nz (accessed 23 December 2008).

Grover, V., Teng, J. & Fiedler, K. D., (2002). Investigating the role of information technology in building buyer-supplier relationships. *Journal of the Association for Information Systems*, 3, 217–245.

Hagel, J. I. (1999). Net gain: expanding markets through virtual communities. *Journal of Interactive Marke*ting, 13(1), 55–65.

Hagel, J. I. & Armstrong, A. (1997). *Net Gain: Expanding Markets Through Virtual Communities*. Cambridge: Harvard Business School Press.

Jeppesen, L. & Frederiksen, L. (2006). Why do users contribute to firm-hosted user communities? The case of computer-controlled music instruments. *Organization Science*, 17(1), 45–63.

Kepes, B. (2008). If you build it will they come? *New Zealand Herald*, 29 October. Available online at: http://www.nzherald.co.nz/smallbusiness (accessed 19 November 2008).

Klein, H. K. & Myers, M. D. (1999). A set of principles for conducting and evaluating interpretive field studies in information systems. *MIS Quarterly*, 23(1), 67–93.

Kozinets, R. V., Hemetsberger, A. & Schau, H. J. (2008) The wisdom of consumer crowds. Collective innovation in the age of networked marketing. *Journal of Macromarketing*. 28(4), 339–353.

MacManus, R. (2006) TradeMe: Big fish in a small pond. ReadWriteWeb. Available online at http://www.readwriteweb.com/archives/trademe_big_fish_small_pond.php (accessed 30 March 2009).

McMillan, J. (2002). *Reinventing the Bazaar*. New York: Norton & Co Ltd.

McWilliam, G. (2000). Building stronger brands through online communities. *Sloan Management Review*, 41(3), 43–54.

Miller, K. D., Fabian, F. & Lin, S-J. (2009). Strategies for online communities. *Strategic Management Journal*, 30, 305–322.

Molesworth, M. & Denegri-Knott, J. (2008). The playfulness of eBay and the implications for business as a game-maker. *Journal of Macromarketing*, 28(4), 369–380.

Murray, A. J. & Greenes, K. A. (2006). In search of the enterprise of the future. *The Journal of Information and Knowledge Management Systems*, 36(3), 231–237.

Ou, X. C. & Davison, R. M. (2009). Why eBay lost to TaoBao in China; the global advantage. *Communications of the ACM*, 52(1), 145–148.

Paterson, L. (2009). Online customer communities. *Business Information Review*, 26(1), 44–50.

Powell, W. (1990). Neither market nor hierarchy: networked forms of organistion. In Straw, B. & Cummunigs, L. (eds.), *Research in Organizational Behavior*, Greenwich, CT: JAI Press, 295–336.

Preece, J (2000). *Online Communities, Designing Usability, Supporting Sociability*. Wiley: New York.

Preece, J. & Maloney-Krichmar, D. (2003). Online communities: focusing on sociability and usability. In Jacko & Sears (eds.), *Handbook of Human-Computer Interaction*, Lawrence Erlbaum Assoc.

Ross, E. & Holland, A. (2007). *50 Great E-Businesses and the Minds Behind Them*. Sydney: Random House.

Saarinen, J. (2005). *TradeMe, Your Ultimate Guide to New Zealand's Biggest Online Auction Site*. Auckland: Penguin.

Schultze, U. & Orlikowski, W. (2004). A practice perspection on technology mediated network relations: the use of internet based self-service technologies. *Information Systems Research*, 15(1), 87–106.

Standing, S., Standing, C. & Love, P. (2008). A review of research on e-marketplaces 1997–2007. *Proceedings of the Pacific Asia Conference on Information Systems*, 809–820.

Standing, C. Stockdale R. & Love P. (2007). Hybrid buyer-supplier relationships in global electronic markets. *Information and Organization*, 17, 89–109.

Stockdale, R. (2008). Peer-to-peer online communities for people with chronic diseases; a conceptual framework. *Journal of Systems and Information Technology*, 10(1), 39–55.

Stockdale, R. & Borovicka, M. C. (2006). Ghost towns or vibrant villages? Constructing business-sponsored online communities. *International Journal of Communications, Law and Policy*, 11(Autumn). Available online at: http://ijclp. org/11_2006/

Walden, E. (2000). Some value propositions of online communities. *Electronic Markets*, 10(4), 244–249.

Wang, Y. & Fesenmaier, D. (2004). Modeling participation in an online travel community. *Journal of Travel Research*, 42, 261–270.

Wasko, M. M. & Faraj, S. (2005). Why should I share? Examining social capital and knowledge contribution in electronic networks of practice. *MIS Quarterly*, 29(1), 35–57.

Wiertz, C. & de Ruyter, K. (2007). Beyond the call of duty: why customers contribute to firm-hosted commercial online communities. *Organization Studies*, 28(3), 347–376.

Williams, R. L. & Cothrel, J. (2000). Four smart ways to run online communities. *Sloan Management Review*, 41(1), 81–92.

11
The Role of Trust in the Success and Failure of Regional Internet Community Portals in Promoting SME E-Commerce Adoption

Denise E. Gengatharen

Introduction

In the late 1990s there was a growing fear in Australia (Curtin, 2001; Small Enterprise Telecommunications Limited [Setel], 2001) and other countries of a digital divide between SMEs (Small and Medium Enterprises) and their larger counterparts, and also between regional and suburban SMEs, in the uptake of e-commerce. Australia's responded to this fear with a number of government-funded IT projects which were targeted at increasing access to and adoption of IT and e-commerce in the regional and SME communities. Many of these projects were developed at the local level through collaborative community-based programs. This reflected the federal government's view that 'the best and most workable solutions and ideas emerge from the grass roots, rather than being delivered, fully formed, from on high [as] community and non-profit groups and local-government authorities are attuned to the pulse of their communities [and] are best placed to know what their own needs and circumstances are' (Williams, 2004). Some of these programs were led by local governments. These initiatives included setting up regional e-marketplaces (REMs) and internet trading platforms that would improve SME e-commerce uptake and lead to economic development. According to Standing et al., (2004) and Zimmerman (1998) the motivation behind such initiatives is the expectation of community benefits like raised levels of e-business knowledge, skills and technology within the community. These community benefits can lead to the community or region becoming an attractive location for business and for skilled labour. A regional e-marketplace can also provide the benefits of efficient showcasing of regional offerings. Australian examples of such initiatives are the discontinued BizeWest (Tatnall & Burgess, 2002) and Tasmania Business Online (Hayes, 2004) and the Regional Electronic Trade Facilitation Centre (Wilkins et al., 2003). In Western Australia, some regional portals were developed with the dual purpose of bringing local communities online and encouraging e-commerce uptake among SMEs. This enabled the receipt of government funding under programmes like ITOL (Information Technology On-Line see http://www.dcita.gov.au/ie/). While these portals had different e-commerce models and owner arrangements, most had some level of local community participation. In Europe, public-funded trading platforms like Rakat in Denmark, Achatville in France and Empower.ie in Ireland were established to give SMEs the opportunity to participate in e-marketplace trading in a trusted environment (E-Business Policy Group, 2002).

In an effort to examine the factors that relate to the success or failure of such initiatives and to determine their benefits, if any, a study of three government-funded regional community portals in Western Australia (WA) was undertaken. These portals were used to promote e-commerce among SMEs and while two were located in regional or rural WA, the third was set up in a metropolitan area. The two regional portals continue to operate while the metropolitan one failed and was discontinued in 2004. While there were a number of factors that contributed to the success of the regional portals and the failure of the portal in metropolitan WA, the study indicated that trust was a critical factor on a number of different levels. The success and failure of the portals will now be examined from a trust perspective. The following sections are structured as follows: first, perspectives from the literature on the role of trust in e-marketplaces and in SME uptake of e-commerce and participation in e-marketplaces are highlighted. The three cases are then discussed in order to demonstrate the roles played by trust in the success of the two portals in country WA and the failure of the metropolitan portal. The chapter concludes with some recommendations for those considering similar initiatives.

The role of trust in e-marketplaces

As a critical success factor of e-marketplaces, trust has received much attention in the academic literature. Given the impersonal nature of the online environment, trust in online transactions is even more crucial than in traditional exchange transactions (Ba and Pavlou, 2002; Bakos, 1998). Pavlou (2002) examined how institution-based trust can be developed in online B2B marketplaces to facilitate inter-organizational trust between buyers and sellers. He proposed five specific institution-based mechanisms: perceived monitoring, perceived legal bonds, perceived accreditation, perceived feedback, and perceived cooperative norms. Pavlou & Gefen (2002) showed that the presence of structural assurances alone in a B2B marketplace does not necessarily engender trust, unless buyers perceive these mechanisms as reliable and credible. Ratnasingam et al., (2005) viewed institutional trust as the lubricant of B2B e-marketplaces and trust-building facilitating conditions proposed for such entities are IT connectivity, standards, security and uniform product descriptions.

According to Hsiao (2003), distrust as a barrier to e-marketplace adoption can be in the forms of reliability-related and value-oriented distrust. While the former can be reduced by technical remedies, the latter may be rooted in the cultural beliefs of the would-be adopters targeted by the e-marketplace. As such, there is a need to be sensitive to value-oriented fears in order to break down the distrust barriers to e-marketplace participation.

The role of trust in SME adoption of e-commerce and participation in e-marketplaces

Although Kumar et al., (1998) examined the failure of a large inter-organizational information system and not an e-marketplace per se, their research is also pertinent as the SPRINTEL system in the textile industry in Prato, Italy had all the hallmarks of a regional e-marketplace. An important finding from the SPRINTEL case was that recognition of the existence of trust and relationships can lead to cooperative strategies and a view of IT as a collaborative advantage. Kumar et al., refer to their approach as a 'trust-based rationalism' for examining the role of IT in organizations and networks.

Ba et al., (2001) looked at the role of trust on two levels in enabling SMEs to successfully grow and compete in e-marketplaces. Firstly, asymmetric information available in e-marketplaces meant that SMEs faced the risk of misinterpretation of information due to a lack of trust in web-based sites. Secondly, given their lack of size and resources for brand building, it was difficult for SMEs to get the trust of buyers. The authors proposed digital intermediaries and trusted third parties as one way to overcome these trust issues. Brown & Lockett (2001) also considered the role of trusted intermediaries within eClusters of SMEs. They viewed eClusters as a future type of digital enterprise community which could be interconnected e-marketplaces, guaranteed e-markets, internet business communities or community-centric application service providers. Underpinning eClusters would be a Trust Platform which will comprise structure, services and governance provided by three kinds of intermediaries: technology, enterprise and community. Empirical research found that trusted local and regional third-party community intermediaries can play a critical role in influencing SME involvement in e-commerce and that 'existing trusted offline relationships, be they a lead company in a business network or a trade association, could be important in recruiting SMEs to online services' (Lockett & Brown, 2006, p. 394). In terms of regional e-commerce, Steinfield & Whitten (1999) showed that 'trust-embeddedness' (existing strong off-line community and business ties) could be leveraged to engender trust and enable locally sensitive e-commerce strategies for businesses in a given community. The successful implementation of Lonxanet, an e-marketplace in Galatia, Spain which was created to address issues of fragmentation, inefficiencies, income inequalities and economic and biological sustainability in the Galician artisanal fisheries industry, was attributed to trust in the system and the governance structure of partnerships created to run the e-marketplace (Dans & Freire, 2002). Fisher & Craig's (2004) research on a SME business portal in Victoria, Australia showed that trust in the portal sponsors was responsible for the initial support of the portal but there was no effort to bring together the participants during the portal development to engender trust among them. In the case of the RETFC (Wilkins et al., 2003), the governance process and trust between stakeholders ensured that all parties had a sense of ownership of the e-marketplace and were therefore committed to its success.

The cases

Tables 11.1 to 11.3 give the details of three cases of regional community portals in WA that have been used to promote e-commerce among SMEs. (Note: Pseudonyms have been used.)

Data collection and research methodology

Informal data for TwinTowns.com was collected over a one and a half year period beginning early 2003 from a variety of sources including the portal website, historical documents, minutes of meetings, internal

Table 11.1   Background details of the portals

	TwinTowns.com	RegWa.net	CountryWA.com
Year initiative first conceived and by whom	1999. Mooted by the Business Enterprise Centre of one of the towns, supported by some people in the two local governments.	1999. Committee of a few people in the chamber of commerce of the largest town in the region, resident website developers and internet service providers, a couple of the larger businesses in the region.	1999, consortium of representatives from IBM, the WA Office of Information and Communication, the regional development commission, the Business Enterprise Centre of the largest town in the region, a local university and a major IT company.
Ownership structure	Not-for-profit organization comprising local governments of two neighbouring towns, their business associations and a university in the region.	The Chamber of Commerce (CoC) of the largest town. In June 2003, purchased by the Regional Development Commission. Not-for-profit organization (Connect RegWa) formed to own it.	In 2001, the portal became a cooperative with locals owning shares, overseen by a board of community representatives.
Details of the area served by the community portal	Two neighbouring towns in metropolitan WA covering 900 km², having about 220,000 residents and 7000 small businesses. Major industries: manufacturing, agriculture, retail trade, services, tourism.	A regional area of WA covering 24,000 km², having a population of 132,000 and 10,500 small businesses. Major industries: manufacturing, mining, agriculture, retail trade, services, tourism.	A regional area of WA covering 44,000 km², having a population of 53,000 and approximately 4800 small businesses. Major industries: agriculture/livestock farming, viticulture, horticulture, timber, retail, manufacturing, wholesaling, construction, services, tourism.

memos, e-mail communications, meetings with portal staff and via observation by attendance at board meetings. Informal data collected from RegWa.net and CountryWa.com was from the REM/portal website and published documents.

Table 11.2 Funding and costs of the portals

	TwinTowns.com	RegWa.net	CountryWA.com
Funding 1999/2000 2001/2002 2003/2004 TOTAL	A$ 20,000 (state government) A$ 90,660 (federal government)	A$6,000 (regional development corp.) A$30,000 (state government)	A$75,000 (ITOL)
	A$ 108,000 (local governments of the two towns and university) A$ 92,000 (state government–for training SMEs)	A$75,000 (ITOL) A$126,000 (state government)	A$100,000 (federal government under the Networking the Nation Program)
	A$50,000 (local governments of the towns). *Request for further federal and state government funding declined in 2001/2002.	A$2,200,000 (state government, for the portal and for training SMEs, etc.)	A$68,500 (ITOL–part of A$174,000 awarded to a joint consortia to develop an intelligent e-business search system for SMEs in the region)
	A$360,660	A$2,437,000	A$243,500 (ITOL application for additional A$50,000 declined)
Technical development	Outsourced for A$70,000	Developed by local IT company who hosted RegWa. net for free. Initial portal development costs not available. Development of REM about A$30,000. A$200,000 paid for upgrade in 2004.	Total estimated amount spent on technical development to date A$100,000
Operating costs Direct income	A$4000 per month (by this time only one staff and only REM operating)	Ongoing monthly operating costs A$28000 (for the whole portal including training costs).	Ongoing monthly operating costs approximately A$5000
	A$600 per month from participation fees	A$7000 per month from participation fees.	Slightly less than A$5000 per month from all sources

Constructs from the literature on SME adoption of IT/e-commerce/ e-marketplace trading, community portals and IS evaluation were used to esign a case protocol for the gathering of formal data. This involved semi-structured interviews of 1–1½ hours with nine REM owner

Table 11.3   Features and status of the portals

	TwinTowns.com	RegWa.net	CountryWA.com
Portal and e-commerce features	• Internet-based community portal catering for B2B, B2C, B2G and C2C activity. • REM with business directory. Request-for-quote (RFQ) mechanism. Quotes can only be received by registered users. Notification of quote by e-mail, fax or SMS but user has to log onto system to retrieve quote and reply. • Community groups listed for free. • Businesses listed for free but pay A$199 p.a. for RFQ-enabled REM link and an additional A$99 for a flyer page. Live links to user's websites if registered and paying. • Corporate sponsorship of site is available.	• Internet-based community portal catering for B2B, B2C, B2G and C2C activity. • REM with business directory. RFQ mechanism. Quotes can only be received by registered users. Notification and RFQ sent by e-mail, fax or SMS. User does not have to log onto the system to retrieve the quote. • Community groups listed for free. • Businesses listed for free but members pay A$22 p.a. for an e-mail link A$66 p.a. for e-mail/web link A$150 p.a. for preferential listing (shuffled up the page in a search) A$199 p.a. for e-mail, web and five-page website template (additional A$11 p.a. to be listed in more than one business category). A$250 p.a. for e-commerce solution (shopping cart) • Corporate sponsorship of site is available. • Monthly e-newsletter	• Internet-based community portal catering for B2B, B2C, B2G and C2C activity. • Business listings (members and non-members) and members listing (businesses and other organizations like schools etc.). No RFQs. • Community groups listed for free. • Businesses listed (via free link to the online directory of the Chamber of Commerce [CCI]of the largest town in the region) but participants pay: (with discounts for shareholders) A$77 p.a. for a premium listing (live e-mail and web link, listing under business and member listings, listing under up to three product/service categories and one town or topic category. A$198 p.a. for premium listing and 1 fully editable web page (A$220 p.a. to include shopping cart /Order Form) A$605 p.a. for premium listing and five fully editable web pages (A$880 p.a. to include shopping cart/Order Form). A$990 p.a. for premium listing and 10 fully editable web pages (A$1650 p.a. to include shopping cart /Order Form. • Corporate sponsorship of site is available. • Regular e-newsletter.

Continued

Table 11.3 Continued

	TwinTowns.com	RegWa.net	CountryWA.com
Date portal/ e-commerce features launched	December 2002 portal & REM (with business directory) launched. December 2003 development on the community and B2C part of the portal abandoned in favour of B2G/B2B.	Regional portal and business directory launched March 2000. REM page launched November 2002. Technical upgrade and shopping cart (Nov' 2004).	Regional portal launched May 2000. Shopping Mall page (collection of businesses with shopping cart facilities provided by the portal) launched in 2003. End 2003–four merchants on the mall. 2004–shopping mall page removed.
Marketing efforts	A few seminars prior to development; a handful of newspaper write-ups in local community newspapers, marketing manager employed late 2003.	Promoted to the community via television and newspaper advertising. Sales personnel hired when it was launched. Seminars and talks given to both the business and social communities.	Promoted to the community via television (for free in exchange for a live link on the portal to the television station's page), seminars and talks. Currently part-time sales consultant for participation and advertising space on the portal.
Statistics Business listings Community listings Government listings Portal hits RFQs	(April 2004) Approx. 1000 (of which 219 had REM links but only 157 were paying participants) Total not available but 35 had web pages Not available Monthly average 500 Monthly average of 11 (based on 2 months activity before closure and based on 3 to 4 RFQs issued per job – these were from town 1)	(June 2004) 9800. (1790 paying participants of whom 273 had full e-mail/web and REM links) 1770 (1155 had web/e-mail links). 142 (69 had web/ e-mail links). Monthly average 7000 Monthly average 33	(May 2005) Approx. 1500 (2001–165 paying participants. 230 cooperative members who pay a min. $50 each) Approximately 100 (four are members) Approx. 15 (nine are members). 28 towns, 15 schools listed Monthly average 1.2 million N/A. No statistics available on business channelled to participants via the portal.
Current status	Ceased operations mid 2004 and wound up in Oct' 2004.	Continues to operate.	Continues to operate.

representatives and nine SME participants of TwinTowns.com between February and August of 2004. Interviews were audiotaped, transcribed and transcripts were shared with participants to omit errors and to validate interpretations of the participants' views (Klein & Myers, 1999). Field notes and transcripts were made within 24 hours of each interview. All project and case data was maintained in a database, was coded according to the constructs identified in the literature and was checked by another researcher. Data was then analyzed and additional constructs were added or existing ones modified as new themes emerged from the analysis and from the extant literature (Carroll & Swatman, 2000). The revised conceptual framework was then used to collect data by way of in-depth interviews between August 2004 and November 2004 with four owner representatives of RegWa.net and six RegWa.net SME participants. The data was analyzed and the conceptual framework updated. Shorter interviews were then conducted via telephone with fourteen SME participants in June 2005. Formal data collection on CountryWa.com was done via in-depth telephone interviews and e-mail communications with four portal board members and shorter telephone interviews with 20 SME participants between May and June of 2005. In all, 66 interviews were conducted. A comparative analysis of the data from the three portals was then conducted.

Case analysis and discussion from a trust perspective

All three portals were created to encourage SME uptake of e-commerce in the hope that such a move could lead to regional development. Although the technology model and funding were similar prior to 2003/2004, the two rural portals (RegWa.net and CountryWa.com) achieved some positive outcomes compared to the failed TwinTowns.com. Results of the research indicated that trust had a major role in the outcomes of the three portals. In this study, trust is examined at the following levels: trust among owner-stakeholders, trust between SME participants and the third-party community intermediaries; trust between buyers and sellers on the portal and trust in the e-marketplace mechanism (or technology).

Trust among stakeholders

Collaborative endeavours like the ones in this study bring together diverse groups with different interests and motivation. They are complex environments due to the many stakeholders who are representatives but not end users. Conflict is likely to evolve and stakeholders do not have as much legitimacy as in an intra-organizational project. Trust and openness are therefore required among participants. Collaboration in these types of coalitions is easier to achieve when all stakeholders feel that they will personally benefit from the project. However, benefits are more difficult (though not impossible) to identify, as the stakeholders originate from different formal organizations and as such 'do not have a sense of shared destiny that involves them personally prior to the project' (Johnsen & Normann, 2004).

Evidence from TownTowns.com indicates that although the owner-stakeholders appeared to hold the collective view that the portal would be a regional development tool that would consider both the business and community aspects of the region, the owners had their own agenda and were seeking their own personal benefits from the project. This lack of trust and openness among the owner-stakeholders negatively affected the portal's progress. Although the two towns appeared to be spearheading the project, it was more Town 1 that was driving it and the staff of Town 2 appeared to view the partnership in a negative light.

I don't think we built a team in the first place, I don't think we had team spirit (Strategic Development Manager, Town 2).

To the frustration of certain people at [Town 2]...because [TownTowns. com] is designated as a regional portal, they cannot do anything with the council name or leverage the local business, so they're hamstrung in that sense as well (Strategic Development Officer, Town 2)

Lack of action and cooperation from [Town 2]. They doubt capacity of the REM to deliver...Part of problem is that [Town 2] want their staff to have a 'one stop shop' system for purchasing, and are not keen to add another system. They have also raised the issue of possible confidentiality breaches (Minutes of TwinTowns.com Board meeting dated 27 March 2003).

Evidence also indicates that the towns viewed the portal as a means to gain legitimacy to be viewed as being progressive by emulating the online initiatives of other structurally equivalent organizations:

A couple of people...were also looking after themselves in that this project would give them a name, a presence and would give them work (Strategic Development Manager, Town 2)

It was the result of the hubris and excitement of what has become known as the dot.com boom, when every person and their dog thought that the world was going to change because of the Internet. The then Regional Department of Commerce & Trade was quite instrumental in sponsoring a number of regional portals...but I think they were created with a view that they would be a community resource...those people who were part of [Towns 1 and 2] aspired to emulate those portal developments but in order to successfully get funding I presume there was an onus to sell the package on the grounds that it would actually make a profit. (Strategic Development Officer, Town 2).

While the towns appeared to want to help small businesses in the region in the uptake of e-commerce, they were not prepared to support them in a big way by being major buyers on the e-marketplace. All the requests for quotes (RFQs) issued via the TwinTowns.com REM (these averaged 11 over the last 2 months of operation) were issued by Town 1 based on three to four RFQs issued per tender.

If Town 2 was to go and deliberately facilitate small business, it will cost a lot more & who will fork out the much higher rates? To some extent I think that's what the local Business Associations want...but they do it in nowhere near the volumes. In time they might. (Purchasing Manager, Town 2).

So the CEOs [of the Towns] attend [TownTowns.com] committee meetings, maintaining face, making sure they don't upset the local business associations but at the same time they know that if they were to start throwing their weight around, it will also be detrimental to their own positions in their own organisations. So there is that façade that they maintain (Strategic Development Officer, Town 2 in response to why the towns were not mandating their purchasing via the portal).

Evidence suggests that the business associations appeared to be in the coalition to legitimize their positions as representatives for businesses in the area by attempting to use the RFQ feature of the portal to bring some form of transparency to the tendering process of the towns.

What I see the use of the RFQ facility for is discretionary purchasing of the councils where without hesitation they pluck 1 or 2 out of the listings & give them the chance to quote...I know for a fact that there are excuses that can be used for not allowing the best quote to win...The culture thing has got to be broken down as well...what this [the portal] should do, is that it should be transparent and give the opportunity to the other people. I'd be interested to find out from the council who were the people that used it, how many did they put out, who they put it out to & how many of the quotes did they accept (Chairman, Business Association Town 1).

The university's role in the coalition was to provide research-based advice on the project and viewed it as an opportunity to itself obtain funding for the research. This required TownTowns.com to pay the university AU$8,000 a year for three years as part of the research partner contribution. The other owner-stakeholders viewed this as a payment that would buy them some of the researcher's time for administration on the portal but this issue was 'skirted around' as follows and only resurfaced when the project was in crisis:

The distrust and lack of openness among owner-stakeholders came to a head when the project was in crisis and the coalition was forced to examine the way forward for the portal. Options for a new business plan included a) selling the portal and RFQ technology; b) taking the running of the portal and RFQ system under the towns; or c) maintaining the status quo but appointing a marketing person on a commission basis and going for an all-out marketing campaign. The latter was proposed and favoured by the business associations which felt that not enough was done to promote the portal and RFQ system and that if management of the portal was taken internally to the towns, it would become a bureaucratic exercise and the business associations would step aside. They felt that there may be difficulty with transparency should the portal be run internally by the towns. Towards the end, the relationships on the portal among owner-stakeholders deteriorated as evidenced below:

> *I get very frustrated at these meetings. When I'm in the real world and I'm the only real world person there ... sorry ... but I'm not an academic, I'm not a council employee, I'm actually there at the coal face, spending my dollars, paying people to do things ... I don't sit behind a desk ...* (Chairman of Business Association, Town 1).

> *It all comes down to people, those who want to make it happen. We can make it happen. You need champions. In the Board as well ... you also need trust, respect.* (Chairman of TownTowns.com and CEO of Town 1).

Unlike TwinTowns.com, there were no issues of distrust between the owners/stakeholders or partners of RegWa.net as participants and users were considered partners and their input was used in the initial and ongoing development of the portal. The close working relationship between Connect RegWa, the CoC, the software developer and the advisory board members were also observed during visits to the region for the research. The importance of partner-trust and stakeholder input has been highlighted in the literature on portals (Fisher & Craig, 2005)

Table 11.4   Minutes of towntown.com board meeting

TownTowns.com Board Meeting Nov 1999	Excerpt of Minutes
17 April 2002	The research grant application describes the role of the research student as purely research. The position will need to include a strong business management focus (CEO of Town 1).
	The application had an emphasis placed on research, to allow the best possible evaluation. In reality the role would have a management focus. (University representative)
10 October 2002	4.1 Research Council Grant.
	University research grant application successful. A research student will be appointed next year. The grant total is A$120,000. A$69,000 cash component and A$51,000 in-kind. [TownTowns.com] is committed to a cash component of A$8,000 per year for the three year term of the project. A panel will be appointed to select the person for the role of which [TownTowns.com] has the option to be a part of. **[TownTowns.com] will have ownership of half the person's time–20 hours per week. This time may be used on training, sales, administration etc.**
31 October 2002	2. MINUTES OF PREVIOUS MEETING.
	[The University representative] requested to remove the last point made on 4.1. **The research student's job role and hours may become flexible and varied.**

and regional online community initiatives (Thompson, 2005). In RegWa. net, one SME equated participation with being a member of an online chamber of commerce. In addition, the initial involvement of the chamber of commerce, the local ISPs and other local businesses in RegWa.net created strong institutional pressures for businesses to join the portal.

In the case of CountryWa.com, theoretically the loose ownership structure prior to 2001 allowed access to the expertise of the Perth Consortia while still having the administration of the portal in the hands of the local steering committee. The reality, however, was that having the dual committee and loose ownership structure in some ways hindered the development of the portal. Scarce resources were stretched in an effort to meet the differing agendas of the committees. This reflects the parallels between CountryWa.com and TwinTowns.com. The difference however, in terms of the effect of ownership structure and governance style, was that in CountryWa.com the structure was more loosely arranged and the project manager was passionate about what the region needed.

> *But, if anything, I found the conflicts between those people who were chest-bumping over positioning held me up more than anything so I would just go ahead with whatever it was they thought I should be doing but I must admit I went ahead with what intuitively felt right* (Original Project Manager, CountryWa.com).

> *It was asking far too much too quickly of the Project to attempt this component in the region. Businesses were barely adopting e-mail and web sites as a functionality of their businesses, let alone having the idea or ability to become 'e-commerced up'. Members of the Perth consortia, who tended to come down here in their advisory capacity with theory and postulation, pushed this ... The local businesses were interested but definitely NOT ready* (Excerpt from the thesis of the original project manager).

> *In the first meeting with the Perth consortia I had suggested a survey of the region to specifically identify computer and Internet use, skills levels etc., but I had been dissuaded. The Perth consortia wanted the project to quickly get underway, to produce something to show as a model in community online development for government funding bodies, as soon as possible* (Excerpt from the thesis of the original project manager).

The loose ownership structure enabled the project manager to carry on with the community side of the portal despite the misgivings of the Perth Consortia and by eventually creating a cooperative to own CountryWa.com, the ownership of the portal was vested in the ultimate stakeholders, the inhabitants of the region and trust between the portal owners was no longer an issue.

Trust between SMEs and the third-party community intermediaries

The owners of RegWa.net used the trust embedded in the local business and community relationships (Steinfield & Whitten, 1999) to foster trust and therefore participation in the initiative. In the outlying towns, the local telecentres were used to identify potential micro SMEs which would benefit from one-on-one IT advice and coaching. As with RegWa.com trust embedded in the local relationships was used to promote participation in CountryWa.com. In CountryWa.com some SMEs joined because they wanted to show their support of the community initiative and because some personally knew the people who were involved in the project. This finding supports the research findings of Lockett & Brown (2006) that trusted local and regional third-party community intermediaries can play a critical role in influencing SME involvement in e-commerce.

In the case of TwinTowns.com, however, although the business associations were involved in the governance of the portal, their distrust of the other owner-stakeholders was echoed by their members who were participants on the portal. Evidence to support this is as follows:

> *There's always going to be this friction between the two towns and to mix the two of them together in a business association type of relationship is never going to work* (SME participant from Town 1).

> *We've got a situation where we've got Town 2 and Town 1 and they sometimes appear to be at loggerheads. They don't seem to be working together and you get the 'them and us' type of thing* (SME participant from Town 1).

> *It did smell of local government. People knew they were dealing with the local government and it wasn't a player in the commercial world and didn't have credibility … if [Town 1] decided to help every business in its area advertise, then by all means set it up, but make sure you're using people with outside expertise to actually run it* (SME in Town 1).

There is a need therefore to ensure that the owners or sponsors of initiatives like the ones in this study are in actual fact trusted third-party community intermediaries and are in one accord as to the motives behind such endeavours.

Trust between buyers and sellers on the portal

Trust building between buyers and sellers in an e-commerce environment is a much researched topic especially where SMEs are involved. SMEs receiving online RFQs could be unsure of the authenticity of the requester. Online buyers of SME products could be wary of the authenticity of the SME supplier. In TwinTowns.com, there were some initial attempts at system-induced trust measures with buyers required to be authenticated before they were allowed to issue RFQs (the owners felt that the registering of SME suppliers and the regional nature of the trading platform would to some extent reduce buyer mistrust). The proposal was to sight some form of identification (e.g., business registration for companies, drivers' licenses for individuals) before registering buyers. Due to the lack of resources needed to practice this authentication process and in an effort to 'break down the barriers to public usage of the REM' (TwinTowns.com internal document), the need to authenticate buyers on the REM was abandoned in mid-2003. As none of the SMEs interviewed from TwinTowns.com had received a RFQ from anyone other than a local government department, trust in the requester was not an issue for them.

In RegWa.net, the trading model on the portal was initially similar to that of TwinTowns.com (RFQs via a REM). RegWa.net had for four years been locally focused and trust between buyers and local SME sellers was not considered an issue. However, it became obvious after four years of operation that the 'buy local' focus and REM were not going to sustain the portal. According to the e-commerce manager of Connect RegWa:

> [According to purchasing officers of regional major buyers] 99% of their purchases are locked in to contracts, so they don't issue quotes. They all agree in principle with the concept and they all support the buy local idea ... but most of them don't have small purchasing power any more.

When Connect RegWa assumed ownership of RegWa.net, the focus shifted to include using the portal to sell the region online to buyers outside the region, a move supported by all stakeholders. RegWa.net now regards its target market as those who will be purchasing from the region via the portal, not those who will be selling on the portal. The portal now caters for both virtual and hybrid 'click and mortar' (Steinfield et al., 2002; Steinfield et al., 1999) sales approaches. The community and local content on the portal has increased with competitions for visitors to the site and specials offered in niche areas like accommodation, tourism and agriculture, for which the area is renowned. In addition, each town in the region has its own version or 'view' of the portal under the name of the town. Visitors can go to the main portal (RegWa.net) or into a town version of the portal (MyTown1, MyTown2 etc.). The reason for this move was that research undertaken by the e-commerce manager of Connect RegWa showed that the smaller the 'catchment area' of a community portal, the greater the usage of the portal. By increasing buyer traffic and stickiness of the portal, the owners of RegWa.net hope to make it an attractive place for sellers to list and be able to sell online. In order to facilitate smaller SMEs to sell online, shopping cart facilities are being offered by RegWa.net to suppliers for a flat fee of AU$250 per annum. Through the stronger buyer focus, the e-commerce uptake by SMEs is also being fostered. The e-commerce and community sides of RegWa.net are now being inextricably intertwined with B2C business being the driving force for e-commerce on the portal. This is why the separate REM page was removed and replaced in late 2004 with a 'shopping' page (with shopping carts) organized by categories of goods or services (although the ability to search the directory and issue RFQs has been retained). Although the portal is now outward looking for its buyers, buyer-seller trust issues have not yet surfaced to warrant facilities like trust certificates for SME sellers. On the sellers' side though, the risk to micro businesses of accepting financial payments by credit card over the internet has been absorbed by RegWa.net for a small fee and this drew a number of them to the portal:

> *The main thing that they offered a small business was the facility to take money by credit card. All the sales go through them and ... they take a really small percentage off. But this is one of the things that had stopped me. The step that you had to take before you can market on the Internet is to be able to take money on a secure side and they did that and I thought it was a real advantage'* (SME in RegWa.net providing specialty apparel).

In CountryWa.com, most of the businesses participating on the portal were micro businesses (less than five employees) that were using only the advertising aspect of the portal and most did not have online trading. There are no RFQ facilities available and although a shopping mall page was tried in 2003, this was discontinued in 2004. Apart from being listed on the portal, businesses thus manage their own e-commerce endeavours. Trust between buyers and sellers was therefore not an issue that needed to be addressed by the portal owners.

Trust in the e-marketplace mechanism (the technology aspect)

In TwinTowns.com the issues of distrust of the REM system by SME participants stemmed not from cultural issues (as in the case of the REM in Singapore investigated by Hsiao [2003]), but from flaws with the system, lack of adequate technical support and lack of feedback on project progress.

Those who actually went in to try and retrieve RFQs, viewed the system as non-user-friendly because of the technical problems and the slow connections.

> *It was so complicated in the way that it was set up ... Look at what hard-nosed free enterprise businesses are doing out there & take a page out of*

*their books and keep it simple, because if Mum at home can't go in there &
use it simply, she won't use it* (SME in Town 1).

*I never really got to learn how it worked exactly even in spite of it appear-
ing to be simple, the way they showed us the demo when we went for the
evening. I don't know whether they changed the system subsequent to that
but it was incredibly difficult to use both from the point of view of trying
to log on and get the info about the quotes that had supposedly been sent
to you ... I never actually managed to do that, and also in terms of finding
your way around it* (SME in Town 1).

*Support was offered but again it's the marketing officer who did that ... the
problem is that one person is trying to do all the things. Specifically, what
should have been set up was some form of help desk that is equally business
related as it is technical. That doesn't appear to be there* (SME in Town 1).

*We couldn't get through & I think he might have come once but his answer
was 'Well, its working here ... mine's OK'; but I said 'I'm a customer &
mine's not. I got to the point where I just thought forget it, just go to the
local paper-based directory & it was quicker ...* (SME in Town 1).

In TwinTowns.com, launching the REM before technical problems were
fully addressed and not having adequate technical support for participants did great damage to the image of the portal and REM. In examining a failed government-supported B2B portal for SMEs in Victoria,
Fisher & Craig (2004) found that the technology did not have the promised functionality when it was launched, which was detrimental to the
management of SME participants' expectations and led to their eventual mistrust of the technology and portal.

Trust in the e-marketplace technology of RegWa.net was rated positively by the majority of SMEs with comments ranging from *'absolutely'*
to *'no issues with that'*. Given that the RegWa.net system was simple and
didn't require any integration with back-office systems of SMEs, there
were no issues relating to trust in the integrity or security of data. The
level of technical support provided by RegWa.net was also viewed favour-
ably by SME participants. There appeared to be a lot of two-way communication between RegWa.net staff and SMEs especially when problems
occurred or even when the SMEs had suggestions for improvements.
This helped to engender trust by the participants in the system.

SMEs in CountryWa.com did not have any grievances with training,
advice, technical support, account maintenance and feedback (in terms
of communication with owners). Trust in CountryWa.com was rated
positively by the majority of SMEs with comments like ' *"it's all right"*;

"It is good considering a lot of it is voluntary"; "Very good, for a portal with no money they do extremely well"; "it's OK so far" and "Because I wasn't doing any financial transactions, no problems"'.

Conclusion

This research shows that in the case of collaboratively developed regional portals or e-marketplaces that are created to aid regional development by encouraging e-commerce uptake by SMEs, trust is a critical success factor on a number of levels viz trust between owner-stakeholders, trust between SME participants and the portal owners, and trust in the portal or e-marketplace technology. While trust between buyers and sellers on the portal has not been as critical as other levels of trust, it is only the nature of this sort of e-marketplace (a regional portal for SMEs to take their first e-commerce steps) that makes it less critical. Trust between buyers and sellers and facilitators to build this trust will be important when SMEs join independent privately funded e-marketplaces. Trust at all the other levels needs to be engendered for the portal to have any chance of fulfilling the purpose for which it was intended. All stakeholders in the initiative (participants, owners, developers and the communities) need to have a shared vision of the roles that such initiatives will play in encouraging e-commerce uptake by SMEs in the region.

While the role of the local trusted third-party community intermediary (Lockett & Brown, 2006) in promoting e-commerce among SMEs can be leveraged by capitalizing on the 'trust-embeddedness' in existing off-line local relationships and networks (Steinfield & Whitten, 1999), care needs to be taken that the ownership structure of such portals is one where all owners have a mutual sense of trust and openness. This will have an effect on the trust between the SMEs and the owner or sponsor of the portal or e-marketplace. A broadly consultative governance style coupled with solidarity among owner -stakeholders would go a long way towards engendering trust of SMEs. In terms of trust between buyers and sellers on the portals, the nature of the two surviving portals is such that there has been no need for trust measures like third-party certification or escrows (Ratnasingam et al., 2005). However, given the motive behind such portals (i.e., introducing SMEs to e-business in a trusted and inexpensive environment) a move like that by RegWa.net in accepting and processing credit card payments on behalf of the participants for a small fee would enable micro businesses to venture into online trading without the associated risks. Finally, it is important to build SME trust in the market mechanism or technology by ensuring that the technology is rolled out to users with the promised functionality and that users have access to good technical support.

References

Ba, S. & Pavlou, P. A. (2002). Evidence of the effect of trust building technology in electronic markets: price premiums and buyer behavior. *MIS Quarterly, 26*(3), 243–268.

Ba, S., Whinston, A. B. & Zhang, H. (2001). Small digital business in electronic markets: a blueprint for survival [Electronic Version]. *Electronic Markets, 11*(1), 59–63.

Bakos, Y. (1998). The emerging role of electronic marketplaces on the internet. *Communications of the ACM, 41*(8), 49–55.

Brown, D. & Lockett, N. (2001). Engaging SMEs in e-commerce: The role of intermediaries within eclusters, *Electronic Markets: The International Journal,* 11(1), 52–58.

Carroll, J. & Swatman, P. (2000). Structured-case: A methodological framework for building theory in information systems research, *Proceedings of the 8th European Conference on Information Systems,* 116–123, Vienna University, Vienna, Austria

Curtin, J. (2001). *A Digital Divide in Rural and Regional Australia? Current Issues Brief 1 2001–2002, Department of the Parliamentary Library, Information and Research Services.* Retrieved May 10, 2005 (last accessed) from http://www.aph.gov.au/library/pubs/CIB/2001–02/02cib01.pdf

Dans, E. & Freire, J. (2002). IT as an agent of social change: Lonxanet and the case of the Galician artisanal fisheries. *Proceedings of the Twenty-Third International Conference on Information Systems* (769–777). Barcelona, Spain: Association for Information Systems. Retrieved November 2, 2003 from http://aisel.isworld.org/

E-Business Policy Group. (2002). *eEurope Go Digital: Benchmarking National and Regional e-Business Policies for SMEs.* Retrieved May 7, 2003 from http://europa.eu.int/comm/enterprise/ict/policy/benchmarking/final-report.pdf

Fisher, J. & Craig, A. (2004). From websites to portals: success factors for business community portals. *Proceedings of the 12th European Conference on Information Systems (The European IS Profession in the Global Networking Environment)* (CD-ROM). Turku, Finland: Turku School of Economics and Business Administration.

Fisher, J. & Craig, A. (2005). Developing business community portals for SMEs – issues of design, development and sustainability [Electronic Version]. *Electronic Markets, 15*(2), 135–145.

Hayes, S. (2004). Island's $ 1.8m e-mart crashes. Australian, June 01, 2004. Available from http://mailman.anu.edu.au/pipermail/link/2004–June/056990.html

Hsiao, R.-L. (2003). Technology fears: Distrust and cultural persistence in electronic marketplace adoption, *The Journal of Strategic Information Systems* 12 (3), 169–199.

Johnsen, H. C. G. & Normann, R. (June 2004). When research and practice collide: the role of action research when there is a conflict of interest with stakeholders. *Systemic Practice and Action Research,* 17(3), 207–235.

Klein, H. K. & Myers, M. D.(1999). A set of principles for conducting and evaluating interpretative field studies in information systems, *MIS Quarterly,* 23(1),67–94.

Kumar, K., van Dissel, H. G. & Bielli, P. (1998). The merchant of Prato – revisited: toward a third rationality of information systems. *MIS Quarterly,* 22(2), 199–226.

Lockett, N. J. & Brown, D. (2006). Aggregation and the role of trusted third parties in SME e-business engagement – a regional policy issue. *International Small Business Journal,* 24(4), 379–404.

Pavlou, P. A. (2002). Institution-based trust in interorganizational exchange relationships: the role of online B2B marketplaces on trust formation. *The Journal of Strategic Information Systems,* 11(3–4), 215–243.

Pavlou, P. A. & Gefen, D. (2002). Building effective online exchange networks with institutional trust. *Proceedings of the Twenty Third International Conference on Information Systems,* Barcelona, Spain: Association for Information Systems. Retrieved September 26, 2003 from http://aisel.isworld.org/

Ratnasingam, P., Gefen, D. & Pavlou, P. A. (2005). The role of facilitating conditions and institutional trust in electronic marketplaces. *Journal of Electronic Commerce in Organizations,* 3(3), 69–82.

Small Enterprise Telecommunications Limited (Setel). (2001). *The Other Digital Divide: E-commerce and Australian Small Business. SETEL Position Paper No 3, August 2001 (Revised).* Retrieved May 10, 2005 (last accessed) from http://www.setel.com.au/publications/public/papers/003.htm

Standing, C., Sims, I., Stockdale, R., Gengatharen, D. E., Standing, S. & Wassenaar, A. (2004). Can e-marketplaces bridge the digital divide? An analysis of two western Australian cases. *The Electronic Journal on Information Systems in Developing Countries,* 20(3), 1–14. Retrieved January 14, 2005 from http://www.ejisdc.org

Steinfield, C., Bouwman, H. & Adelaar, T. (Fall 2002). The dynamics of click-and-mortar electronic commerce: opportunities and management strategies. *International Journal of Electronic Commerce,* 7(1), 93–119.

Steinfield, C., Mahler, A. & Bauer, J. (1999). Electronic commerce and the local merchant: opportunities for synergy between physical and web presence. *Electronic Markets,* 9(1/2), 51–57.

Steinfield, C. & Whitten, P. (1999). *Community Level Socio-Economic Impacts of Electronic Commerce.* White paper presented to the Telecommunications Policy Research Conference, Washington D.C., Sept. 25–27, 1999. Retrieved January 14, 2005 from http://www.tprc.org/ABSTRACTS99/steinwhitepap.PDF

Thompson, H. (2005). Using cluster theory as the lens through which the results of government funded online service initiatives can be examined. *Proceedings of the CRIC Cluster Conference. Beyond Cluster – Current Practices & Future Strategies* [CD-ROM]. Ballarat: University of Ballarat.

Wilkins, L., Swatman, P. M. C. & Castleman, T. (2003). *Electronic Markets and Service Delivery: Governance and Related Competencies in Virtual Environments.* School Working Papers – Series 2003, SWP 2003/02. School of Information Systems, Deakin University, Melbourne, Australia. Retrieved February 9, 2005 (last accessed) from http://www.deakin.edu.au/buslaw/infosys/docs/workingpapers/papers/2003_02_Wilkins.pdf

Willlaiis, D. (2004). Keynote opening address. *Presented at the Connecting Up Conference,* South Australia, May 3, 2004. Retrieved May 10, 2005, from http://www.dcita.gov.au/Article/0,,0_7–2_4011–4_118562,00.html

Zimmerman, H.-D. (1998). Regional electronic marketplaces for electronic commerce and beyond. *Proceedings of International Telecommunications Society ITS 1998,* Stockholm, June 21–24, 1998. Retrieved May 23, 2005 (last accessed) from http://www.businessmedia.org/modules/pub/view.php/businessmedia-51

Index